Destiny at Bay

By the same author

Streamlined Bridge
Card-Play Technique (*with Nico Gardener*)
Bridge for Beginners (*with Nico Gardener*)
Bridge Psychology
Will You Be My Partner?
Bridge: Modern Bidding
Success at Bridge
Bridge in the Menagerie
Confessions of an Addict
The Bridge Immortals
Victor Mollo's Winning Double
Bridge: Case for the Defence
Best of Bridge (*with E. Jannersten*)
Bridge in the Fourth Dimension
Instant Bridge
Defence at Bridge (*with Aksel J. Nielsen*)
Bridge Unlimited
Bridge Course Complete
The Finer Arts of Bridge
Masters and Monsters
Streamline Your Bidding
Streamline Your Card-Play
Bridge à la Carte
Winning Bridge
You Need Never Lose at Bridge
I Challenge You
The Other Side of Bridge
Tomorrow's Textbook
The Compleat Bridge Player

Pocket Guides (published by Bibliagora):

Winning Bidding (Acol)
Winning Defence
Winning Conventions

Destiny at Bay

THE LATEST FROM
THE BRIDGE MENAGERIE

VICTOR MOLLO

METHUEN

First published in Great Britain 1987
by Methuen London Ltd
11 New Fetter Lane, London EC4P 4EE
Copyright © 1987 Victor Mollo

British Library Cataloguing in Publication Data

Mollo, Victor
    Destiny at bay: the latest from the
    Bridge menagerie.
    1. Contract bridge — Collections of games
    I. Title
    795.41'58   GV1282.5

ISBN 0-413-17150-7

Typeset by Words & Pictures Ltd
Thornton Heath, Surrey
Printed in Great Britain by
Richard Clay (The Chaucer Press) Ltd,
Bungay, Suffolk

Contents

Author's Preface

Among our members at the Griffins Club you will recognise many of your friends. And you will meet yourself, too, though here identification may not be so easy.

> 'Oh wad some Pow'r the giftie gie us
> To see ourselves as others see us'

Bridge is a faithful mirror of life, and as the Griffins hold it for you, reflected in the glass you will see the follies and foibles of man shorn of the veils which so carefully hide his ego away from the card table.

On the technical plane there is nothing new in bridge. There never can be. It is the human side which provides inexhaustible material, for the simple finesse, no less than the subtle bidding sequence or savant squeeze, can release the springs, setting in motion the duels, the clash of personalities, the battles of wits and will which make bridge the greatest game in the world.

Most of the hands in these pages will be new to most readers. A few with long memories may recognise a bid or play featured in one of my Menagerie articles ten to fifteen years ago. None are of more recent vintage, with one exception — a deal from Aksel J. Nielsen's collection, gathered over forty years, which he put at my disposal when we collaborated on *Defence at Bridge*. I adapted a hand for an article I contributed to *Popular Bridge*. It was, however, Aksel J. Nielsen's discovery and in 1978 he used it himself in *Bridge With The Three Musketeers*. I am happy to acknowledge my debt.

Overleaf, Oscar the Owl, our Senior Kibitzer, will introduce you to the leading members of our club. All are alive and well at the time of writing, and we are all young, too, whatever our years, for bridge keeps us so. Victors or vanquished we rise from every deal, like a phoenix from the ashes, spoiling for the next one.

As you get to know us you will soon see that ours is an exhilarating existence. Never boring and never bored we enjoy every turn of Fortune's wheel. *Joie de Vivre*, the art of savouring every sparkling moment — that is the way of the Griffins. We invite you to join us.

CHAPTER ONE

Overture

"If only they'd had bridge in times gone by! They didn't know what they were missing."

Oscar the Owl, our Senior Kibitzer at the Griffins, was in a mellow mood. The Taylor '27, following the Latour '61 with the *bécasse au fumet*, brought a warm glow to his amber eyes as he philosophised.

"Think of the agonies they endured over that great controversy between free will and predestination, the plots and conspiracies of the Jansenists and the Jesuits, the ruined lives, the feuds and vendettas, spilling over from this world into the next. A game of bridge and they could have put their beliefs to the test without a single soul being damned, reserving all their anathemas for the post-mortems, as we do."

H. H.

"Which side would win?" I asked.

"They'd both win, of course," replied the Owl. "First the Hideous Hog, champion of free will, would deftly side-step Nemesis and set destiny's designs at nought, then . . ."

"But that's a contradiction in terms," broke in Peregrine the Penguin, Oscar's opposite number at the Unicorn where the Griffins play duplicate on Thursdays.

"If something is predestined, it happens. If it doesn't, it wasn't predestined."

"You are leaving free will out of account," objected O.O. "Suppose that destiny intends a contract to succeed. Declarer in, say, 4♠ has ten top tricks. The lead is favourable. There are no snags, but the Hog introduces a new dimension, imposes his will and causes declarer to go down. We've seen it happen so often."

"He cheats fate?" I suggested.

The Owl nodded in approval.

1

"So you don't believe in predestination," interjected the Penguin. "You are on the side of the Jansenists?"

THE RABBIT

"I didn't say that," protested O.O. "I said that both sides would win, free will one day, destiny the next. Outpointed by the Hog, destiny gets her own back through the Rueful Rabbit. Friendly, gentle and unassuming, but scatterbrained beyond belief, the Rabbit rarely knows what he is doing and sometimes forgets the contract he is trying to make or break, but fate decrees, that despite his best endeavours, he should produce an inspired bid or else, without malice aforethought, by the purest chance, the right sequence of plays, and lo and behold, he does. He can't help himself. There's a force he cannot control."

THE GUARDIAN ANGEL

"Perhaps his Guardian Angel . . ." I began.

"True," agreed the Owl, "as we all know R.R. has the most gifted, as well as the most unscrupulous Guardian Angel in the business, but he is, after all, only destiny's agent. He is not a principal."

"Doesn't he at times exceed his instructions?" I ventured.

"Why not forget all about angels, Jesuits, free will and predestination, and accept the fact that the Rabbit is infernally lucky," said P.P.

"I do," rejoined O.O., "but luck is a dispensation granted by fate. If you believe in luck you believe in predestination. Free will won't stop you being as lucky as the Rabbit or as unlucky as . . . as . . ."

KARAPET

"Karapet," I suggested.

"Yes, a perfect example," agreed the Owl. "Karapet Djoulikyan, the Free Armenian, looks upon himself as the embodiment of misfortune. It all started, as we have so often been told, with the evil spell cast on his family by the witch of Ararat in 1453 or thereabouts. Everything has gone wrong for the Djoulikyans ever since."

"Poor Karapet," I said. "Perhaps one day his luck will turn."

"I sincerely hope not. Don't do him out of his simple pleasures," warned O.O. "Karapet is a masochist and takes as much pleasure in recounting his woes over a Fernet Branca, as does the Hog gloating over his Bollinger. *Chacun à son goût.* You know what they say, that only a sadist would be kind to a masochist. So don't deprive Karapet of his cherished miseries."

PAPA

"What, then, about his friend, Papa the Greek, a fine player who would be better still if he weren't so clever. How does his free will fare against predestination?" asked P.P.

"He usually comes off second best, I fear," replied the Owl. "But then Papa's greatest pleasure isn't to win but to see the Hog lose and so prove that he is the better player. It doesn't happen very often, but he's a glutton for punishment and keeps on trying. An exhibitionist to the tips of his long tapering fingers he would rather go down by being too clever than make his contract without being clever at all. He does his own thing and so do all the Griffins. We've no inhibitions. 'This above all else, to thine own self be true'. That's our motto and we all live up to it."

THE SECRETARY BIRD

"Even the Secretary Bird?" asked Penguin incredulously.

"Of course," replied the Owl. "The Emeritus Professor of Bio-Sophistry is first and foremost a lawyer and sues for the sake of suing. The result is of secondary importance. 'Tis better to have sued and lost than never to have sued at all,' is his proud device.

"He dislikes everyone and everyone dislikes him. So no one is inhibited and we can all be happy, in a negative sort of way."

THE WALRUS

"And is the Walrus also uninhibited?" I asked.

"Certainly," said O.O. "Points are to Walter the Walrus what the law is to the Secretary Bird. He doesn't play bridge, he counts it, and would as soon give a dud cheque as make game without the requisite number of points. It's a moral issue and the Walrus has the highest principles and lowest IQ of any of our members."

"Lower than the Toucan's?" asked Peregrine in surprise.

THE TOUCAN

"The Toucan has no IQ," rejoined the Owl. "Some men, as Malvolio has it, are born to greatness. Timothy the Toucan is born to insignificance. That's his part in life and he plays it very well. Meek and humble, he will never inherit the earth, but he is contented, bouncing in his chair, his long nose aglow with Burgundy. 'They also serve who only stand and wait' " quoted O.O. "The Toucan, modest, deferential to his betters, which means to everyone, is the best of his kind, and that makes him a worthy Griffin, a member of the élite like the rest of us."

THE CHIMP

"The élite?" The Penguin sat up with a jerk. The second decanter was draining away and P.P. was beginning to look distinctly drowsy and to slur his words.

"The élite?" he repeated. "How does that fit in with the Chimp?" The combination seemed incongruous.

"Where would we be without Charlie the Chimp?" retorted O.O.

"Bridge is a microcosm of society and who has ever heard of a society without its Chimps, sailing close to the wind, yet not quite close enough to be blown off course?

"Cunning, crafty, always giving himself the benefit of the doubt, yes, but no more so, surely, than many a man in pin-striped trousers you see driving in a Rolls to the Bank of England. He is not above suspicion, I grant you that, but he is not Caesar's wife and when all's said and done, the best families in the land have their black sheep. We Griffins wouldn't be truly representative without one of our own."

"B .. best ...... black .. she-ep," muttered the Penguin before subsiding finally into the arms of Morpheus.

THE SUNLIT PRESENT

"In *vino veritas*. Very well put," applauded the Owl. "We Griffins have the best of everything — the best exponents of free will and of predestination, the best angels and the best witches, even the best black sheep. Someone," pursued O.O. giving me a meaning look, "should bring our club's history up to date."

GOING BACK TO THE PRESENT

The Owl drained his glass before resuming. "Founded by the Master of the King's Pleasures to provide amusement for Charles II at ombre and faro, our early days in Vauxhall are shrouded in mist. As a coffee house in St. James's we were, perhaps, a shade better than the others. Whist later raised us to the fore, but it is to bridge, so true a mirror of life, that we owe our fame and glory. So leave the checkered past behind. Think only of the sunlit present. For many years now," went on the Owl, "you have been recording in *The Griffins Chronicle*, and elsewhere too, I believe, the daily exploits in our cardroom. Go through them. Select the episodes which highlight the personalities behind the cards, so typical of the world outside, yet so much more vibrant, more colourful, and just as comical in their vanities and their pretensions. Be kind, be stern, be cruel if you like, but keep nothing back in doing justice to the Griffins. Sleep on it," concluded the Owl with a wistful look at the empty decanter.

The following morning I repaired to our library to look up early copies of *The Griffins Chronicle*. It wasn't long before I came across a series of telling blows struck by the Hog in his war on destiny. I reproduce the articles as I wrote them at the time, setting the scene with the usual preamble which began so often at the Griffins Bar. This was one of the first:

CHAPTER TWO

The Hog in Charge

BENDING THE ODDS

The Hog threw the book aside in disgust. "The ignoramus!" he exclaimed. "Starts with finessing, one of the most advanced subjects in bridge, and winds up with smother plays and quintuple grand coups, as if they mattered."

"But wouldn't you say . . ." began Oscar the Owl.

"No, I wouldn't," snapped the Hog.

Mellowed by a glass of Delaforce '60, he continued in friendlier vein.

"There are too many players chasing too few coups. What if you do catch a smother or a criss-cross? You won't find one more than once a year, so where's the profit? Finesses, on the other hand, are there to take all the time and the good player makes a point of bringing them off, while the bad one is, perforce, unlucky."

"But surely," protested O.O., "a card is either right or wrong. The ace is or isn't over the king. The king is or isn't under the ace-queen and there's nothing anyone can do about it. They are fifty-fifty chances, so where does the skill come in?"

"When I take fifty-fifty chances," replied the Hog with hauteur, "I expect them to come off at least four times out of five. After all, it's only a question of bending the odds."

Searching through his pockets for a bit of paper, he produced a crumpled letter, which someone had asked him to post, and scribbled quickly on the back of the air mail envelope.

Dlr. North   ♠ J 10 2
Both Vul: ♡ A K J 10 3
                    ◊ 6 3
                    ♣ K Q 8

```
        N
    W       E
        S
```

                    ♠ A K 8 7 6 4
                    ♡ Q 2
                    ◊ 8 7 5
                    ♣ 5 2

West	North	East	South
–	1♡	Pass	1♠
2◊	2♡	Pass	3♠
Pass	4♠		

"Like the contract?" asked H.H.

"There's little to choose between 4♠ and 4♡," replied the Owl after due reflection. "Both contracts depend on not losing a spade, though . . ."

"No, no," broke in the Hog, "when this hand came up the Rabbit was North and as you know, he seldom makes ten tricks. So play it in spades. That ♠Q may be bare or else East may have started with ♠Qx, in which case the contract will fall into your lap. Obviously, it's better than a fifty-fifty chance."

"And did you bend the odds still further?" enquired O.O. politely.

"Naturally," replied H.H., "but perhaps you would like to go through the motions with me. West leads the ◊K, then the ◊Q, East signalling with the ◊10, followed by the ◊2. Next comes the ◊A. Over to you."

The Owl pondered. "If East over-ruffs dummy's jack of spades, there's nothing I can do about it. Did he?"

"You go up with dummy's jack? Very well, East follows with the ◊4. Continue."

As the Owl took in the situation, his heart-shaped face relaxed into a smile. "I rather think," he said, "that we've been there before. East gives a false signal because he wants declarer to put up the jack. He is sitting with Q9x and hopes to promote his nine. It's a brilliant defence, but by no means original."

"Please play," said H.H.

The Owl pointed to the ♠10.

"East covers with the queen," said the Hog.

O.O. nodded. "As expected. I cross to dummy with a heart and lead the ♠2."

"The three from East," announced H.H. The Owl nodded once more. "Quite so, and this is where I bend the odds, as you call it, by inserting the eight, and East's manoeuvre gets him nowhere. Now had he played normally, I might well have gone for the drop and lost the contract. Too clever that East of yours. I suppose it wasn't our friend, Papa, by any chance?"

"No," replied the Hog. "Papa was South and played exactly as you did, as I intended him to play. I happened to be East." As he spoke the Hog filled in the other hands.

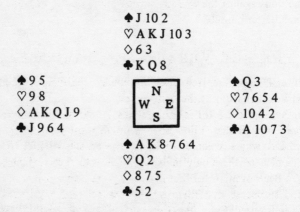

```
                        ♠ J 10 2
                        ♡ A K J 10 3
                        ◇ 6 3
                        ♣ K Q 8
        ♠ 9 5                              ♠ Q 3
        ♡ 9 8              N               ♡ 7 6 5 4
        ◇ A K Q J 9     W     E            ◇ 10 4 2
        ♣ J 9 6 4          S               ♣ A 10 7 3
                        ♠ A K 8 7 6 4
                        ♡ Q 2
                        ◇ 8 7 5
                        ♣ 5 2
```

"I forgot to add just now," went on the Hog, " that while I expect my own fifty-fifty chances to come off four times out of five, so I expect them to fail no less frequently when they are taken against me. Bending the odds, you see, works both ways.

"Consider the position from East's angle," continued H.H. "Without the false signal, West will take two top diamonds and switch to a club. Now, whether declarer takes the trump finesse or plays for the drop, he is bound to succeed. There's just one chance for the defence — that West has the ♠9. Then East can bend the odds, for a declarer familiar with the classics will say as you did 'We've been there before' and play accordingly. Of course, Papa recognised the situation and he gave me quite a pitying look as he took the 'marked finesse'."

"Mind you," added the Hog as an afterthought, "a subtle defence like that could never succeed against the Rabbit. He isn't nearly good enough to be fooled."

"In fact," ventured O.O., "the hand should have been played by him after all. No hope of promoting, bending . . ."

"That," broke in the Hog, "would have been at best a fifty–fifty chance." Seeing the Owl's puzzled look, he went on to explain. "Playing in 4♡, the Rabbit ruffs the third diamond, draws trumps and turns to the spades . . ."

"Bringing down the queen," interjected O.O.

"Certainly," agreed H.H., "but observe how easy it is to block the suit, for unless the jack and ten are played to the first two tricks, dummy's long spades are dead and declarer loses two clubs."

"It is true," concluded the Hog philosophically, "that you can't bend the odds against the Rabbit, but then why bother when he can do it so much better himself?"

THE HOG VERSUS THE COMPUTER

"Computers!" said the Hog contemptuously, grabbing a handful of olives as we sat chatting at the Griffins bar.

"All they are good for is misdirecting letters and sending men to the moon, though that, mind you, is where most of them should be anyway. But when it comes to the higher aspects of life, to art, to beauty, which of these ugly monsters could ever rival a Michelangelo, a Keats, a Beethoven, or for that matter, a great bridge player?"

"Ah, I suspected that there might be a personal angle to it somewhere," murmured Colin the Corgi, the facetious young man from Oxbridge.

"I only wish," went on the Hideous Hog, ignoring him, "that some philanthropist would sponsor a team of computers to take me on at bridge. They could be programmed to cheat, for all I care. I bet they'd be found out the first time!"

He searched his pockets for a piece of paper. Extracting a cheque which had seen better days, he scribbled on the back.

Dlr. West   ♠ A Q 10 4
E/W Vul: ♡ 8 5
                                   ◇ A 4
                                   ♣ A 10 7 5 2

```
        N
     W     E
        S
```

                                   ♠ K 5 3
                                   ♡ Q 10 9
                                   ◇ K Q 8 7
                                   ♣ K 6 4

West	North	East	South
Pass	1♣	Pass	1◇
1♡	1♠	Pass	3NT

"There," he said. "West leads the ♡K, sees East's deuce and switches to the ◇J. Pick your computer, Oscar, and make nine tricks."

Oscar the Owl studied dummy and assessed his prospects. "So long as I keep out East," he mused aloud, "I shouldn't have too much trouble. Even if the clubs are 4–1, I . . ."

"They aren't," broke in the Hog "they split 3–2 nicely."

"I go up with dummy's ◇A," went on O.O., "and I lead a low club hoping to duck the trick into West's hand. What's East's card?"

"The ♣9," replied H.H.

"Then obviously I can't afford to duck. I go up with the ♣K and . . ."

"West drops the ♣Q," announced the Hog.

The Owl pondered. "If it's a singleton, there's no future in clubs. But, of course, West may have the ♣QJ bare." Anyway, I lead another club. What happens?"

"West," the Hog told him, "follows with the ♣3 and East with the ♣8 on dummy's ace."

O.O. hooted softly. "Our West, I see, is a technician and knows his business. He realises, of course, that had I the ♣KJ I would have finessed in perfect safety, so he jettisons his queen to create an entry for partner with the jack. It's in all the textbooks. However," went on Oscar, "I haven't lost yet, not by any means. Before I tackle the spades, I'll test the diamonds. At trick five I lead the ◇K."

"The ◇10 from West," said the Hog.

"So far, so good," observed O.O. "I continue with the ♢Q. Maybe the ♢9 will drop. Does it?"

The Hog shook his head. "West," he replied, "throws the ♡3."

The Owl reflected for a moment, then a smile formed slowly around the corners of his mouth.

"I consult that much-maligned computer," he pursued, now smiling broadly. "It registers doubletons in both minors in West's hand and it records 11 points — the ♡AKJ, the ♢J and the ♣Q. We haven't actually seen the ♡J, it is true, but the lead, East's deuce and the switch at trick two, show up that card clearly enough. West passed as dealer. With a six-card suit and an 11 count he might have opened, even at the vulnerability, and any self-respecting computer can be programmed to work that out. It follows that West's shape is 4-5-2-2. Thereupon that pretty little monster cashes dummy's ♠A, crosses to the ♠K and takes the marked finesse against West's ♠J. How's that?"

"Two down," replied H.H., filling in the diagram.

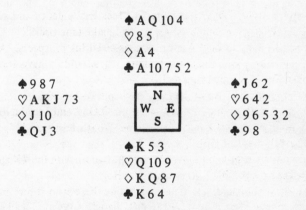

```
            ♠ A Q 10 4
            ♡ 8 5
            ♢ A 4
            ♣ A 10 7 5 2
♠ 9 8 7            N            ♠ J 6 2
♡ A K J 7 3    W     E          ♡ 6 4 2
♢ J 10            S             ♢ 9 6 5 3 2
♣ Q J 3                         ♣ 9 8
            ♠ K 5 3
            ♡ Q 10 9
            ♢ K Q 8 7
            ♣ K 6 4
```

"Against any other computer," said the Hog, "yours would have won the day, for as you can see, there are ten cold tricks, and no computer in the world could do anything about it. But West wasn't a computer. Far from it. He was an artist, an er . . ."

"Who was this illustrious West?" asked Colin the Corgi, arching an eyebrow.

The Hog gave him a withering look. "I invite you, Oscar," he went on, "to view the hand from West's seat. I usually open on such hands but with that Walrus opposite it's best to have something in reserve. For his jump to 3NT, Papa, yes, Themistocles was South — should have at least 13 points. What does that leave East? At best, one miserable point — the ♠J, for nothing else is missing.

My first concern, of course," continued H.H., "was to kill the clubs. Hence the pseudo unblocking play. How do you programme a computer to do that?" asked the Hog rhetorically. "But note the effect. Once declarer places me with two clubs, he miscounts the hand automatically, so by jettisoning the ♣Q I create an entry for partner, not with the ♣J, but with the ♠J!" Absentmindedly, the Hog emptied Oscar's glass.

"Very pretty defence," rejoined the Owl, "but why blame the computer? What could Michelangelo or Beethoven do about it, or even you yourself, H.H.?"

"I'm not sure about Michelangelo or Beethoven," replied the Hog, "but for my part, I would have drawn an inference from the order in which East followed in clubs, first the ♣9, then the ♣8. It would mean nothing if East were the Toucan, for all cards below the rank of ace and king are much the same to him. Neither would it help much in the case of an expert since he would take care to play the card nearest his thumb, giving nothing away. But East happened to be the Walrus, who firmly believes that the means justify the end and that so long as you count the points in the bidding and signal scrupulously in the play, the tricks you subsequently gather are of secondary importance.

"Your computer, needless to say, doesn't ask who's who at the table and makes no distinction between Jupiter and the Bull. But for me that ♣9-8 sequence would have carried a message and I might have guessed."

The Hog tore up the cheque. Seeing the Owl's puzzled look, he explained. "I had intended it originally for my wine merchant, but I've had second thoughts. Good customers, like I am, shouldn't pay too promptly. It's undignified. Bad form."

7NT ON ONE OF TWO FINESSES

"I hear that you brought home an iniquitous grand slam this afternoon," said Oscar the Owl, as we sat chatting in the bar.

"It couldn't have been as bad as all that," countered the Hideous Hog. "After all, it depended at worst on one of two finesses."

"A grand slam on one of two finesses?" repeated O.O. incredulously. "Impossible. What if the first one fails?"

"Then I don't take it, of course," retorted the Hog. "Who do you think I am? Papa?"

The Owl wasn't convinced. "Even if you somehow divined which finesse to take, a grand slam on a finesse . . ."

"No, no," broke in the Hog, "I said that the contract was *at worst* on one of two finesses. In the event, both were wrong."

"Then how did you know what not to do?" persisted the Owl.

"I tried both finesses," explained H.H., who was beginning to grow impatient with Oscar's unimaginative approach, "but since both were wrong, I rejected them and . . ."

"I didn't see the hand," interjected O.O., "I only heard about it, but I still don't understand how you took two finesses, found them wrong, untook them, so to speak, and still made the grand slam. Perhaps you'd show me the hand."

The Hog searched his pockets for a bit of paper. Dismissing a couple of crumpled bills in favour of a charity appeal, he put down the North-South hands.

Dlr. North
N/S Vul:

♠ Q
♡ Q
◇ A Q 10 8 6 3 2
♣ K 7 5 2

```
    N
 W     E
    S
```

♠ A J 10
♡ A J 10
◇ K J 4
♣ A 6 4 3

North	South
1◇	3♣
4♣	4NT
5◇	5NT
6◇	6♡
6♠	7NT

"Too ambitious," observed O.O.. "Surely 6◇ would have been enough."

"If you expect partner to make twelve tricks, you will, I hope, give me credit for making one more," rejoined the Hog with spirit. "We can hardly play in diamonds, though, since that would make partner declarer. Mind you, my 6♡ gave him the chance to call 7♣ if his clubs were good enough. No one can accuse me of being selfish."

"Who was partner?" enquired O.O.

"Immaterial," replied the Hog, "some honest plodder who bids what he thinks he's got and is right half the time. Can't remember the name though I expect he had one. What's more important is that I had Walter the Walrus on my right and on my left, none other than Papa the Greek."

"I can see only eleven tricks," said O.O. studying the hands.

"True," agreed the Hog, "eleven tricks, plus the Walrus, and that should suffice, especially as Papa usually manages to find a clever lead. This time he didn't. He picked on a diamond which didn't help at all. So I started with the spade finesse."

"But . . ." began O.O.

"Exactly," agreed the Hog, "the king was wrong. The Walrus, who regards covering honours as a matter of moral rectitude, like revering one's parents or leading the fourth highest or paying one's taxes, that is within reason, of course, well, the Walrus didn't so much as blink. So I went up with the ♠A, crossed to dummy with a diamond and tried the heart finesse. Again the Walrus played smoothly with that vacuous, bovine look which a more subtle player might put on to conceal something. Clearly, he didn't have the ♡K either, so once more I had to go up with the ace."

The Owl shook his head. "Not so good now," he remarked.

"On the contrary," retorted the Hog, "prospects have improved visibly. Had the Walrus been endowed with the king in either major, he might have just had the sense, after a long trance, not to cover and that would have left me a trick short. But once I knew that Papa had both kings, the contract became little worse than an even-money chance. And for once there was a speck of justice in the world for he did have three clubs.

"Can't think why people use up so much space with print," murmured H.H. filling in the East-West hands.

This was the full deal:

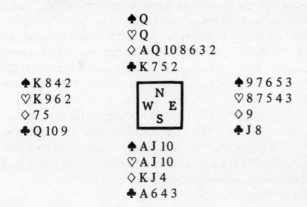

```
                    ♠ Q
                    ♡ Q
                    ◇ A Q 10 8 6 3 2
                    ♣ K 7 5 2
    ♠ K 8 4 2              N          ♠ 9 7 6 5 3
    ♡ K 9 6 2         W        E      ♡ 8 7 5 4 3
    ◇ 7 5                 S          ◇ 9
    ♣ Q 10 9                          ♣ J 8
                    ♠ A J 10
                    ♡ A J 10
                    ◇ K J 4
                    ♣ A 6 4 3
```

"As you can see," went on the Hog, "all I had to do was to play out the diamonds, leaving dummy with four clubs and myself with the ♠J ♡J and ♣A6. The last diamond reduced Papa to four cards and to keep three clubs he had to part with one of his kings. Whichever it was, I would cash the jack of that suit and squeeze him again."

"What did Papa say?" asked O.O.

"He called it an elementary automatic progressive squeeze which he foresaw as soon as dummy went down," replied H.H. "The Walrus went one better. Having one miserable point, he knew his fate, he said, even before seeing dummy."

A SADLY NEGLECTED ART

"Doubling cue-bids, that's virgin soil, you know," said the Hog as we sat sipping Madeira. "People know no more about it today than they did in Culbertson's time. There's been no study, no research, no . . . I thought you were in New York," broke off H.H. seeing Colin the Corgi saunter into the bar.

"Just got back," replied C.C., "landed at Heathrow an hour ago."

The Hideous Hog bared his teeth in what was probably intended as a smile.

"In that case," he told the Corgi, "I will show you a remarkable hand. I had it on Wednesday. Stop me if you've heard about it already," added the Hog, scribbling on the bar bill.

"You're looking very pleased with yourself," rejoined C.C., "more so than usual, that is, so no doubt it was a devastating performance, but I saw nothing about it in the American papers. Mind you, they're very parochial over there ... seemed more interested in their Presidential election than in your superb artistry. No sense of news value."

"There," said the Hog, ignoring the banter. "Game All and this is your hand."

♠ A Q
♡ 9 7 5 4
◇ Q
♣ A K Q 10 8 6

"Bidding or play?" enquired the Corgi.

"Sophisticated bidding, advanced play," replied H.H.

"The auction is uncontested," he went on. "You bid 1♣ and then 3♣ over partner's 1◇. What action do you take when he calls 4♣?"

"He's obviously looking for a slam," reflected C.C., "and that hinges seemingly on not losing two hearts. Very well, I bid 4◇. What happens?"

"Partner duly bids 4♡," replied the Hog. "You can now settle for 6♣, but it costs nothing to bid 4♠. Agreed?"

Oscar the Owl, our Senior Kibitzer, was about to blink but the Hog quickly silenced him.

"Please don't interrupt, Oscar," he told him severely, "you know what happened. I want to see if Colin draws the same inferences."

Before the Corgi could say anything, the Hog went on. "Over 4♡, South bid 4♠ which West promptly doubled. Now North bid 5◇. What do you make of that?"

"He could have passed," pointed out C.C., "so presumably he's showing extra values. Still, what more can I do than bid 6♣?"

"You can bid 7♣," rejoined the Hog. "If he is showing a good diamond suit, your ◇Q is invaluable. A little imagination ..."

"Very well," agreed C.C. "I'll bid 7♣, not because I think it is right, mind you, but because you're licking your chops, so obviously you made it in some devious way and you want to see if I can do the same. So I am in 7♣. Proceed."

"Dummy," said the Hog, jotting down North's hand, "was a great disappointment."

♠ 2
♡ A K 3
◇ A 10 3 2
♣ J 9 7 5 3

"Apparently, partner was bent on showing the ◇A. With the ♡K to spare and a second round control in spades, he felt that he had to do something big. A questionable manoeuvre with so feeble a suit, but there it is. You're in a grand slam and West leads the ♡Q. Kindly make thirteen tricks."

The Corgi pondered. "I can see eleven tricks — six clubs, the ♡AK, the ◇A and a spade ruff. I told you that I didn't want the grand slam. In 6♣ I give up a heart and ruff one for my twelfth trick. Now I must hope for a revoke or two. So I play at breathtaking speed, switching suddenly from suit to suit and . . ."

"This is no time to be facetious," broke in the Hog, "or to miscount your tricks. You have twelve on top, not eleven, for with all those entri entries a dummy reversal presents no problem. You ruff three diamonds in your hand and need just one more trick. The spade finesse, perhaps . . ."

The Hog left the sentence unfinished, waiting for the obvious rejoinder.

The Corgi shook his head. "Much as you may like to be in grand slams on finesses, this one, after West's double is a non-starter."

The Hog nodded sympathetically.

"Quite so," he agreed. "Declarer, a very fine player, let me tell you, took the same view. But if the spade finesse was doomed, West might have four or more hearts, and if so, he would surely be squeezed. South played on that assumption.

"One round disposed of the trumps. Then came the dummy reversal, the ◇A and three ruffs in the closed hand, dummy's trumps providing two entries. Next declarer cashed the ♡K — the ♡A had gone on the first round — and finally dummy's two remaining trumps."

"Who discarded what?" enquired the Corgi.

The Hog told him. "Both defenders followed to the diamonds which split 4-4. On the clubs East threw four spades, to be precise, the 6543. West shed the ♠987 and the ♡10. He had followed with the ♡J to the ♡K, but the ♡4 was still out. When declarer played dummy's last trump, this was the position.

```
          ♠ 2
          ♡ 3
          ◇ —
          ♣ —

          ┌─────────┐
          │    N    │
          │  W   E  │
          │    S    │
          └─────────┘

          ♠ A Q
          ♡ —
          ◇ —
          ♣ —
```

"If West had the last heart, he could only have one spade. Need I say more?" concluded H.H., draining someone's glass.

"Very well, so the ♠K, now bare, drops on the ♠A. What of it?" scoffed C.C. "A dummy reversal, followed by a squeeze, indicated by the revealing double of a cue-bid. Good technique, if you like, but I would expect any expert to make your grand slam."

"Except against me," retorted the Hog triumphantly.

"*Against* you?" asked the Corgi, "but weren't you the brilliant South who . . ."

"You seem to be under a slight misapprehension," retorted the Hog. "The brilliant South was Papa. I was the brilliant West who beat the unbeatable grand slam before it had even been bid. This, you see, was the deal:

```
                          ♠ 2
                          ♡ A K 3
                          ◇ A 10 3 2
                          ♣ J 9 7 5 3
    ♠ J 9 8 7                              ♠ K 10 6 5 4 3
    ♡ Q J 10 2          ┌─────────┐        ♡ 8 6
    ◇ J 9 8 7           │    N    │        ◇ K 6 5 4
    ♣ 2                 │  W   E  │        ♣ 4
                        │    S    │
                        └─────────┘
                          ♠ A Q
                          ♡ 9 7 5 4
                          ◇ Q
                          ♣ A K Q 10 8 6
```

South	West	North	East
1♣	Pass	1◇	Pass
3♣	Pass	4♣	Pass
4◇	Pass	4♡	Pass
4♠	Dble.	5◇	Pass
7♣			

"You look nonplussed Colin, surprised no doubt, by my double of 4♠. Evidently you have never considered what is involved in doubling cue-bids.

"East," went on H.H., "doubles to indicate a lead. But when West knows, as in this case, that it will be his own lead, should he really double to place the high cards for declarer?

"Of course not. If the slam is a lay down, it doesn't matter what West does. If it isn't, he should try to mislead declarer, not to provide him with helpful information. In this context a false double is the equivalent of a false card.

"Without my double," continued the Hog, pointing a fat, pink forefinger at the Corgi's midriff, "Papa would have taken the spade finesse, a fifty-fifty chance, and made his grand slam. The squeeze required not only the same fifty-fifty chance, but also length in hearts with West. Much as Papa likes to be spectacular, he wouldn't have bent the odds against himself to that extent. I had to do it for him.

"Remind me," added the Hog, pocketing absent-mindedly Oscar's cigar piercer "to write a monograph sometime on doubling cue-bids. It's a sadly neglected art."

Destiny had had the worst of the opening exchanges, but it wasn't long before a series of deadly counter-attacks, led by the Guardian Angel, put her ahead on points.

CHAPTER THREE

The Guardian Angel

THE TRUMP DISCARD

"If a little learning is a dangerous thing, too much can be fatal," said Peregrine the Penguin, Senior Kibitzer at the Unicorn and one of the most loyal supporters of the Griffins Bar.

"Yes," agreed Oscar the Owl. "He thinks it's more honourable to go down, trying to engineer a smother play, than to make his contract by a simple finesse."

We were discussing the Rabbit's new-found zest for esoteric bridge, his disdain for ordinary plays and his search on every deal for complex stratagems and coups.

Rare books from Bibliagora appeared on his bookshelves. *Existentialist Squeezes* in the original Mandarin had a place of honour next to the *Predictions of Nostradamus*. Achilles Heal's *The Hundred Greatest Plays* — by the *player who made them*, was on his bedside table.

And as the Rabbit acquired higher knowledge, so he sought eagerly for opportunities to put it into practice. A good occasion was this hand which came up at the club recently.

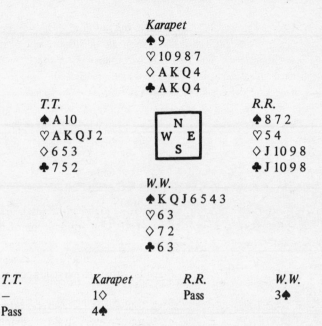

Karapet
♠ 9
♡ 10 9 8 7
♢ A K Q 4
♣ A K Q 4

T.T.
♠ A 10
♡ A K Q J 2
♢ 6 5 3
♣ 7 5 2

R.R.
♠ 8 7 2
♡ 5 4
♢ J 10 9 8
♣ J 10 9 8

W.W.
♠ K Q J 6 5 4 3
♡ 6 3
♢ 7 2
♣ 6 3

T.T.	Karapet	R.R.	W.W.
—	1♢	Pass	3♠
Pass	4♠		

The Hideous Hog, who had been waiting to cut in for several minutes, walked impatiently round the table to look at all four hands.

"You should be in after this," whispered O.O. encouragingly.

"On the contrary," retorted H.H., "I shouldn't, but I probably will be."

Before he could explain this cryptic remark, the Toucan led out the ♡K, then the ♡A. As he was gathering the trick, the steward came in to call the Rabbit to the telephone.

"As any child or Toucan can see," resumed the Hog, "the contract is unbeatable unless the defence can come to two trump tricks. The Toucan's best chance, therefore, is to find the Rabbit with the ♠J and to make him ruff a heart with it."

"But he hasn't got the ♠J," objected the Owl.

"True," agreed the Hog, "but his actual trump holding is just as good, for he can ruff twice, with the seven and eight, driving out an honour each time."

"A double uppercut?" suggested O.O.

"Precisely," agreed the Hog. "But that, of course, requires a modicum of intelligence on the Toucan's part, for if he continues with the ♡Q the Rabbit will have no inducement to ruff a winner. To ensure the promotion he should lead the deuce, but, of course, he will never think of it, and even if he did, the Rabbit would doubtless ruff low. So, you see, the contract will be made. An injustice, on the face of it, but I will be in and you will be able to watch me instead of my having to watch them, and the good will outweigh the bad, so to speak."

"Excuse me," apologised the Rabbit, returning to the fold, "that was my City astrologer telling me which shares I should have bought yesterday. They've gone up already. With Jupiter in the ascendant, and Mars . . ."

The ♡Q from the Toucan interrupted the soliloquy.

The Hog snorted as if to say, "I told you so."

Suddenly R.R. stopped talking to himself. Dipping his left ear, his nostrils aquiver, he extracted the ♣8 and with a trembling hand placed it on the ♡Q.

The Walrus over-ruffed and played the ♠J. Rising with the ace the Toucan continued with the ♡J. Unhesitatingly, the Rabbit ruffed wtih the ♠7, driving out W.W.'s third honour and promoting the Toucan's ♠10 to set the contract.

"Well played," said Oscar the Owl.

"Brilliant," cried a junior kibitzer.

"It could only happen to me," sighed Karapet. "With eleven cards to choose from he had to pick the right one."

The Hog, who had expected the rubber to be up, wasn't amused. "Brilliant, my foot! He probably didn't know what trumps were or maybe," he jeered, "his astrologer told him that eight was today's lucky number," and with that as his parting remark, the Hog strode angrily out of the room.

The Rabbit's play was certainly out of character. He must have had some strange reason for doing the right thing, and as he drove me back home that night, I brought up the subject tactfully.

"That was an imaginative defence R.R.," I said reminding him of the hand.

The Rabbit blushed. "Yes," he agreed. "I confess that I'm rather pleased with myself, but then I recognised the situation at once. It's one of Achilles Heal's great plays. He made it in Amsterdam or it may have been in Addis Ababa. East and dummy have the same four-card suits, so East is squeezed from the start and the answer is to discard a trump. Then all is well because . . ."

"So that's what it was!" I couldn't help exclaiming. "You were discarding a trump to avoid being squeezed. But then why did you discard the eight and not the deuce?"

"Though it didn't matter in this case," explained the Rabbit, "with three trumps it is correct to signal by playing high-low. In the long run," he added "it pays to play correctly."

PROBLEMS TOO EASY TO SOLVE

"Would you like me to show you a double-dummy problem?" asked the Hideous Hog.

We assured him that we wouldn't.

"Here you are then," he went on, and diving into his pocket he produced a crumpled letter which he proceeded to smooth out. "Don't worry," he prattled on as he scribbled, "it's not one of those problems where you make a slam by jettisoning all the aces and throwing someone in with a deuce. Quite the contrary.

"Mind you," chuckled the Hog, enjoying a private joke with himself, "I had warned him more than once about those chocolate almond biscuits of his. Ha! ha!" That was clearly a reference to the Rabbit, but in what context wasn't apparent.

Dlr. West
N/S Vul:

	♠ A 10 6 5 4
	♡ 7 6 4
	◇ 10 8 3
	♣ 8 4

```
      N
   W     E
      S
```

♠ K Q 2
♡ A K 5
◇ K Q 6
♣ Q J 10 9

West	North	East	South
Pass	Pass	1♡	Dble.
Pass	1♠	Pass	2NT
Pass	3NT		

"West leads the ♡Q which you allow to hold. Next come the ♡2. Proceed." The Hog sat back.

Oscar the Owl was the first to speak.

"If we could count on the spades for five tricks we would have seven on top, but since this is a problem, East doubtless has four spades to the jack and . . ."

"Don't look for snags," said H.H., breaking in. "East hasn't got four spades and every card is right, just where you want it," chortled the Hog "that's what makes it so unusual a double-dummy problem."

"So we can reckon on five spades," resumed O.O. "There's no time to drive out the ♣AK, but we can easily set up a diamond for our eighth trick, and if East has the ◇A . . ."

"He has," interjected the Hog.

". . . he will soon be squirming."

"Exactly," agreed Peregrine the Penguin, taking up the analysis. "After two hearts and five spades East is down to six cards. He must retain the ♣AK and two hearts. Otherwise we can play on clubs. That leaves room for only two diamonds, so we use our one chance of playing from dummy to lead a diamond. We score the ◇K and lead the ◇6, fetching the ace. The ◇Q now becomes our ninth trick."

"It's just possible," cautioned O.O., "that West has the ♣K. Third in hand at favourable vulnerability, East might still open on . . ."

"Why don't you play on?" interrupted the Hog "you'll never find yourselves in an easier contract."

The Owl nodded. "Very well," he said. "Call the cards. Peregrine and I'll count the tricks."

Looking every inch a penguin in his black alpaca jacket, snow-white shirt and orange bow tie, P.P. began to call the cards.

"The ♠K."

"The ♠7 from West, the ♠3 from East," said H.H.

"The ♠Q," continued the Penguin.

"The ♠J from West," said the Hog.

The Owl and the Penguin looked perplexed. "I don't like it. It's too easy," murmured O.O.

"Much too easy," echoed P.P. "With two entries to dummy we can make certain of two diamonds, regardless of the ♣K — or er anything else."

Detecting a slight hesitation in P.P.'s voice, the Hog hastened to reassure him. "Without a doubt," the Hog told him, "you can make certain of two diamond tricks. I've already told you that everything is right."

"You know," ventured Timothy the Toucan, who had joined our

table, "I believe that even I could make this contract."

"Play on," commanded the Hog with an imperious gesture.

"I overtake the ♠Q with the ♠A and lead a . . ."

"The ♣3 from East" announced H.H., smiling broadly as he filled in the diagram.

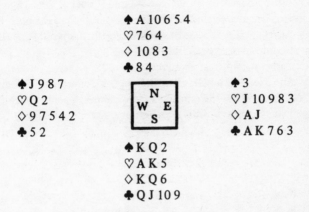

A couple of minutes later O.O. and P.P. conceded defeat. Declarer had seven tricks — three spades, two hearts and two diamonds — but in no way could he make any more.

The Hog was in his element. "Didn't I tell you that it was a double-dummy problem? If you look at all four hands you'll never find a way of going down, and yet, against that defence, who wouldn't?

"The beauty of it is that it's so simple," pursued the Hog. "A moment's thought will show you that the ♠J on the ♠Q should be an automatic false card. If, as here, declarer has three spades, East will show out and the ♠J will be picked up on the marked finesse. On the other hand, if declarer has two spades only, he cannot bring the suit in anyway, so sacrificing the jack will cost at most one trick. And, of course, West needs no crystal to see how much declarer would like a second entry in dummy and how irresistible will be the temptation to overtake his ♠Q."

"It's a brilliant defence," agreed O.O., "and yet, as you say, it's simple when you think of it. I congratulate you, H.H."

"I'll second that. Congratulations," said P.P. admiringly.

"Me?" the Hog sounded surprised. "But I was only kibitzing."

"Who, then, was West?" The Owl, the Penguin and the Toucan all spoke at once.

"The Rueful Rabbit," replied the Hog, puffing contentedly at the Toucan's cigar. "You wonder, no doubt, how so short-sighted a player came to hit on so far-sighted a defence. The explanation is as simple as the play itself. It's those chocolate almond biscuits. They're sticky, and the ♠J was firmly stuck to the ♠8. The Rabbit didn't know that he had it until he began to detach the ♠8 and suddenly the jack appeared in its place. No one was more surprised to see it than the poor Rabbit. Mind you," added the Hog, "it could happen to anyone — if they ate chocolate almond biscuits."

The barman came to clear the table. "Yes, yes, you can take it away," the Hog told him, pointing to the letter with the diagram. "It's from a nephew," he explained. "He's expecting a birthday present and sends me his new address. I've been trying to lose it all day."

THE GUARDIAN ANGEL WORKS OVERTIME

Someone ordered another bottle of Bollinger and soon the Hog was in full spate again.

"That Rabbit, you know, bears a charmed life. But then he's got the best Guardian Angel in the dirty tricks department," he added enviously, writing on the back of the bar bill.

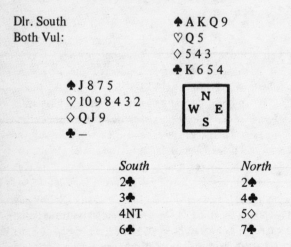

Dlr. South
Both Vul:

♠ A K Q 9
♡ Q 5
◇ 5 4 3
♣ K 6 5 4

♠ J 8 7 5
♡ 10 9 8 4 3 2
◇ Q J 9
♣ —

South	North
2♣	2♠
3♣	4♣
4NT	5◇
6♣	7♣

"You lead the ♡10, low from dummy, the ♡7 from partner and the ♡A from declarer," began the Hog. "Next comes the ♣A, a club to dummy's ♣K, East following, and five more clubs. What do you keep?"

"What has East been throwing?" asked the Penguin.

The Hog told him. "After following twice, he let go the ♡6, the ♡J, the ♠2 and the ◊6, in that order."

Oscar nodded. "We can count twelve tricks — seven clubs, the ♡A, three spades and obviously the ◊A. Declarer cannot have a red king as well, for that would give him thirteen top tricks."

"Yes," agreed the Penguin, "it all fits in. East's last six cards are three spades, the ♡K and the ◊Kx. He could have two spades and the ◊Kxx, but that doesn't really matter, does it?"

"You still haven't told me what you are keeping," pointed out H.H. "Let me remind you that as you follow to the seventh club you come down to five cards. Which will they be?"

"I've kept my four spades and the ◊QJ, so I throw the ◊J," replied O.O.

"Don't tell me," cried P.P. in mock alarm, "that East has been munching chocolate almond biscuits again and now suddenly discovers the ◊A sticking to the back of the ♡K, and discards it by mistake."

"No," rejoined the Hog, "he discovers, however, and so do you, that declarer has no spade at all. In fact, the Guardian Angel has played the hand with diabolical cunning. Look at the full deal:

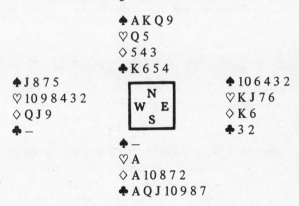

```
                    ♠ A K Q 9
                    ♡ Q 5
                    ◊ 5 4 3
                    ♣ K 6 5 4
  ♠ J 8 7 5                          ♠ 10 6 4 3 2
  ♡ 10 9 8 4 3 2        N            ♡ K J 7 6
  ◊ Q J 9           W       E        ◊ K 6
  ♣ —                   S            ♣ 3 2
                    ♠ —
                    ♡ A
                    ◊ A 10 8 7 2
                    ♣ A Q J 10 9 8 7
```

"Note that subtle 4NT bid," observed the Hog. "For the Rabbit it's merely a sign of exuberance, the normal reaction of the sub-normal player who bids 4NT because he's excited and can't think of anything else to say. But here, R.R. is only the mouth-piece of his Guardian Angel, who uses Blackwood to camouflage his void. He wouldn't invoke Blackwood with a void. So he must have a spade. That's how he intends opponents to reason."

"North," continued H.H., "was Walter the Walrus, the great points merchant, and it's hardly surprising that he called the grand slam. Mind you, I don't blame him. I blame the Guardian Angel for not making his protegé choke on one of his biscuits during so much over-bidding. However, G.A. fully made up for it in the play.

"The Rabbit," went on H.H., "had every intention of cashing the spades. That way he couldn't go more than one down and there was always the hope of bringing down the ♠J10. What he didn't realise was, that apart from the ♣K, all his clubs were higher than dummy's. The Rabbit, as you know, doesn't worry overmuch about the pips and his G.A. made sure that this wouldn't be the exception to prove the rule.

"That pseudo-squeeze was a beauty," said H.H. admiringly. "Had he been my partner I would have bought him a new harp. You saw how impossible it was for West to shed a spade. It was just as bad for East. Assuming, as he must, that declarer has one, he must keep four spades, relying on West for the ◇Q. If declarer has ◇AQ, East is genuinely squeezed — or so it seems to him. In short, both defenders are mes-merised by dummy's spades, unable to imagine that declarer has no access to them. And so, clinging on to their useless spades, they let go their precious diamonds. The G.A. waves his wand and all the Rabbit's geese turn into swans."

THE RABBIT'S PERCENTAGE PLAY

At the bar of the Griffins, the Rueful Rabbit and his friend, Timothy the Toucan were holding a council of war.

"Admittedly," the Rabbit was saying, "when it comes to what they call 'flair', we may not be as good as some of the others. But we can easily make up for it by using modern scientific weapons. Do you know, Timothy," went on R.R. in hushed tones, "that Amalya Kearse's *Bridge Conventions Complete* runs to 624 pages and there's sometimes more than one convention per page. Now if we only took up half of them . . ."

"Wouldn't it be a little confusing?" objected T.T.

"Yes," agreed R.R., "but it would confuse all alike and it would pay us in the end. What do you say?" asked the Rabbit, turning to Colin the Corgi who had joined them two glasses earlier. "Wouldn't we gain more on the swings than we lost on the roundabouts?"

"Without a doubt," agreed C.C. "After all, you need no conventions to confuse you, so you would still be playing your usual game, while your opponents, less accustomed to confusion, wouldn't feel so much at home. By and large," concluded the Corgi, "there's nothing like a thick fog to redress the imbalance of flair."

One of the first sophisticated weapons to be adopted by the partnership was South African Texas, and before long a hand tailor-made for the convention came up in a rubber in which R.R. and T.T. faced Papa the Greek and Karapet Djoulikyan, the unluckiest player in modern times — and before that too, of course.

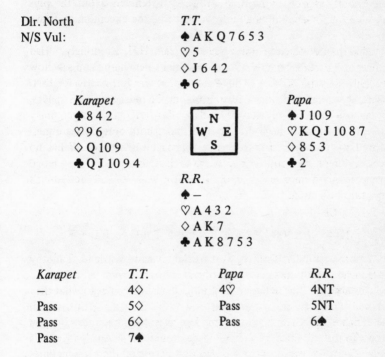

Dlr. North
N/S Vul:

T.T.
♠ A K Q 7 6 5 3
♡ 5
◊ J 6 4 2
♣ 6

Karapet
♠ 8 4 2
♡ 9 6
◊ Q 10 9
♣ Q J 10 9 4

N
W E
S

Papa
♠ J 10 9
♡ K Q J 10 8 7
◊ 8 5 3
♣ 2

R.R.
♠ —
♡ A 4 3 2
◊ A K 7
♣ A K 8 7 5 3

Karapet	T.T.	Papa	R.R.
—	4◊	4♡	4NT
Pass	5◊	Pass	5NT
Pass	6◊	Pass	6♠
Pass	7♠		

As with all transfer bids, South African Texas seeks to make the lead run up to the hand with the presumed tenaces. The variation consists in making clubs transferable to hearts and diamonds to spades. The Toucan's opening bid of 4◊ was, therefore, the equivalent of 4♠.

"With first round controls in all four suits," explained the Rabbit later, "I had to do something big. I couldn't bid seven on my own, though, in case it required a trump finesse. I mean, one doesn't want to be in a grand slam on a trump finesse, does one . . . ?"

The Toucan had no such inhibitions. He liked his singletons and it didn't occur to him that there might be a trump loser.

Karapet opened the ♡9 to the Rabbit's ace. A quick glance at dummy told R.R. that a prerequisite to the grand slam was a 3–3 trump break. Assuming such to be the case, he could see twelve winners. One more could surely be developed in clubs.

The first step was to draw trumps and that, owing to the unusual nature of the trump fit, required crossing to dummy.

What was the best way to get there? A heart ruff was dangerous because Karapet might well have started with a singleton and a ruff by him, in front of dummy, with some seemingly innocuous eight or nine, would have the effect of a deadly uppercut.

A club ruff looked more promising, and yet, if Papa had seven hearts and three spades, he could easily have a singleton club. Seeing it as the lesser risk, however, the Rabbit began by laying down the ♣A. When the Greek followed with the ♣2, the Rabbit's ears twitched and his nostrils quivered with suspicion.

What was it that he had read about the theory of restricted choice? If a player had two cards to choose from, he might play either, but if he had only one his choice was restricted. Yes, that was it.

Now would Papa play a deuce if he had a queen or a jack or a ten to spare? Of course not. If he played a true card it could only be because he had no other. Changing course, the Rabbit decided to cross to dummy by ruffing a heart and was much relieved when Karapet followed suit.

The trumps duly breaking 3–3, all that remained was to find somewhere a thirteenth trick. Fortunately, there was no immediate hurry, so while he was in the swing of it, R.R. took two more rounds of trumps. From his hand he threw two hearts, two clubs and the ◇7. Papa was in no trouble, but Karapet, having to keep as many clubs as declarer, had to let go the ◇9.

With five cards left, this was the position.

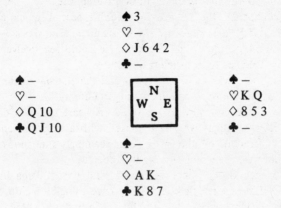

The Rabbit crossed to his hand with the ◊A and cashed the ♣K. When Papa threw on it the ♡K, he smiled. How right he had been to diagnose that ♣2 as a singleton! The smile soon turned into a frown, however, as he reflected that with all the clubs bunched in one hand it might be more difficult to set one up as his thirteenth trick. Had Karapet discarded one club or two? He couldn't be sure, but either way the clubs somehow ceased to look attractive.

The only other hope was to bring down the ◊Q. That wasn't too promising either, but it seemed to be the better percentage play. Stoically, the Rabbit cashed the ◊K and when the queen fell, it was all over.

"Extraordinary," he told me as we drove home that night, "that so careful a player as Karapet should have discarded a diamond. Of course, he couldn't tell that I had both the ace and king. That's the beauty of South African Texas. It keeps the strong hand concealed, and there's a better chance of a slip in defence.

"I'm still not sure though," went on the Rabbit, "that I was right to play on the diamonds rather than on the clubs. Pretty close, I suppose. What would you say were the odds?"

"The exact odds against bringing off a trump squeeze entirely by accident have never been worked out," I told him, "but in your case, R.R., I should say that they were no worse than 50-50."

THE RABBIT PHILOSOPHISES

"Too many people play too well these days," the Rueful Rabbit told me in confidence as we drove back together from the club, "and good play can boomerang, you know. If everyone always does the right thing, everyone else knows what it's going to be, and as in chess, there's a gambit for every move — or is it the other way? Whichever it is, the less expert player has an advantage. Now take me. How can anyone counter my moves when I often don't know where I'm moving myself?

"It's true," went on the Rabbit, "that I sometimes make mistakes, but they don't know *which* mistakes, do they? So they defend in the dark. The blind man looking for a black cat ... you know what I mean."

These philosophic reflections were prompted by a hand which came up during the last rubber of the afternoon. Timothy the Toucan was R.R.'s partner.

Dlr. South
Both Vul:

```
                    ♠ Q 10 5
                    ♡ 3
                    ◇ A K Q J 10 8 7
                    ♣ 6 4
    ♠ J 9 7                          ♠ K 4 3 2
    ♡ A J 10 9          N            ♡ 4 2
    ◇ 2              W     E          ◇ 9 6 5 4 3
    ♣ Q 10 9 3 2        S            ♣ 8 5
                    ♠ A 8 6
                    ♡ K Q 8 7 6 5
                    ◇ —
                    ♣ A K J 7
```

R.R.	Papa	T.T.	Karapet
South	West	North	East
1♡	Pass	2◇	Pass
3♣	Pass	4◇	Pass
4♡	Pass	5◇	Pass
5♠	Pass	6◇	Pass
6♡	Dble.	6♠	Dble.
6NT	Dble.	7◇	Dble.
7NT	Dble.		

There was nothing noteworthy about the opening three rounds of bidding. The first diversion was the Rabbit's 5♠, a 'waiting bid', as he explained later – waiting for something to turn up. After all, the Toucan wasn't bound to go on bidding diamonds 'til closing time. The Rabbit freely admitted that there was a case for passing 6◇ and with the Hog as partner, he would have done so without hesitation, but with Timothy it was different. He had the natural urge of the strong to protect the weak and it went against the grain to leave that poor Toucan in 6◇ facing a dummy bereft of trumps.

With Papa doubling in a voice of thunder, and even Karapet looking as if he meant it, the last two rounds of bidding were motivated by panic rather than science, and by the time the partnership found refuge in seven notrumps, it wasn't so much a question of choosing the best contract as the cheapest.

Coolly Papa surveyed the scene. With a four figure penalty in prospect, his one concern was to find the most lethal lead. A diamond was too passive. A heart was out of the question, that being declarer's six or seven card suit. So it had to be a club or a spade, and since Karapet had doubled 6♠ – presumably a cue-bid showing second round control – that seemed the obvious choice. The spade seven was the carefully selected card.

It was R.R.'s custom to play quickly to the first trick or two and to meditate later – or not at all. So he promptly inserted dummy's ♠10, captured Karapet's king with his ace and began to count his tricks. The total came to eleven, so at worst the deal would cost 500, a much better result than seemed likely during that cross-fire of machine gun doubles.

Going over to dummy with a spade, Papa's nine falling to the queen, the Rabbit hastened to release that avalanche of luscious diamonds. On the first five he threw hearts, while Papa discarded two hearts, followed by the ♣10 and ♣3, to help Karapet. The Armenian reciprocated by discarding on dummy's last two diamonds the ♡4 and ♡2, giving the Greek an exact count of the hearts. The Rabbit shed his last heart and a spade, retaining four clubs. As the last of the diamonds was called, this was the five-card end position:

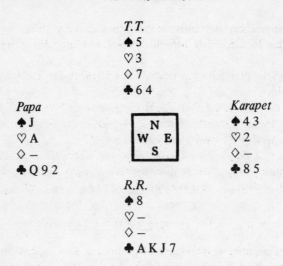

                              T.T.
                              ♠ 5
                              ♡ 3
                              ◇ 7
                              ♣ 6 4

Papa   *Karapet*
♠ J   ┌─────────┐   ♠ 4 3
♡ A   │   N   │   ♡ 2
◇ —   │ W   E │   ◇ —
♣ Q 9 2   │   S   │   ♣ 8 5
                             └─────────┘
                              R.R.
                              ♠ 8
                              ♡ —
                              ◇ —
                              ♣ A K J 7

The cold, calculated discard of the ♡4 on the previous trick had exposed
Papa to a deadly three-suit squeeze and he was now looking at Karapet
as Prometheus must have looked at the eagle pecking at his liver.
Fortunately the Rabbit didn't know and wasn't likely to guess that the
lowly ♡3 could be a threat to anyone. So, trying to look imperturbable,
Papa parted with his ♡A.

The Rabbit wasn't impressed. He had seen people throw aces and
kings before, retaining less conspicuous winners for use later, and he
didn't doubt for a moment that Papa still had the best heart. Suddenly
he had a brainwave and his ears tingled with excitement. Instead of
going two down, which once seemed such an attractive prospect, he
would do as the experts did, throw a loser on a loser and end-play
Papa, forcing him to lead a club away from his queen. That way he
would go only one down, a truly remarkable achievement on so tragic
a misfit.

The ♡3 was the ideal throw-in card and never was the Rabbit happier
to lose a trick.

It took him a little while to realise that it was a winner and he
barely noticed Papa's ♠J. For a moment he was tempted to cash his
ace-king of clubs and call it a day. It was an unworthy impulse and
he quickly suppressed it, for there was now a chance of actually making
the contract. It came down to what pundits call a percentage play.
There were two chances. The club finesse might be right or the ♠5
might be good. Since Papa had thrown all his hearts, he was clearly

guarding something and what could it be but the ♣Q! So the finesse was unlikely to succeed and the little spade was, on balance, the better chance.

"It pays to play with the odds," cried the Rabbit exultantly when the ♠5 held.

"Why did you throw that ♡4, the key to the whole hand?" fumed Papa, snarling at Karapet. "What's the use of complaining about your luck when you wantonly discard your winners?"

"When you play with me, Papa," rejoined the Armenian, shaking his head sorrowfully, "please don't double 7NT just because you have an ace — especially if you don't intend to lead it."

AN AUTO-SMOTHER PLAY

It is doubtless true, as the Hog is never tired of saying, that success at bridge is the reward for not playing badly rather than for playing well. For all that, there are results to which only a true master can aspire. A case in point was this hand which came up in the weekly duplicate at the Unicorn. As usual, most of the competitors were members of our own club, and as happens when rubber bridge players turn, for a change, to duplicate, the atmosphere was easy and relaxed. Rich men can't afford to lose money, for it makes them look foolish, but what are matchpoints to men of means?

Behind a green kipper tie, criss-crossed with wide orange zigzags, sat Papa the Greek, coolly appraising the kibitzers. Were they good enough to watch him? Sitting opposite was Karapet the Unlucky, looking resigned to the misfortunes which he knew to be in store for him. When all was said and done, why should they be any worse than those he had left behind? Facing Timothy the Toucan, bouncing happily, if a little unsteadily, in his chair, was the Rueful Rabbit, sipping Cherry Brandy and munching his favourite chocolate almond biscuits. The stage was set for an ordinary hand with an extraordinary sequel.

Dlr. West   ♠ A 3 2
Both Vul: ♡ K Q J
                             ◊ A K 3 2
                             ♣ Q 10 8

```
        N
    W       E
        S
```

                             ♠ Q J 10 9
                             ♡ 4 3 2
                             ◊ J 5 4
                             ♣ A K J

T.T.	Karapet	R.R.	Papa
West	North	East	South
Pass	1◊	Pass	1♠
Pass	2NT	Pass	3◊
Pass	3♠	Pass	4♠

A purist might argue that 3NT was the obvious contract on the combined hands and that Papa had no reason to bid 3◊, much less to call the game in spades on a known 4-3 fit.

Replying to this criticism in the post-mortem, Papa explained that, with nothing in the red suits, he saw no need to run needless risks, and with so much high-card strength he could easily afford the luxury of a 4-2 trump break. The fact that in a spade contract he would have the limelight as declarer was, of course, purely incidental.

The Toucan led the ♡A, followed by the ♡9 to dummy's king. Papa crossed to his hand with a club to take the finesse in trumps and ran the ♠Q. It held. So did the jack, both defenders following. The Greek drew the inescapable conclusion. With ♠Kxx West would have naturally covered the jack, if not the queen, so clearly the trumps were divided 4-2, in accordance with the odds.

Papa was prepared for it and at rubber bridge or in a match it wouldn't have mattered, for the contract was in no danger. But with matchpoint scoring, the situation was radically different. Other Souths, lacking Papa's finesse, would doubtless bid a crude unsophisticated 3NT, and with ten certain tricks, their side would score 630, maybe even 660, though that would require a favourable diamond break and correct timing. Playing in spades, the score at other tables would be

620, declarer losing a spade, a heart and a diamond. To do likewise would bring a poor result. Was it possible to do better? Having lost a heart already, which of his two other unavoidable losers could Papa avoid?

There was one chance. If West had the same distribution as he did and East had the ♢Q, it would be possible to produce this three-card ending:

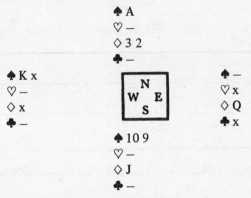

Now a diamond would put East on play and whether he exited with the thirteenth heart or the thirteenth club, West would be forced to under-ruff or to throw his king in the jaws of dummy's ace.

An added attraction to this line of play was that if it didn't succeed, nothing would be lost. If West ruffed, while Papa stripped the hand, it would be with a winning trump and ten tricks would still be there.

At trick six, Papa led a diamond to dummy's ace, then a club to his hand and another diamond to the king. This way, even had West started with a singleton diamond, he could have only ruffed a loser. The last club was cashed and now came dummy's heart, the penultimate hurdle. Alas, not only did the Toucan ruff, he cashed the ♢Q, the Rabbit discarding a heart, and continued with the thirteenth club.

His cheeks a deep magenta, his ears twitching guiltily, the Rabbit ruffed with the ♠K. This was the full deal:

```
                    ♠ A 3 2
                    ♡ K Q J
                    ◇ A K 3 2
                    ♣ Q 10 8
    ♠ 8 7 6                              ♠ K 5 4
    ♡ A 9              N                 ♡ 10 8 7 6 5
    ◇ Q 10 8 6      W     E              ◇ 9 7
    ♣ 7 4 3 2          S                 ♣ 9 6 5
                    ♠ Q J 10 9
                    ♡ 4 3 2
                    ◇ J 5 4
                    ♣ A K J
```

"You can't have that king. It isn't true. Look again," cried Papa in anguish.

"I didn't mean to revoke. I couldn't see. That is, I wouldn't er . . ." dithered the Rabbit.

"I suppose it's those chocolate almond biscuits again," said the Owl reprovingly.

"No, no," protested the Rabbit. "It's nothing to do with the biscuits. When I sorted my hand I thought that I had the ♣K, but when I parted with my second diamond the spades were next to the clubs, both black suits together, and in moving the hearts in between the king must have got caught up in the wrong suit — only for a second, mind you, but then it was too late. It was careless of me, of course, but fortunately it made no difference. I mean, I would have made my king anyway, wouldn't I?"

DECLARER'S MARKET

"How very odd," observed Oscar the Owl, "on board 27 both sides made game in spades."

"I've only got the hands, not the bidding," rejoined Peregrine the Penguin, "but I can't see why either side should contemplate game in spades on this lot."

A meeting of senior kibitzers had been summoned at the close of the annual match between the Dionysians and the Bacchanalians to deal with the customary spate of protests. The results were impossible. Therefore the hands must have been misboarded. That was the usual argument.

We found no irregularities in the first half of the match — except, of course, in the bidding and in the play. Board 27, however, required investigation and this is what transpired.

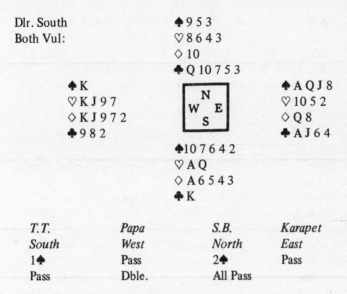

Dlr. South
Both Vul:

♠ 9 5 3
♡ 8 6 4 3
◇ 10
♣ Q 10 7 5 3

♠ K
♡ K J 9 7
◇ K J 9 7 2
♣ 9 8 2

♠ A Q J 8
♡ 10 5 2
◇ Q 8
♣ A J 6 4

♠ 10 7 6 4 2
♡ A Q
◇ A 6 5 4 3
♣ K

T.T.	Papa	S.B.	Karapet
South	West	North	East
1♠	Pass	2♠	Pass
Pass	Dble.	All Pass	

Papa led the ♣9. Karapet went up with the ♣A, dropping declarer's ♣K, and returned a heart. The Toucan, his red nose aglow with excitement, bounced in his chair. Ruffing was the best part of his game and he was now in his element.

Going up with the ♡A, he cashed the ◇A, ruffed a diamond, cashed the ♣Q, discarding his ♡Q, and ruffed a heart. A third diamond, ruffed in dummy, was over-ruffed by Karapet who persisted with another heart.

The Toucan ruffed and continued with a fourth diamond on which Papa played the ◇K, a fateful card as was to emerge later. This was again ruffed in dummy with the ♠9 and over-ruffed by Karapet with the ♠Q.

Shutting his eyes, the Armenian tried to visualise the distribution. Slowly every card came into view.

On T.T.'s ruffs and discards Papa was marked with four hearts and three clubs. His ◇K on the fourth round indicated four diamonds. Therefore he had two trumps. It followed that the Toucan remained with the king and a low spade and the last two diamonds.

All that Karapet had to do was to force T.T. for the last time with
a club. If he exited with a diamond, as seemed likely, Karapet would
ruff, lay down the ♠A, dropping the ♠K, and leave Papa to score the
last trick by ruffing a club.

As he led his ♣J the Armenian came close to not looking lugubrious.

Timothy the Toucan ruffed gleefully, for he could now see a way
of going only one down. A splendid result. What he did next didn't
matter much, but the ♣10 seemed as good as anything else.

Papa's ♠K came as a surprise. Declarer's fate was sealed anyway,
but Karapet was taking no chances. If, by some mischance, Papa
played a trump, Karapet would have to overtake and concede a club.
So, to make assurance doubly sure, he overtook the ♠K and led his
last club for the Greek to ruff.

Alas, Papa had no trump to ruff with. No sooner had the Toucan
gathered his eighth trick with dummy's ♣10, than Papa and Karapet
were at each other's throats.

"Why didn't you leave me on play with my ♠K to cash my winning
diamond?" cried Papa.

"Because you told me that you didn't have it. Your ◇K expressly
denied . . ."

"That was to give you a count, to show you that we had no diamond
losers, so that you could underlead your ♠A instead of playing that
crazy ♣J. But, anyway, that's beside the point. If you really thought
that I could have another trump — which would put the Toucan's bidding on a level with your play — why didn't you let me cash my ♡K?"

"Just in case you er didn't, that is . . ." Karapet knew that he was no
longer on firm ground.

"What!" roared Papa, "you thought that I might make a mistake?
Me! It's an outrage."

This was the remarkable bidding sequence in the other room.

Ch. Ch.	H.H.	W.W.	R.R.
South	*West*	*North*	*East*
1♠	Pass	Pass	4♠
Dble.	Pass	Pass	Redble.

An explanation was sought from the parties concerned and this is what
came to light.

Charlie the Chimp, sitting South, was discussing, as usual, the
previous hand.

"When your partner bid 1♠," he was saying, "I was marked with a doubleton, so . . ."

"It's your bid," said Walter the Walrus, the Hideous Hog and two young kibitzers.

"Yes, I know, 1♠. Besides," went on the Chimp, "if I had the ♡A . . ."

"No bid," said the Hog.

"Keep quiet," roared the Walrus.

Dazed and dizzy with the chatter, the Rabbit counted his points and found more than enough for a raise to 4♠. That he was raising the wrong man didn't dawn on him 'til later.

Before redoubling, the Rabbit asked the Walrus politely what he understood by the double. "Take-out or penalty?"

"Penalty, of course," bellowed W.W., "what d'you suppose I can take him out into?"

The Chimp led a trump. "Lead out of turn, I think," burbled R.R., who was about to table his hand.

"You may not have come across it before," observed the Hog acidly, "but it's not unusual for the opening lead to be made by the player sitting on declarer's left. And now," went on H.H., "if your bid and your redouble are justified, you should make at least two overtricks."

Beads of perspiration stood out on the Rabbit's forehead as the enormity of his gaffe became clear to him. Single-handed, on that one board he was about to lose the match.

And yet, they were 21 IMPs up at half-time. If he could only get out of it for, say, three down, 1600 or so, maybe they would still have a chance.

Steadying his nerves with a chocolate almond biscuit, he won the first trick in dummy with the ♠K and crossed to his hand with the ♣A to take three more rounds of trumps. With five tricks stacked neatly in front of him, he felt better, and while he still had the chance, he led a heart towards dummy.

The Chimp detached the ♡A, then the ♡Q, but it didn't seem to make any difference. Somehow his tricks had ebbed away and whatever he did, he could only score his long trump and his two aces.

The Rabbit doesn't know to this day what happened.

The Walrus wasn't surprised. "With my miserable two points I expected a slam," was his only comment.

"No doubt your other pair will bid it," snorted H.H.

A RASPBERRY FOR THE RABBIT

"I love Paris," said the Rabbit enthusiastically as we sat reminiscing over a recent visit. "Those beautiful brioches, the Louvre and palaces, the Beaujolais and shows, the shops and the Champs Elysées.

"But there's another side to it, you know. Take the traffic. It isn't just that they drive on the wrong side of the road, for they all do that abroad anyway, but they seem to have the death wish. Why else should they keep driving at each other? And I must say I don't like their funny French cards. Why can't they have the same as we do?"

A creature of habit, the Rabbit liked to stick to the things he knew and to play bridge with people who knew him. He looked rueful and forlorn when we strolled into a club and found no Hog or Papa to revile him and make him feel at home.

We didn't have to wait long before a table was up. R.R. promptly cut in, while I decided to get the feel of things by kibitzing a young man who had been introduced to me as Andorra's top international.

This was the first hand.

Dlr. North
Vul: Neither

♠ Q 8
♡ 8 7 4
◇ A J
♣ A Q 10 8 7 5

```
        N
   W         E        R.R.
        S
```

Andorran
♠ A 10 6 3
♡ A K J 10 9 2
◇ 2
♣ 9 2

North	South
1♣	1♡
2♣	2♠
4♡	4NT
5♡	6♡

The auction was straightforward and there was nothing much wrong with the contract.

West led the ◊5, removing a precious entry from dummy, and now the play became more interesting.

How could declarer give himself the best chance?

The Andorran began by laying down the ♡A. Then he led the ♣9 to dummy's ♣Q.

That was surely the right play. If the finesse lost, the only hope would be a 2-2 trump break, providing a trump entry to dummy's clubs which could be established — assuming the likely 3-2 split — after one ruff.

Should the club finesse succeed, declarer would take the finesse in trumps. If it failed, dummy's third trump would serve as an entry to the clubs. Finding East with three trumps would be more embarrassing, but declarer would still have every chance of bringing home his contract by losing one trick only in spades. The ♠K could be right or the ♠J might come down after a ruff.

The ♣Q held the third trick, East following with the ♣J. The Andorran paused, but only for a moment. With the ♣10 in dummy, he had no reason to fear a 4-1 break. The trump finesse would put him in the same happy position as before and he proceeded to take it.

West produced the ♡Q and returned a diamond. The Andorran ruffed and took the marked finesse against the ♣K. With the ♡8 as a certain entry, he would set up three winners in clubs to take care of the spades.

On the ♣10, however, the Rabbit, who was sitting East, played the ♣K. His left ear twitched uneasily, while a rich red glow suffused his plump pink cheeks.

This was the deal in full:

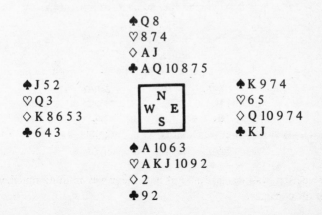

```
                    ♠ Q 8
                    ♡ 8 7 4
                    ◊ A J
                    ♣ A Q 10 8 7 5
  ♠ J 5 2                              ♠ K 9 7 4
  ♡ Q 3              N                 ♡ 6 5
  ◊ K 8 6 5 3     W     E              ◊ Q 10 9 7 4
  ♣ 6 4 3            S                 ♣ K J
                    ♠ A 10 6 3
                    ♡ A K J 10 9 2
                    ◊ 2
                    ♣ 9 2
```

There was a gasp from the kibitzers. Andorra's top international looked at R.R. in awe. He was deeply impressed.

"Magnificent deception," he said admiringly. "*Spectaculaire*. Have we not encountered together before? At the Championat . . ."

"No, no," broke in the Rabbit hastily. "I wasn't there. I mean, it wasn't me you encountered."

He was immensely flattered to be mistaken for someone else, but for how many deals could he hope to keep up the deception?

"You played so naturally," said an elderly kibitzer. "What gave you the idea? Was it because declarer laid down the ♡A before testing the clubs? Did that suggest that your partner had the doubleton queen? A brilliant analysis, Monsieur, I congratulate you."

How could the Rabbit tell them that he had been himself the victim of deception, mistaking the ♣J for the ♣K? Those funny French cards had got him into a muddle.

"Oh dear," he sighed, "I'd like a liqueur, a Framboise d'Alsace, like I had for lunch at the Tour d'Argent. What is the French for framboise?"

MYSTERY OF THE MISSING ACE

"It isn't *his* good luck, it's *my* bad luck," protested Karapet, the Free Armenian, indignantly. No one seemed to realise that he was much the unluckiest man since Job. At times, he suspected that people were too selfish to care.

The Rueful Rabbit and his friend, Timothy the Toucan, had won our weekly duplicate at the Unicorn and in the general view their success wasn't entirely due to their skill.

"That Rabbit is much too lucky," said Walter the Walrus. "If I had his luck . . ."

The Hideous Hog, who joined us at the bar as the results were being announced, nodded in agreement. "Yes," he said, "it was fortunate for him that I couldn't get back in time to play, but when all's said and done, all the other competitors had the same advantage. Even you, Karapet. Admittedly you were unlucky to be playing with Papa, though you brought it on yourself, mind you, but did you have to give the winners four tops on three boards? Poor Papa! Ha! ha!"

Everyone was talking about that last set of boards on which Papa the Greek and Karapet faced R.R. and T.T.

This was the first one.

Dlr. North
N/S Vul:

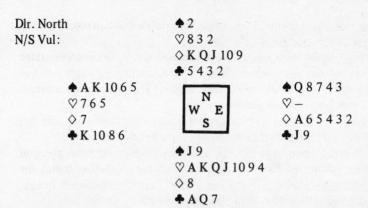

```
                        ♠ 2
                        ♡ 8 3 2
                        ◇ K Q J 10 9
                        ♣ 5 4 3 2
  ♠ A K 10 6 5              N              ♠ Q 8 7 4 3
  ♡ 7 6 5               W       E          ♡ –
  ◇ 7                       S              ◇ A 6 5 4 3 2
  ♣ K 10 8 6                                ♣ J 9
                        ♠ J 9
                        ♡ A K Q J 10 9 4
                        ◇ 8
                        ♣ A Q 7
```

Though East–West can make 6♠, it is difficult for them to come into
the bidding. After North's pass, South has little fear of missing a slam
by pre-empting and 4♡ was everywhere the final contract.

What would be the par result? The verdict of leading kibitzers was,
that though declarer has four losers, inspired play can bring home the
contract even against inspired defence.

To preserve communications, in the event of a 3-0 trump break,
declarer refuses to ruff a second spade. West switches to a trump,
but South has time to lead a diamond and he can draw trumps, ending
with the ♡8 in dummy.

East counters by refusing to go up with the ◇A. Declarer plays a
second diamond, discarding a club, and West ruffs. The ◇A is still out
and South remains with a losing club.

Declarer, however, has the last word. Before leading his diamond,
he draws a second round of trumps. As before, East holds up his ◇A,
then West ruffs. But now, having no trump left, he is end-played.
A spade, presenting declarer with a ruff and discard, or a club into the
AQ yields South his tenth trick.

When the board reached Papa's table there was a slight variation in
the bidding and a more important one in the play.

T.T.	*Karapet*	*R.R.*	*Papa*
West	*North*	*East*	*South*
–	Pass	Pass	4♡
Pass	Pass	Dble.	

Looking for a cheap sacrifice, at favourable vulnerability, R.R. doubled for a take out. Having passed originally, he felt that there was no room for a misunderstanding.

The Toucan, on the other hand, reasoned that a partner who couldn't bid at the one level, wouldn't want to compete at the level of five. So, bouncing excitedly in his chair, his long red nose aglow, he left the double in, expecting a luscious penalty.

Like all other Wests in the room, T.T. opened the ♠K and continued with the ace. Papa, of course, was too good a player to ruff.

At trick three, the Toucan switched to his singleton diamond, hoping to find the Rabbit with the ace. After all, he had to have something for his double.

It came as a severe disappointment to him to see the Rabbit's ◇2. Papa continued with a second diamond, but again R.R. played low. The Toucan couldn't make out why no one had the ◇A and seeing Papa throw a club, he half suspected him of revoking. So he ruffed and exited with a trump.

There was nothing the Greek could do to avoid the unsuccessful club finesse — and a cold bottom.

"What a fiendishly clever defence!" said a young kibitzer who was sitting behind the Toucan. "If you go up with the ace of diamonds, R.R., as I saw them do at other tables, declarer ruffs the next diamond with an honour, and draws trumps, ending in dummy. That hold up..."

"What hold up?" asked the Rabbit, thoroughly bemused. "Which ◇A?"

As he was about to replace his hand in the board, he noticed that a card had been left behind in the east slot. "Belongs to me, I suppose," he murmured softly, picking up the ◇A.

THE RABBIT'S SACRIFICE

It's all very well," said the Rabbit, sipping his favourite cherry brandy as we sat chatting after dinner in the Griffins bar, "but difficult plays are much simpler really than the easy ones. I mean, one can read books and study smother plays and squeezes and get used to throwing aces and trumps away, but can you always be sure that the ♡8 is master or that there are no more clubs out? At times," went on R.R., "I can get a count on opponents' hands and yet retain legitimate doubts about my own, if you see what I mean."

The Rabbit's reflections were prompted by a brilliantly played grand slam during the afternoon session. The momentous deal found

the Rueful Rabbit and Timothy the Toucan facing Papa the Greek and
Karapet, the Free Armenian, the unluckiest player North of the Equa-
tor – and South of it, too, of course.

The Griffins, much against their better judgment, were trying out
goulashes. After a throw-in, the cards, without being shuffled, are
dealt in three lots of three, then four, or else twice five at a time,
then three. Exotic distributions abound and this deal was no exception.

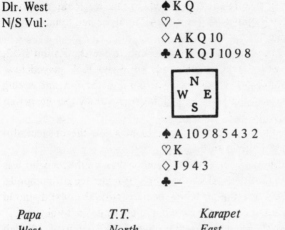

Dlr. West   ♠ K Q
N/S Vul: ♡ –
                   ◊ A K Q 10
                   ♣ A K Q J 10 9 8

                   ♠ A 10 9 8 5 4 3 2
                   ♡ K
                   ◊ J 9 4 3
                   ♣ –

Papa	*T.T.*	*Karapet*	*R.R.*
West	*North*	*East*	*South*
Pass	2♣	Pass	2♠
3♡	4♡	Dble.	4♠
5♡	6♠	Pass	Pass
7♡	Pass	Pass	7♠

The final contract was due to a misunderstanding. The Toucan felt that
he had done enough by soaring to 6♠ with only two prospective
trumps, and if they were going to end up in 7♠, he didn't want the
responsibility for bidding it.

The Rabbit, on the other hand, took the view that if the Toucan
couldn't double 7♡, neither could he, while if T.T. didn't mind 6♠,
it would make a difference of only one trick to bid 7♠.

Papa led the ♡Q, and as dummy went down, R.R. counted nineteen
tricks. A recount, allowing for the heart ruff at trick one, brought the
tally to twenty.

The Rabbit duly ruffed the ♡Q and was startled to see Karapet
drop the ♡A. Now why should he do a thing like that? After all, he

couldn't know that R.R.'s ♡K was bare. Papa jettisoned aces because he was brilliant or at least he thought so, but Karapet wasn't, so the only explanation was that his ♡A was as bare as R.R.'s ♡K. If so, Papa had been dealt eleven hearts.

"An unthinkable thought," murmured R.R. to himself, "and yet it could account for his bidding. First he passes, next minute he's in 7♡. Ridiculous, but then in a goulash anything could happen."

If Papa had a trump, all would be well. If not, R.R. would have to perform a multiple Grand Coup and kill winners to dispose of losers. Fortunately, the Rabbit had studied the technique and felt confident that he could handle the situation pretty well. He had twenty tricks and he needed thirteen, so he would have to reduce his winners by seven.

The first step was to ruff a club. Papa followed. Next came a spade on which Papa discarded a heart. The Rabbit had expected as much, but he wasn't unduly depressed for now he would have a chance to show what he could do.

Ruffing another club, R.R. noted that Papa had no more. That left him with one card which wasn't a heart, a club or a spade. The Rabbit deduced that it was probably a diamond and that Karapet would, therefore, have four diamonds. Consequently, dummy had four entries and R.R. could go on killing winners for some time without let or hindrance. The entire deal was an open book.

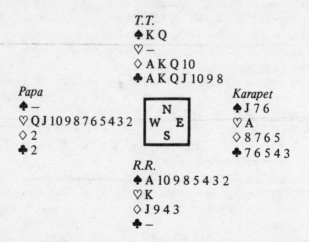

Three times the Rabbit crossed to dummy with diamonds, ruffing clubs

on the way back. This left

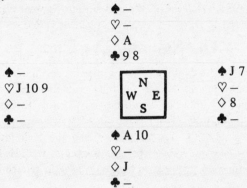

```
                ♠ —
                ♡ —
                ◇ A
                ♣ 9 8
♠ —                             ♠ J 7
♡ J 10 9      ┌─────────┐       ♡ —
◇ —           │   N     │       ◇ 8
♣ —           │ W   E   │       ♣ —
              │   S     │
              └─────────┘
                ♠ A 10
                ♡ —
                ◇ J
                ♣ —
```

The ◇A provided the vital entry for a quintuple Grand Coup. "Why did you push them into a grand slam?" cried Karapet in anguish. "You could have shut them out early on or left them in 6♠, maybe even 4♠. It was sheer sadism."

"How could I guess," retorted Papa with dignity, "that at unfavourable vulnerability they would choose to sacrifice at that level?"

No more was heard at the Griffins about goulashes for a long time to come.

As for the Guardian Angel, he appeared to be strictly impartial — unscrupulous and ruthless against all alike. But would he exert his magic the same way if H.H. and R.R. were on the same side? This, as the Hog would be the first to admit, was rarely the case when they were partners. But what if they were in the same team?

I looked up the records.

CHAPTER FOUR

The Salamander Cup

THE RABBIT LEARNS AMERICAN

In the first match of the season the Pterodactyls met the Salamanders, donors of the Cup which bears their name, the most cherished trophy in clubland.

Foreseeing the unforeseeable, the sole constant feature of this event, the committee insisted that only our Senior Kibitzer, Oscar the Owl, should be allowed to deal, and that the Rabbit should be barred from replacing the cards in the slots, even his own. There had been too many accidents in the past.

The Toucan, who had been excited for days at being chosen to play for the Pterodactyls, overslept and missed the first part of the match, his place as R.R.'s partner being taken by a distinguished visitor from the States.

"What's been happening?" asked T.T. breathlessly, bouncing in at halftime.

"You've had a 1700 swing in your favour on the last board," replied the Owl. "Game to the Pterodactyls in both rooms. Here you are," he added, taking out the curtain cards for T.T. to see the full deal:

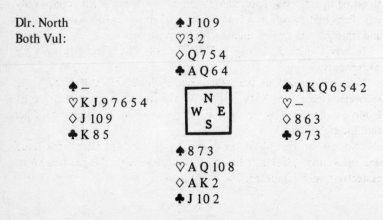

```
Dlr. North              ♠ J 10 9
Both Vul:               ♡ 3 2
                        ◇ Q 7 5 4
                        ♣ A Q 6 4
    ♠ —                           ♠ A K Q 6 5 4 2
    ♡ K J 9 7 6 5 4        N      ♡ —
    ◇ J 10 9            W     E   ◇ 8 6 3
    ♣ K 8 5                S      ♣ 9 7 3
                        ♠ 8 7 3
                        ♡ A Q 10 8
                        ◇ A K 2
                        ♣ J 10 2
```

Sitting South, the Rabbit became declarer in 4♡ redoubled after this sequence.

Papa	American	Karapet	R.R.
West	North	East	South
—	Pass	3♠	4♡
Dble.	Pass	Pass	Redble.

"But that's absurd!" exclaimed the Toucan. "No sane South would bid 4♡, let alone redouble, and neither would R.R."

"On the contrary," rejoined O.O., with an inscrutable smile, "the bidding cannot be faulted. Neither can the play, nor the defence, nor for that matter, the opening lead."

Seeing the Toucan's look of bewilderment, the Owl explained.

"As you know our Rabbit is no linguist. Having said No Bid all his life, it didn't occur to him that an American would say Pass. To the Rabbit it sounded like 1♡. Over Karapet's 3♠ he felt too good for a simple raise to 4♡, but he was cramped for space. Happily, Papa's double solved the problem.

"It wasn't 'til Papa led the ◊J and the American began to table the dummy that the awesome truth dawned on him.

"Mind you," went on O.O., "the Greek was very sympathetic. Had they been playing ordinary money bridge, he declared, he would insist on throwing the hand in. In a match, however, one had a duty, an obligation . . ."

"Well, as you can see," pursued the Owl, "the contract is unbeatable. It's virtually Rabbit-proof. He grabbed his six winners in the minors, finessing in clubs en route, and exited with a spade. With trumps only left, Papa had to ruff and lead a trump. Three times he was end-played and finished making just three of his seven trumps."

It was a minute or two before Timothy the Toucan caught up with events.

"What happened in the other room?" he asked, still dizzy as he recovered from the shock. "Did you say we made game there, too? I don't quite see how. Even if someone doubled 2♠, where did East find the eighth trick?"

"No, no, no one played in spades," explained the Owl. "The hand was once more played in hearts, this time with the Hog sitting West, as declarer, in 2♡ doubled. The bidding was:

H.H.	W.W.	S.B.	Ch. Ch.
West	North	East	South
—	Pass	1♠	Dble.
2♡	Dble.		

Oscar the Owl went on to unfold the story.

The Secretary Bird asked Charlie the Chimp what he understood by his partner's double of 2♡.

"Co-operative," replied the Chimp, "showing at least 8–9 points, but no long suit." Thereupon S.B. passed with a cunning look. So did Charlie the Chimp looking even more cunning. The Professor of Bio-Sophistry hoped to end up defending a minor suit contract. The Chimp, expecting a fruity penalty, intended all along to leave in the double.

One could hardly blame the Walrus for opening a spade. The Hog cashed the ♠AKQ, discarding diamonds, ruffed a diamond and exited with a club. This ran up to the Chimp's ♣10 and back came a diamond.

Of course, another club would have been better, but Charlie the Chimp placed the Hog with six hearts and four clubs and he wanted to prevent him from setting up the fourth club.

The Hog ruffed again and exited with a club. If only the Walrus had cashed the ♣A, the contract would have still been beaten, but he, too, placed H.H. with four clubs and when he returned another diamond, the Hog was home. The ruff brought him his sixth trick and he was left with ♡KJ97, and above all, the ♣K as an invaluable exit card.

"A co-operative double, a co-operative defence," murmured Colin the Corgi in that mocking tone which endeared him so much to us all.

"On reflection," the Rueful Rabbit was heard to say as he went in for the second half, "the Americans have got something. There's a lot to be said for 'Pass', you know. I mean 'No Bid' is so, so uninformative, isn't it?"

THE THIRD MAN

In the next round for the Salamander Cup, the Pterodactyls met the Dinosaurs and to this day Papa claims that the match was won for the Pterodactyls, single-handed, by Charlie the Chimp, who was kibitzing for the Dinosaurs.

At halftime, the Dinosaurs, captained by Papa the Greek, were 600 up. A succession of small flat hands, including two throw-ins, followed in the second half, and when the last board was placed on the table,

kibitzers and players alike saw little chance for the Pterodactyls. This
was the last board.

Dlr. North
Both Vul:

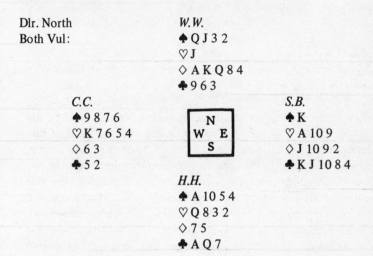

```
                      W.W.
                      ♠ Q J 3 2
                      ♡ J
                      ◇ A K Q 8 4
                      ♣ 9 6 3
C.C.                                        S.B.
♠ 9 8 7 6                 N                 ♠ K
♡ K 7 6 5 4          W         E            ♡ A 10 9
◇ 6 3                     S                 ◇ J 10 9 2
♣ 5 2                                       ♣ K J 10 8 4
                      H.H.
                      ♠ A 10 5 4
                      ♡ Q 8 3 2
                      ◇ 7 5
                      ♣ A Q 7
```

In one room, the Hog and Walter the Walrus, for the Pterodactyls,
faced Colin the Corgi and the Emeritus Professor of Bio-Sophistry,
known as the Secretary Bird. In the other room, Timothy the Toucan
and the Rueful Rabbit opposed Papa and Karapet.

Looking at the diagram, it may appear strange that either North–South
pair should bid a slam. Psychology and tactics, however, proved decisive.

As soon as the Walrus opened the bidding, the Hog could see that a
game would present no difficulty either in the bidding or in the play.
So, to give the Pterodactyls a chance, he had to shoot 6♠. A good
contract being useless, only a bad one could be good.

Papa felt certain that, at the score, the Hog would bid the slam, so
he did likewise. If it failed, it wouldn't matter for the result would be
the same in both rooms. But if there was a play for it, however remote,
he couldn't afford not to be in it.

This was the sequence in the Hog's room:

W.W.	H.H.
North	*South*
1◇	1♠
3♠	4♡
5◇	6♠

Explaining the auction to a junior, the Owl pointed out that, para-
doxically, the textbook response of 1♡ on the South hand would be,
in this case, unprepared. The Walrus might have four spades, and if
so, he would end up as declarer. To guard against this risk and to shut
out 1♠, H.H. had to bid it himself.

Over 3♠ a cue-bid of 4♡ was mere routine. After all, he didn't
want a heart lead.

Colin the Corgi led the ♠9. The Hog played low from dummy and
seeing S.B.'s ♠K, obviously a singleton, pursed his lips. It boded ill
for the prospects of a 3–3 break in diamonds and it made it prohibitive
to ruff two hearts in dummy. Even with the club finesse right, only
ten tricks were visible.

Smoothly the Corgi followed low to a heart at trick two, allowing
the Secretary Bird to win. A club came back. The Hog negotiated
successfully the unavoidable finesse and continued with the ♡Q.
The Professor had shown up with two kings and an ace already and
was hardly likely to have the ♡K as well. In such situations there's
always a chance of slipping through the queen against a careless defender.

There's nothing careless about the Corgi, however. He covered and
the Hog ruffed in dummy. When he saw S.B.'s ♡9 his eyes narrowed.
Maybe the Pterodactyls weren't destined to be extinct after all. On
dummy's ♠Q and ♠J, which followed, the Secretary Bird shed two
clubs, leaving this position.

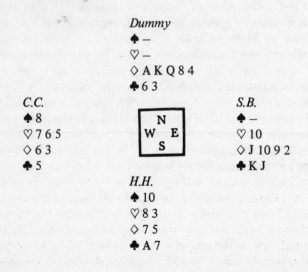

```
                        Dummy
                        ♠ —
                        ♡ —
                        ◊ A K Q 8 4
                        ♣ 6 3
      C.C.                                    S.B.
      ♠ 8                 ┌─────────┐          ♠ —
      ♡ 7 6 5             │   N     │          ♡ 10
      ◊ 6 3             W │  W   E  │ E        ◊ J 10 9 2
      ♣ 5                 │   S     │          ♣ K J
                          └─────────┘
                        H.H.
                        ♠ 10
                        ♡ 8 3
                        ◊ 7 5
                        ♣ A 7
```

After a club to the ace came the ♠10, drawing C.C.'s last trump. The Secretary Bird squirmed.

"Take your time, Professor," jeered the Hog. "It makes all the difference in which order you present me with the last two tricks."

Finally, S.B. let go the ♡10 and the Hog's ♡8, now a master, squeezed him mercilessly in diamonds and clubs.

The Hog grunted happily. "I rather think," he gloated, "that I have, that er we have won the match."

"An execrable contract," hissed the Secretary Bird, "but if they bid it, expecting you to do it, they couldn't help making it. The three-suit squeeze is automatic. Child's play."

"Want a bet?" asked H.H. contemptuously. S.B. hissed loudly.

ENTER THE CHIMP

In the other room, things took a somewhat unexpected turn.

As a kibitzer, no less than as a player, Charlie the Chimp has the gift of being able to concentrate on any hand except the one in progress. As the last board was placed on the table, he was saying to the Rabbit.

"Had you returned a trump you could have broken that contract. Why didn't you?"

Like the Corgi, the Toucan led the ♠9 against 6♠, and like the Hog, Papa played a low heart at trick two. The Toucan detached the ♡K and held it aloft. Then he replaced it, bounced giddily in his chair as was his wont in moments of tension, and took it out again.

All set to follow with the ♡9, the Rabbit turned to the Chimp. "I didn't return a trump because I hoped to give partner a diamond ruff."

"But he was marked with another diamond," retorted the Chimp.

"How could I guess ..." began the Rabbit, when the Toucan, subsiding in his chair, finally replaced the ♡K and produced the ♡5. His mind was still on the hand brought up by the Chimp, R.R. followed automatically with the ♡9 which he had held in his hand for some time.

Papa gathered the trick in surprise, cashed the ♠Q, and took the club finesse. Then he sat back and sighed for in no way would the addition come to twelve. If he ruffed two hearts in dummy, it would cost a trump trick and he would score in all — three trumps, three diamonds, two clubs, a heart and two heart ruffs. Setting up a long diamond, with a high ruff, at the cost of a trump, would lead to the same result. And if he simply cashed his four trumps, R.R. could throw two clubs and a heart with impunity. The count hadn't been rectified and there was no sign of a squeeze anywhere.

A 3-3 diamond break was the only chance and when it failed to materialise, Papa sat back philosophically, consoling himself with the reflection that the Hog, without the present of a heart trick, would make a trick less.

As Peregrine the Penguin, who was directing the match, came to announce the result, the Chimp was saying to the Rabbit. "You surely placed him with six clubs, so . . ."

". . . won by 1230" concluded P.P.

"*Who* has won by 1230?" asked the Rabbit and the Chimp in unison.

Looking back on these two matches I couldn't help feeling that free will and predestination were, for once, on the same side, an irresistible combination. What would happen, I wondered, if predestination stood aside, leaving the Hog unaided to protect the scatter-brained Rabbit? How would he acquit himself as a substitute for the Guardian Angel?

Examining the archives I soon came across these examples.

CHAPTER FIVE

H.H. as Dummy

GRAND SLAM WITH AN OVERTRICK

The Rabbit was dealing the first hand of the rubber. The Emeritus Professor of Bio-Sophistry, better known on account of his appearance as the Secretary Bird, scowled at Charlie the Chimp, who was flicking ash on the table.

"Why must you wave your beastly cigarette over the table?" expostulated S.B. as he scooped up the ash with a joker from the new pack. "Filthy habit," he added in disgust.

"You can insure against floods, earthquakes, quads," muttered the Hog bitterly. "Why can't you insure against cutting homicidal partners? That's the third time I've got him in two rubbers."

Dlr. South
Neither Vul:

H.H.
♠ 6 4
♡ A K 6 3
♢ A J 3
♣ K 10 4 3

Ch. Ch.
♠ 7 5
♡ J 9
♢ K Q 10 8 4
♣ Q 9 7 2

```
   N
 W   E
   S
```

S.B.
♠ 3 2
♡ Q 10 8 7
♢ 9 7 6 5
♣ J 8 5

R.R.
♠ A K Q J 10 9 8
♡ 4 2
♢ 2
♣ A 6

South	North
2♠	3♡
4♠	5♢
6♣	6♡
7♠	

With only four losers, the Rabbit had no hesitation in opening 2♠. The Hog looked at him suspiciously. They always played Acol together and an opening Two Bid promised at least eight playing tricks, but the Rabbit was an enthusiast for new systems, gadgets and conventions, and maybe he was trying one out now, having forgotten to notify partner; it had happened before.

R.R.'s rebid, however, set all doubts at rest. The jump to 4♠, in an already forcing situation, proclaimed a solid suit and three cue-bids later he soared happily into the grand slam.

The Chimp led the ◊K.

"Take your time," said the Hideous Hog, tabling the dummy. "Don't touch a card until you've counted your losers and winners — and don't play from the wrong hand."

The Rabbit studied the dummy carefully. Then he scrutinised closely his own hand. Nowhere could he find a loser of any sort.

"Unless you ruff the ace of diamonds," he said, spreading his cards with a happy smile, "they're all here."

"Just my luck," growled the Chimp. "I was playing social bridge for peanuts over the weekend and I had every card in the pack. Now, of course . . ."

No one listened to him, least of all the Emeritus Professor, who was examining declarer's hand card by card.

"Play on," he said at last. There was a dangerous gleam in his pince-nez.

"But that's absurd," protested the Rabbit. "I draw trumps and all my cards are winners. What trick do you suppose I could lose?"

"That," retorted S.B., "depends on your thirteenth card. So far we have only been privileged to see twelve."

There was general consternation, but a recount confirmed that only twelve cards in declarer's hand were on view.

The Chimp suggested magnanimously that the deal should be washed out, but this brought a vicious snarl from the Hog who insisted that the missing card should be found and restored to its owner.

The Hog looked through the other pack. The Rabbit examined his sleeves and turn-ups, while two junior kibitzers went down on their knees to search under the table. It was left to Oscar the Owl to look into the box from which the new pack had been taken and there he duly found the missing card — the ♡5.

"One down," announced S.B. triumphantly. "Is it too late to double?"

There were beads of perspiration on the Rabbit's forehead as he ruefully shook his head. "Oh dear, oh dear," he was saying to himself aloud, "what can I do with that little heart? I suppose the only hope is to find the queen-jack of clubs bare. It's so unlikely and yet my horoscope for the day couldn't have been better . . ."

"Maybe," sneered S.B., "horoscopes aren't altogether infallible, for as you can see, the queen-jack of clubs are not bare."

Declarer, having made a claim, defenders could expose their cards with impunity and the Professor spread his for the Rabbit to see.

"Well, I mean . . ." began the Rabbit, but with an air of unmistakable authority, the Hog took over.

" 'Too late to double', were you saying Professor. Of course not. What is more I will take the liberty of redoubling," and in what was intended as pleasant banter, he added, "those club honours may come down after all, you know. That horoscope . . ."

"Really?" hissed the Secretary Bird. "You must have been looking at the wrong constellation, H.H., for I can assure you that I will not unguard my ♣J, not even to please you."

"Neither will I unguard my queen," declared the Chimp, taking heart from S.B.'s defiant manner.

"Can I have that in writing, Professor?" asked H.H. in a cold, rasping voice.

"A sworn affadavit, if you like," hissed S.B.

"Me, too," echoed Charlie the Chimp. "I swear."

"Very well," said H.H., pointing his cigar menacingly at each defender in turn. "R.R. has told you how he will play."

"I . . ." began the Rabbit, but the Hog quickly silenced him.

"You've delivered your statement, R.R., so kindly don't interrupt while I make it. As I was saying," he resumed. "Declarer draws trumps and cashes his winners, the two top hearts, the ace of clubs and the trumps. What happens when three cards remain and the last trump hits the table?

This:

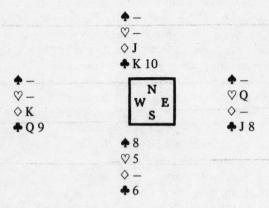

"To keep the ♢K, Charlie must throw a club. To retain the ♡Q the Professor, likewise, must shed a club, and just as R.R. told you, dummy's ♣10 scores the thirteenth trick.

"But," the Hog paused for dramatic effect, then waving his cigar like the conductor's baton in a Wagnerian opera, he went on: "You, Charlie, declared on oath that you will retain your club guard. To do so, you must part with the ♢K, making good dummy's jack. You, Professor, have offered to swear an affadavit that you will keep your ♣J guarded. You cannot, at the same time, keep the ♡Q. So the ♡5, that missing card to which you attached such importance, becomes a master. Count declarer's tricks: seven spades, three hearts, two diamonds and two clubs. That comes to fourteen, bringing the total score, allowing for honours and an overtrick redoubled, to 2540. Correct me if I'm wrong."

NOBLESSE OBLIGE

The Hideous Hog likes to think of the hand below as one of the best examples of his skill in dummy play. It came up recently towards the end of the afternoon session.

"Last hand," announced Timothy the Toucan. "I really shouldn't have stayed to watch even this one."

The Toucan was within his rights, for he had announced the hand before that he had a dinner engagement and could only kibitz two more deals.

Dlr. West
Both Vul:

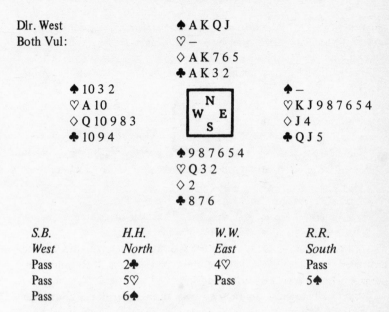

```
                    ♠ A K Q J
                    ♡ –
                    ◇ A K 7 6 5
                    ♣ A K 3 2
  ♠ 10 3 2                             ♠ –
  ♡ A 10               N              ♡ K J 9 8 7 6 5 4
  ◇ Q 10 9 8 3    W         E         ◇ J 4
  ♣ 10 9 4             S               ♣ Q J 5
                    ♠ 9 8 7 6 5 4
                    ♡ Q 3 2
                    ◇ 2
                    ♣ 8 7 6
```

S.B.	H.H.	W.W.	R.R.
West	*North*	*East*	*South*
Pass	2♣	4♡	Pass
Pass	5♡	Pass	5♠
Pass	6♠		

The Emeritus Professor of Bio-Sophistry led the ♡A. As the Rabbit surveyed the dummy, the Toucan glanced nervously at his watch. "It's later than I thought!" he murmured. "Oh dear, I shall be late."

"I'll save time," announced the Rabbit. "I can doubtless make all thirteen tricks by setting up a diamond for a club discard, but since poor Timothy is in a hurry, I'll just take my twelve tricks."

"*Which* twelve tricks?" demanded the Secretary Bird. There was an ominous ring in his voice.

"Well, really Professor," replied the Rabbit. "I mean it's so simple. I ruff your ♡A and another heart, that's two tricks, dummy's two AKs, that's six and my own six trumps."

The Secretary Bird uncrossed his long wiry legs and faced his cards. "Allow me to inform you," he announced triumphantly, "that you go one down. As you can see, I have three trumps, so that if you ruff two hearts in dummy, my spade ten will be promoted to top rank and . . ."

"I don't like to interrupt you," broke in the Hog, who had been studying the layout, "but though you can invoke the laws, you cannot also sit in judgment, deliver the verdict and pass sentence. It's too much for one man, even a distinguished legal scholar such as yourself. All you can do is to ask declarer to play on."

"In accordance with his statement," rejoined the Professor.

The Hog nodded vigorously, perhaps a shade too vigorously. "Yes, you must play in strict accordance with your statement," he told the Rabbit emphasising the operative words.

"I only said that I would ruff two hearts," pleaded the Rabbit ruefully.

"Quite so," agreed H.H., "ruff two hearts, score the two ace-kings and set up the diamonds."

"Impossible, for I have five diamonds, as you can see," declared S.B.

"True, true, but our friend didn't know that when he made his statement. So I am afraid that he must attempt the impossible by ruffing out . . ."

"You are directing him!" hissed the Secretary Bird.

The Hideous Hog looked shocked. "Are you suggesting, Professor, that declarer should depart from his statement?"

"I'll accept no favours," cried the Rabbit whose head was beginning to reel.

He ruffed the ♡A, cashed the ◇AK, discarding a heart, ruffed a diamond in his hand and another heart in dummy, then a fourth diamond in his hand.

"The diamonds er haven't broken," observed the Rabbit weakly. "What must I do next?"

"Noblesse oblige," said the Hog with a lofty look. "Even though you know that you can't set up a diamond, you said something about ruffing them out, and also that you would cash those ace-kings. Honour demands that you carry out your obligations."

The Rabbit duly cashed the ♣AK and ruffed dummy's last diamond.

"Lead a trump," commanded the Secretary Bird.

The Rabbit did as he was told.

"Another trump," persisted S.B.

The Hog, who had been concentrating on looking distrait, came to life quickly and deflected the Rabbit's hand before he could reach dummy's trumps.

"No, no," objected the Hog "the laws do say — there's a footnote, I believe — that declarer can be required to draw or not to draw an outstanding trump, that he may have over-looked. It's in the singular. Nothing to say that he can be directed to draw trumps all night. Besides," purred the Hog in his silkiest voice, "in this instance, he is actually debarred by his own statement from drawing another trump, for if he did, he could only take five trump tricks and he specifically stated six."

"What must I do now?" asked the Rabbit ruefully.

"Anything you like," replied H.H. quickly, "except draw another trump."

This was the position:

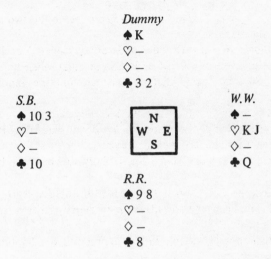

Dummy
♠ K
♡ —
♢ —
♣ 3 2

S.B.
♠ 10 3
♡ —
♢ —
♣ 10

W.W.
♠ —
♡ K J
♢ —
♣ Q

R.R.
♠ 9 8
♡ —
♢ —
♣ 8

"Restricted choice," muttered R.R., playing a club. Winning with the ♣Q, Walter the Walrus had to play a heart, and whether S.B. covered the ♠9 with his ♠10 or under-ruffed, the Rabbit was destined to make the last two tricks and bring home his contract.

"I'm surprised at you Professor," said H.H. sternly. "Fancy trying to talk my friend out of a kindergarten smother play. Mind you," he went on, "you could have broken the contract, even at the end, had you been able to persuade your partner to unblock in clubs, allowing you to win on the third round and lead a trump. You had every right, of course, to consult him about the best defence. Maybe you were not conversant with the laws. As I was saying, noblesse oblige."

I couldn't help reflecting that the Hog's free will had proved no less effective than the magic of destiny's chosen agent, the Guardian Angel. With either in charge every immovable object quickly gave way before the irresistible force of the Rabbit's luck.

Could anyone be as unlucky, I wondered, as R.R. was lucky? My thoughts turned to Karapet.

CHAPTER SIX

Karapet and the Witch

THE GLOATING KIBITZER

The unluckiest player in the Western hemisphere, and elsewhere, too, for that matter, Karapet has an inexhaustible fund of hard luck stories. A meek and humble soul, he doesn't expect people to listen to them, but when they start interrupting to tell him their own, even his gentle nature rebels for surely nobody's woes could match his.

A poignant example is this hand which came up during an ordinary, unfriendly rubber. Karapet and Papa were opposing Timothy the Toucan, the Rueful Rabbit and the Hideous Hog, who was kibitzing against Papa.

"Don't be nervous, Timothy," said R.R. as the Toucan bounced unsteadily in his chair. "We'll play the Hog way. Trust me. I'll be the Hog and you'll be I, er me, if you see what I mean."

This was the deal *in causa*.

Dlr. South
Both Vul:

	♠ 10 2	
	♡ K 7	
	◇ A Q 7 6 5 4	
	♣ 9 7 6	
♠ K Q 9 8		♠ J 7 6 4 3
♡ 4 3	N	♡ 9 8 6 5
◇ J 10 9 8 3	W E	◇ 2
♣ K 8	S	♣ A 3 2
	♠ A 5	
	♡ A Q J 10 2	
	◇ K	
	♣ Q J 10 5 4	

R.R.	*Papa*	*T.T.*	*Karapet*
South	*West*	*North*	*East*
1♣	Pass	1◇	Pass
2♡	Pass	3◇	Pass
3♡	Pass	4♣	Pass
5♣	Dble.	Pass	Pass
Redble.			

The bidding was straightforward and so were the double and redouble. Papa expected to score his ♣K plus a trick in spades, and the Rabbit could surely be relied upon to find a third loser somewhere.

The Rabbit redoubled on principle — the Hog's principle — based on the theory that redoubling improves the odds by rattling defenders, boosting declarer's morale and heartening dummy.

Papa led the ♠K, and as dummy went down, the Rabbit quickly counted twelve tricks — the ♠A, five hearts, three top diamonds and three clubs.

Oscar the Owl and Peregrine the Penguin exchanged meaning looks.

"Three losers," remarked O.O.

"Yes," agreed P.P., "with both red suits breaking badly, he can't get rid of that spade. Now 3NT would have been foolproof."

"But not Rabbit-proof," said the Hog. "With only nine top tricks, there's no game for them anywhere. They should have stayed in a part-score, picked up another good hand next time and clinched the rubber, allowing me to cut in, instead of wasting my time like this. No consideration for other people, no respect . . ."

Interrupting the monologue, the Rabbit went quickly into action.

He won the first trick with the ♠A, cashed the ◇K, and crossing to the
♡K, led the ◇A to discard his spade loser.

The unkind diamond break came as a shock and when Karapet
ruffed, R.R. was forced to over-ruff.

After a pause to regroup, the Rabbit turned to the hearts, hoping
to get rid of dummy's spade on the third round. Ruffing with the ♣K
wouldn't help, so Papa ruffed the ♡Q with the ♣8 to prevent a spade
discard.

The Rabbit frowned. Tricks weren't materialising as intended.
With a harassed look, he over-ruffed in dummy with the ♣9 and continued with the ◇Q, hoping against hope that maybe Karapet would
have no more trumps. This was the position.

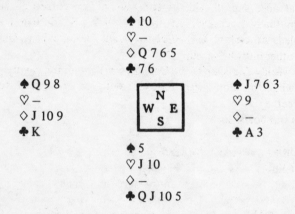

```
                        ♠ 10
                        ♡ –
                        ◇ Q 7 6 5
                        ♣ 7 6
    ♠ Q 9 8                                  ♠ J 7 6 3
    ♡ –              ┌───────────┐           ♡ 9
    ◇ J 10 9         │    N      │           ◇ –
    ♣ K             │ W     E   │           ♣ A 3
                     │    S      │
                     └───────────┘
                        ♠ 5
                        ♡ J 10
                        ◇ –
                        ♣ Q J 10 5
```

If Karapet ruffed with the ♣A, or if he didn't ruff at all, R.R. would
shed his losing spade. So, perforce, he ruffed with the ♣3. The Rabbit
over-ruffed and continued with the ♡10. Papa threw a spade. For all
he knew Karapet might have the ♡J. Besides, not knowing that he was
left with the bare king, the Rabbit would doubtless finesse, so the ♣K
would take the trick anyway.

The Rabbit discarded dummy's ♠10, ruffed a spade and led a trump,
bringing down the ace and king together.

"Why did you double?" asked Karapet in injured tones. "I promised
nothing, yet I produced the ace of trumps and . . ."

"Come, come," broke in the Hog, with a gloating smile and a wink
at the other kibitzers. "You can hardly claim credit for *that* trick.
Papa's king was a certain winner from the start and you scored no
other, anyway. All you can say about that ace of yours is that it didn't

cost a trick, but it didn't win one either, did it?"

The Hog was laughing uproariously. Other people's misfortunes appealed to his fine sense of humour.

PAPA LOSES THE ACE OF TRUMPS

"Tournament Director!" called a choleric gentleman from the table by the bay window.

"Arbitre!" cried his partner, intent on showing that he had played on the continent and knew the language.

The Tournament Director walked over.

"It's impossible . . . ridiculous . . . absurd . . . daft." All four players spoke at once and all said the same thing. Two entries on board 13 were mutually exclusive. At table 4 North-South had made 2◊ redoubled. At table 7 East-West had made 2◊ redoubled. Obviously, one or other must be wrong.

The weekly duplicate at the Unicorn was held up for twenty minutes or so while the scores were checked. Both, however, were found to be correct.

This was board 13.

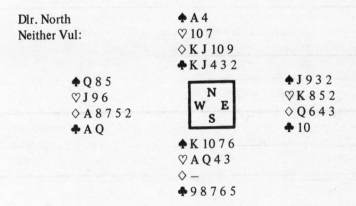

Dlr. North
Neither Vul:

North: ♠ A 4 ♡ 10 7 ◊ K J 10 9 ♣ K J 4 3 2

West: ♠ Q 8 5 ♡ J 9 6 ◊ A 8 7 5 2 ♣ A Q

East: ♠ J 9 3 2 ♡ K 8 5 2 ◊ Q 6 4 3 ♣ 10

South: ♠ K 10 7 6 ♡ A Q 4 3 ◊ — ♣ 9 8 7 6 5

At table 4, Walter the Walrus, the dealer, thinking that he had 11 points only, instead of 12, passed and this was the auction.

H.H.	*W.W.*	*C.C.*	*Ch. Ch.*
West	*North*	*East*	*South*
–	Pass	Pass	1♣
1NT	Dble.	2♣	Dble.
2◊	Dble.	Redble.	

Colin the Corgi, the Hog's partner, bid 2♣ in search of a fit in any one of the other three suits. His redouble of 2◊ was primarily tactical. He didn't expect it to be left in and he was all set to double opponents if they sought refuge in either major. The Hog, no doubt, could look after 3♣.

Charlie the Chimp now bitterly regretted his frail third hand opening, but it was too late to go back. Fearing above all, that if he ventured into a major he might find himself in 3♣, he passed unhappily and 2◊ redoubled became the final contract.

Looking for a safe opening, the Walrus led the ♣K, if only to see the table before deciding on the best line of defence.

The Hog won and led a low trump, taking the trick with dummy's queen. The ♡2 followed. Smoothly the Chimp played the three. If the Hog had the jack, he was bound to make a heart trick anyway, but if he had the J9 he might well misguess.

Influenced perhaps by the Chimp's air of flamboyant indifference, the Hog rose with the jack and continued with the ace and another trump. The Walrus cashed his last trump, drawing two for one, fingered thoughtfully the ♡10, and decided finally to switch to spades, first the ♠A, then the ♠4.

Coming in with the ♠K, on which the Hog jettisoned his ♠Q, the Chimp, exited with his last club, this being the five-card ending:

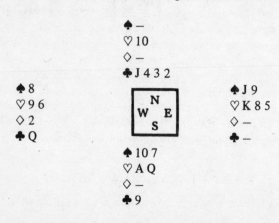

On the ♣Q, the Hog shed one of dummy's hearts and another on the ◇2 which applied the *coup de grâce*. If the Chimp threw a spade, both dummy's spades would be good. If he bared his ♡A, he would be thrown in and forced to lead into the ♠J9. Either way, H.H. would have his eighth trick.

Events took a very different course at table 7 where Timothy the Toucan, playing the weak notrump with the Rueful Rabbit, opened the bidding. This was the sequence:

Papa	T.T.	Karapet	R.R.
West	North	East	South
–	1NT	Pass	Pass
Dble.	Pass	Pass	2◇
Dble.	Pass	Pass	Redble.

Determined to play the hand in anything but diamonds, the Rabbit adopted the classical device of bidding his void suit and redoubling for a rescue.

The Toucan's pass was, in a manner of speaking, two-way. He hoped that perhaps, after all, the Rabbit really had diamonds. Alternatively, if he didn't, maybe he would have enough outside strength to make eight tricks.

Alone at the table, Papa knew exactly what was happening and to stop declarer making cheap ruffs in dummy, he chose what looked like a lethal lead, the ◇2.

The Rabbit inserted dummy's ◇9 and sat back, waiting for someone to pick up the trick. When he finally realised that it was his, he gurgled excitedly, and playing at top speed, embarked on his favourite game, ruffing anything that was ruffable, wherever it might be.

At trick two, he played the ♠A, then a spade to his king and a spade ruff. The heart finesse was followed by another spade ruff, Papa shedding a heart, and then came the ♡A and a third heart. The ◇K scored the eighth trick *en passant*.

"Why didn't you put up your ◇Q?" demanded Papa indignantly.

"Why didn't you open the ◇A?" countered Karapet, "once again, through being too clever, you've lost your ace of trumps."

KARAPET'S LUCKY HAND

The Griffins learned long ago how to take evasive action when Karapet embarked on one of his harrowing hard-luck stories. No one wanted to be unkind, but since his stories were bound to have an unhappy ending, just as they had an unhappy beginning, everything about them was eminently predictable. There was no drama, no suspense.

Oscar the Owl was badly out-manoeuvred the other night, however. The fact that he was cornered in a cul de sac, formed by a small alcove adjoining the card room, was no more than a contributory factor. The Owl might still have escaped had not the Armenian's opening gambit taken him completely by surprise.

"Would you like to hear of a really lucky hand?" he asked O.O.

"Lucky?" repeated Oscar incredulously. Luck and Karapet were strictly incompatible.

"Very lucky," Karapet assured him. "But judge for yourself. Suppose that you picked up a hand on which, as dealer, you would have opened 2♣. Give yourself four aces, a king, two queens. How would you like your vulnerable opponents to mislay four aces and end up in a redoubled slam?"

The Owl hooted softly. Surely no such good fortune could have befallen Karapet.

"It happened at home and you weren't playing for money?" he hazarded.

"On the contrary," retorted Karapet, "the deal came up here last night and we were playing for the usual stakes and the usual side bets."

"Your opponents had the big hand and your side mislaid the aces?" suggested O.O.

"Not at all," replied the Armenian, drawing out of his pocket a piece of crumpled paper with the familiar diagram. "I had the 2♣ hand and here's the bidding."

This is the story behind Karapet's lucky hand.

Dlr. South
N/S Vul: & 30

```
                    ♠ 10 9 8 4 2
                    ♡ K Q J 10 9 8
                    ◇ —
                    ♣ J 10
♠ —                                          ♠ A Q 3
♡ 7 4 3 2          ┌─────────┐              ♡ A 6 5
◇ 8 7 3 2          │    N    │              ◇ A 6 5 4
♣ 9 8 7 6 5        │ W     E │              ♣ A K Q
                   │    S    │
                   └─────────┘
                    ♠ K J 7 6 5
                    ♡ —
                    ◇ K Q J 10 9
                    ♣ 4 3 2
```

H.H.	*W.W.*	*R.R.*	*Karapet*
South	*West*	*North*	*East*
1◇	Pass	1♡	Pass
1♠	Pass	3♣	Pass
3♠	Pass	4NT	Pass
5♣	Pass	6♠	Dble.
Pass	Pass	Redble.	

The part-score explains the Rabbit's second round jump to 3♣. Without it he would have bid 3♠, or maybe 4♠, but now something better
was required, something bold and imaginative to arouse partner.

Over the Hog's rebid of 3♠ he was about to content himself with a
modest 4♠, when suddenly he was struck by a profound thought.
Surely the Hog's sequence showed at least ten and probably eleven
cards in his two suits. If so, and if the spades were good enough, there
might well be a slam about. Much depended on finding him with the
right two aces, and there was always the chance, of course, that he
had three aces.

Could there be a better way of finding out then by bidding 4NT?

Admittedly, purists don't recommend invoking Blackwood with
a void, but this looked very much like the exception that proves the
rule. And when all was said and done, the partnership should be safe
enough at the five level.

Little did the Rabbit dream when he bid 4NT that he would hear 5♣,
showing four aces or none. It could hardly be the latter, for holding four
aces at favourable vulnerability and with a part-score against them, the
least venturesome opponents would have surely come into the auction.

The Hog growled and fidgeted, praying that the Rabbit would make some bid that he could pass. Unconscious of his discomfort, the Rabbit was wondering how best to investigate the prospects of a grand slam. Deciding finally that discretion was the better part of valour, he signed off cautiously in 6♠.

Karapet, who had showed the patience of Job, with whom he had so much in common, decided that the time had come to double.

Ignoring the Hog's hard breathing, pursed lips and malevolent looks, R.R. promptly redoubled. The double, as he explained later, had improved the situation, indicating that if any spade honours were missing they would be conveniently placed.

"Should be cast iron," he remarked cheerfully as Walter the Walrus led the ♡2 and he tabled his hand. Karapet came near to smiling.

Stifling the explosive sounds which were forming at the back of his throat, the Hideous Hog ruffed Karapet's ♡A, crossed to dummy with a diamond ruff and quickly parked two clubs on the hearts. The next heart Karapet was obliged to ruff. Otherwise H.H. would have discarded his last club.

The Hog over-ruffed, trumped another diamond in dummy and again led a heart. Karapet was in the same predicament as before and stoically he ruffed with the ♠Q. Once more the Hog over-ruffed, and going back to the table by ruffing a third diamond, he continued with dummy's last heart. Whether or not Karapet ruffed with his ace was immaterial.

Needless to say, had the Armenian ruffed with the ace at the first opportunity, H.H. would have thrown his remaining club and picked up the queen of trumps by a straightforward finesse.

"Why did you demand a suicidal heart lead?" cried the Walrus indignantly. "Without that lethal Lightner double I would have led a club and they would have gone two down, 1000 to us instead of 2020 to them, a difference of . . ."

"A very thoughtless redouble, R.R.," broke in the Hog, smirking happily. "Karapet might have escaped into 6NT and the best we could do would be to keep them to six tricks, a mere 950 − 1100 less 150 for aces. Lucky that Karapet didn't think of it."

"Lucky!" repeated the dazed Armenian.

The numbness had worn off by the time he came to tell the story to the Owl, but he still felt keenly the grim irony of the situation.

"Here I was with the best hand I'd held for ages," he recalled, sighing softly. "Through a grotesque misunderstanding opponents reach a ridiculous slam and redouble into the bargain. I couldn't have asked for more. And yet, the end product is a catastrophe. I suppose," said Karapet bitterly, "that you might call it a lucky catastrophe. And that," he added with a sardonic laugh, "is as lucky as I am ever likely to be."

THE UNFORGIVEABLE INSULT

"Karapet is about to resign," Oscar the Owl told us as we sat sipping Madeira at the Griffins bar. "All because of the Hog, of course."

"He was rude to him, more so than usual, I mean?" suggested the Rabbit.

"No, not exactly rude," rejoined O.O. "Karapet is used to that, as we all are. H.H. did something far worse. He accused Karapet of being lucky."

There was a stunned silence. Karapet Djoulikyan, the Free Armenian, prided himself on being the world's unluckiest man as his father and grandfather had been before him. It all went back, as we were frequently reminded, to the curse cast on the Djoulikyans by the Witch of Ararat in 1453. Nothing had gone right for them ever since.

Karapet bore his misfortunes stoically, especially when he could get anyone to listen to them. But to be accused of being lucky, that was the final insult.

The hand that was at the root of the trouble had come up the night before at the Unicorn's weekly duplicate.

The Hog was playing with the Rabbit, "to mortify the flesh," as he put it. "One can't go through life without suffering," he explained. "One must atone for one's sins somehow and one of the redeeming features of duplicate is that it doesn't cost money. The Rabbit is free," he added simply.

Colin the Corgi, one of our most talented players, was West. He entered the event too late to get a partner, so he had to play with the Walrus.

Dlr. East
Neither Vul:

	♠Q 5 4 2	
	♡K 6 3	
	◇9 4	
	♣K J 7 6	

♠J 9 8 7 6		♠ —
♡Q 10 8	N	♡J 7 5
◇10 5	W E	◇A Q J 8 7 3 2
♣5 3 2	S	♣10 9 8

	♠A K 10 3	
	♡A 9 4 2	
	◇K 6	
	♣A Q 4	

C.C.	*R.R.*	*W.W.*	*H.H.*
West	*North*	*East*	*South*
—	—	3◇	Dble.
Pass	4◇	Pass	4♠

Colin led the ◇10 to W.W.'s ace and another diamond came back.
The ♠A revealed the 5–0 trump break and it looked as if two trump
losers, in addition to a heart, couldn't be avoided.

Was it possible to set the stage for an end-play? The first step was
to test the clubs, and when all followed three times, H.H. heaved a
sigh of relief. Continuing with dummy's fourth club, he ruffed with
the ♠A, that being his sixth trick.

The Corgi promptly under-ruffed. He could see that if he discarded
a heart, he would have to ruff the third round of hearts, and with
trumps only left, he would be obliged to lead one away from his jack,
presenting declarer with the last two tricks.

The Hog continued with the ♡A, then a low one to the king. With
the four-card ending in mind, the Corgi jettisoned his queen, allowing
the third heart to be won by the Warrus.

This was the position:

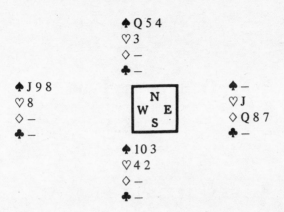

♠ Q 5 4
♡ 3
◇ —
♣ —

♠ J 9 8   ♠ —
♡ 8   ♡ J
◇ —   ◇ Q 8 7
♣ —   ♣ —

♠ 10 3
♡ 4 2
◇ —
♣ —

On W.W.'s ◇Q H.H. threw his last heart and the Corgi inserted the ♠8. The Hog carefully under-ruffed in dummy. Had he won the trick with the queen, he would have lost the last two tricks. As it was, C.C. had to play a spade and the Hog, with eight tricks lined up in front of him, scored the last two.

"That's 420 and a cold top," he remarked confidently as he opened the travelling score-sheet. But there in black and white was the entry for pair 13, Papa and Karapet — ten tricks in 3NT for a score of 430.

The bidding, it transpired later, had gone as follows:

West	North	East	South
—	—	3◇	Dble.
Pass	3♠	Pass	3NT

"Disgraceful!" fumed the Hog when he heard about it. "Themistocles was South, you don't have to tell me, and just so that he should play the hand he didn't support partner with AK103. Why he might as well have opened 3NT out of turn when he picked up his cards. And fancy finding such a dummy! That lucky Karapet. He makes a horrible under-bid, Papa makes a bid still more atrocious and they get a top which nearly robs me of the first prize. The luck of those Djoulikyans. All goes back to that good fairy on Ararat, I suppose . . ."

When I left Karapet, drinking an extra bitter Fernet Branca before dinner, he was on page 11 of his letter of resignation to the Secretary.

CHAPTER SEVEN

H.H. versus Papa

PAPA TEACHES THE HOG A LESSON

The bitter rivalry between the Hog and Papa the Greek was the under-lying motif which dominated many of the hands reported by me in the *Griffins Chronicle*. Their exploits brought out the best of bridge and the worst out of each other. Predestination seemed to stand aside, allowing free will, liberally laced with ill will, to take over. The Guardian Angel was taking a well-earned rest.

The Griffins Bar was often the *avant scène* which saw the prelude to their duels.

As the news spread round the club that Papa the Greek had cut the Hideous Hog, the Griffins left their places at the bar and streamed into the cardroom. No one wanted to miss the next instalment in the feud between these two inveterate enemies.

Pitted against them, contrasting in age and style, were Colin the Corgi and Walter the Walrus. C.C., a gifted but facetious young man, has that urbane disrespect for his elders which can only be acquired through an expensive education. W.W., a pillar of the Establishment, as we all know, upholds moral values, the church, the Stock Exchange and the Milton Work count.

"Anything on TV?" asked H.H. in a loud aside as they sat down. "I expect to be dummy most of the rubber."

"When he was younger," confided Papa in a resonant whisper to his friend Karapet, "he was the second best player in the club. Even now, if he didn't eat so much or drank less . . ."

The first hand was uneventful. The Walrus opened 1NT and was raised to 3NT by the Corgi. The Hog led a spade to Papa's ace. Papa returned a heart. When the Hog was on lead again, he persisted with the spades. Papa, who had a second entry, persevered with hearts.

"A war on two fronts," murmured the Corgi.

"Sorry, partner," said the Walrus, conceding one down. "We had 29. I should have made it. I miscounted the diamonds."

"Don't reproach yourself," replied the Corgi, "there might have been a fourteenth lurking somewhere."

Then this hand came up.

Dlr. South
Neither Vul:

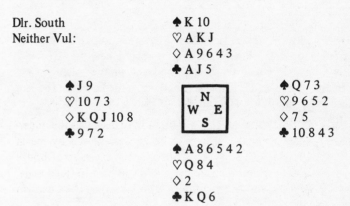

```
                        ♠ K 10
                        ♡ A K J
                        ◇ A 9 6 4 3
                        ♣ A J 5
   ♠ J 9                                 ♠ Q 7 3
   ♡ 10 7 3                              ♡ 9 6 5 2
   ◇ K Q J 10 8           N             ◇ 7 5
   ♣ 9 7 2             W     E          ♣ 10 8 4 3
                          S
                        ♠ A 8 6 5 4 2
                        ♡ Q 8 4
                        ◇ 2
                        ♣ K Q 6
```

The Hog dealt and opened 1♠. The Corgi butted in characteristically with 2◇, a hippy type of bid, expressing contempt for partner and opponents alike, and affirming the will to do his own thing.

Trying to look impassive, his Adam's apple aquiver, his eyes ablaze, the Greek doubled in a muffled voice. Anything but unethical, he kept the decibels down to a bare minimum.

After a pass from the Walrus, who had quickly counted his points and found them wanting, the Hog removed the double to 2♠. Feeling that he was hardly worth another effort, the Corgi passed and it was up to Papa.

There was unspeakable hatred in the Greek's eyes and he was determined to speak it.

Once more the Hog had taken charge. An enormous penalty had been thrown to the winds. Why? Because, had they defended, the spotlight, for once, would have been on Papa, while the Hog would have followed suit.

Very well, Papa would teach him an unforgettable lesson. He wanted the centre of the stage, come what may? He would have it. "7♠!"

This was the complete sequence:

H.H.	*C.C.*	*Papa*	*W.W.*
1♠	2◊	Dble.	Pass
2♠	Pass	7♠	

Everyone was too awed to double. Not a kibitzer stirred as C.C. led the ◊K.

"Thank you er partner," said the Hog while Papa was tabling his hand.

Going up with the ace, H.H. ruffed a diamond, and crossing to the ♡A, ruffed another, on which the Walrus shed a heart. Two rounds of hearts followed, ending in dummy, and yet another diamond was ruffed in the closed hand. This time W.W. discarded a club. The Hog continued with the ♣K, ♣Q and ♣6 to dummy's ace, leaving this three-card position:

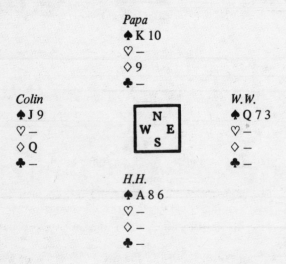

```
                        Papa
                        ♠ K 10
                        ♡ —
                        ◊ 9
                        ♣ —
   Colin                              W.W.
   ♠ J 9          ┌───────────┐       ♠ Q 7 3
   ♡ —            │   N       │       ♡ —
   ◊ Q            │ W   E     │       ◊ —
   ♣ —            │   S       │       ♣ —
                  └───────────┘
                        H.H.
                        ♠ A 8 6
                        ♡ —
                        ◊ —
                        ♣ —
```

The Walrus ruffed the ◊9 with his queen, but the Hog over-ruffed and finessed against the Corgi's jack. There was no other play, for W.W. could only have trumps left and had he started with the queen and jack, there would have been no hope anyway.

The kibitzers gasped.

"The first good bid you have made for a long, long time Themistocles. No wonder you look so surprised," jeered the Hog.

"As I only had two miserable points," protested the Walrus, "I really can't see what all the fuss is about. And, anyway, a grand slam on a finesse is nothing to be proud of."

A SLAM ON A NO-WAY FINESSE

"It's all wrong, you know," began the Hideous Hog, "that saying: 'if it's difficult it will be done at once. If it's impossible it may take a little longer.' It should be the other way round. A difficult situation may require a moment's thought. Why, even I have taken up to thirty seconds at times over a complex squeeze, or smother play. But the impossible must be done immediately. Play first. There's plenty of time to think about it afterwards, but don't let them count to 13. You remember that 6NT last night . . ."

I remembered it well. H.H. had cut an American visitor who wasn't familiar with the Hog count. He knew, of course, that H.H. added 2 points for his play when he was declarer. But he didn't realise that he added two more when Papa was against him.

The Hog dealt, sitting South, and this was the bidding sequence.

South	North
1◇	1♡
3NT	4◇
4♡	4NT
6NT	

What should Papa, sitting West, lead from: ♠K53 ♡J532 ◇Q ♣A9642?

Everything, in turn, looked attractive. A club was, perhaps, the least of all evils, but which one? No one would lead a true card against a slam, so Papa picked delicately on the deuce, false yet not flamboyant.

This was the full deal:

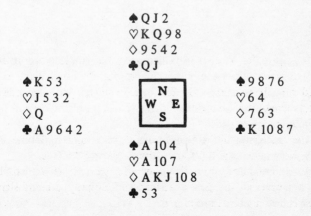

```
            ♠ Q J 2
            ♡ K Q 9 8
            ◇ 9 5 4 2
            ♣ Q J
♠ K 5 3        N        ♠ 9 8 7 6
♡ J 5 3 2   W     E     ♡ 6 4
◇ Q            S        ◇ 7 6 3
♣ A 9 6 4 2            ♣ K 10 8 7
            ♠ A 10 4
            ♡ A 10 7
            ◇ A K J 10 8
            ♣ 5 3
```

As the American began to spread his hand, the clubs came down first. Quick as lightning, before the rest of the cards had been tabled, the Hog pounced on the ♣Q.

Maybe, Walter the Walrus, Papa's luckless partner, wouldn't have covered anyway. Maybe he would. The 'third hand high' adage had been instilled in him since early childhood. But he had also been taught how not to cover touching honours.

Caught off balance, mentally breathless as he tried to follow the Hog's feverish rhythm, the Walrus let go the ♣8.

With the air of a man who had brought off a successful finesse, H.H. sat back and looked malevolently at Papa. Why had he found so eccentric a lead? Clearly, because nothing better had presented itself. The obvious inference was that the Greek had honours in every suit. The Hog decided to play accordingly.

Greeting the ◇Q on his ◇A, at trick two, with a sigh of relief, H.H. turned to hearts. First the ♡K, the Hog unblocking with the ♡10, then the ♡A and the ♡7, overtaken by the ♡8 in dummy.

Papa growled. The Hog chortled.

After discarding the ♣4 on the ♡Q, H.H. played out the diamonds.

What should Papa keep as his last three cards? Looking in his crystal, he could see H.H. sitting with ♠A10 and the ♣K, and reading his mind, he knew exactly what would happen or rather what the Hog intended to happen. Papa would be thrown in with the ♣A and forced to lead a spade away from his ♠K.

Papa end-played? Perish the thought. Following quickly and smoothly, he discarded the ♠3, the ♠5, then the ♣6 and ♣9.

The ♣J was thrown from dummy, while the Walrus left himself with the ♠9 and the ♣K10.

The Hog closed his eyes the better to see through the backs of the cards.

Where was the ♣10? If Papa had it, he must have bared his ♠K, for his other card was the ♣A.

If the ♣10 flanked W.W.'s ♣K he surely wouldn't have kept a third club. Even he knew enough to retain a spade, if only to prevent declarer counting the entire hand.

And, of course, if the Walrus had a spade, it left only one spade for Papa. Either way, his ♠K must drop.

Waiting for that king, the Hog allowed his ♣A to float gently down on the table. Then he claimed thirteen tricks.

"Should we have been in it?" asked the American, looking up

from his paper. "Was it cold?"

"Not entirely," the Hog assured him. "It depended on the lead and on the er club finesse," he added with a friendly leer.

THE SNIPPER SNIPPED

"Who was it that said that the distance from A to B isn't the same as from B to A? Einstein was it? Or Marconi? Ah, no, I remember now. I said it myself."

The speaker was the Hideous Hog. He was explaining to us at the Griffins Bar his method of breaking unbreakable contracts.

"But if you break it, then it can't be unbreakable," argued Peregrine the Penguin, who had inherited from his French grandmother a keen sense of logic.

"Superficial reasoning," retorted the Hog. "Declarer may have ten top tricks to rattle off, in, say, 4♠. The contract is, therefore, unbreakable. But not seeing defenders' cards, not knowing that an honour will fall or a suit will break, he tries to protect himself against the loss of a fourth trick and in so doing loses one of the other ten. So the contract is broken."

"But why should declarer do any such thing?" asked P.P. suspiciously.

"Because you project an illusion," rejoined the Hog. "By conjuring up in his mind the threat of an imaginary loser you induce him to give up a winner."

Firmly grasping my glass in one hand, the Hog scribbled with the other.

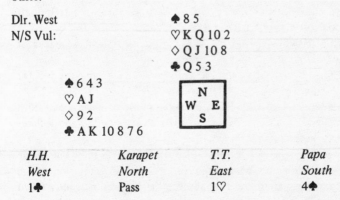

Dlr. West
N/S Vul:

	♠ 8 5
	♡ K Q 10 2
	◇ Q J 10 8
	♣ Q 5 3

♠ 6 4 3
♡ A J
◇ 9 2
♣ A K 10 8 7 6

H.H.	Karapet	T.T.	Papa
West	North	East	South
1♣	Pass	1♡	4♠

"This came up the other day," said H.H. "There's no mystery about the dramatis personae. I was West. Papa was South with Karapet, the Free Armenian, as his partner. I had a partner, too, in a manner of speaking, but it was only the Toucan, so we can skip over it."

"Quite a formidable dummy. A lot better than he could expect," observed the Penguin.

"You led the ♣K, I suppose?" asked Oscar the Owl.

The Hog nodded. "Yes I did. The Toucan followed with the deuce and Papa with the four."

The Owl blinked.

"I know what you are thinking," went on the Hog, "but no, that deuce could hardly have been a singleton. At unfavourable vulnerability I wouldn't expect Papa to soar into 4♠ with three club losers. Besides, the Toucan didn't bounce in his chair or look shifty or anything. No, you can take it that there was no future in clubs."

"Partner must have something," mused the Owl.

"Certainly," agreed the Hog. "He probably has six hearts, the ♣J we know about, and an ace, no doubt. If he hasn't that much, declarer has eleven tricks and we can't stop him from making them."

We all pondered.

"Could the Toucan have both the ace and king of diamonds?" ventured O.O. hesitantly.

"Improbable," replied the Hog. "With an ace and a king even a worm or a Toucan would double."

"Then I can't see where the fourth trick can come from," confessed P.P.

A TRICK OUT OF THE BLUE

"Have you considered a ruff?" asked the Hog.

"But there's nothing to ruff," objected the Penguin.

"How about a diamond?" persisted the Hog. "If I lead my singleton . . ."

"But you haven't got a singleton," protested O.O. and P.P. in unison.

"True," conceded the Hog, "but that's only because you can see my hand. Papa can't, you know, so if I switch to the ◇2 he will have reason to suspect a singleton, won't he?"

"But what good will it do you?" rejoined the Penguin. "Papa will have a nasty moment when the Toucan goes up with the ace and returns the suit, but unless you intend to revoke, you'll have to follow, so . . ."

"No, no," broke in H.H., "you've got it all wrong. If the Toucan has the ◇A there's no defence, for then Papa would need eight solid spades to justify his bid. The ◇K, without the ace, wouldn't look good to him, and he's vulnerable don't forget. No, it's the ♠A I am expecting to save the day."

"How?" asked the Penguin, looking increasingly perplexed.

"Put yourself in Papa's place," the Hog told him, "and you'll soon see. You know his hand, don't you? No?" resumed the Hog without waiting for a reply, "then I'll tell you. If he's missing the ace he must have the other seven spades and, of course, the ◇AK. Nothing else would add up to eight playing tricks with which we must credit him. That leaves five miserable points for the Toucan and confirms my guess that he has six hearts. With seven he might have pre-empted. And now everything is in place. Papa's shape is 7-1-4-1 and we know every card that matters.

"He fears a diamond ruff and two aces are missing. If Timothy the Toucan has the ♠A there's nothing he can do about it. But he bid a heart and that's the ace he is likely to have. Now Peregrine you can surely see how the unbreakable contract is about to be broken."

The Hog filled in the other hands.

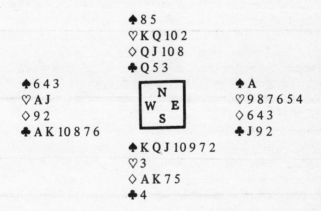

```
                    ♠ 8 5
                    ♡ K Q 10 2
                    ◇ Q J 10 8
                    ♣ Q 5 3
  ♠ 6 4 3         ┌─────────┐        ♠ A
  ♡ A J           │    N    │        ♡ 9 8 7 6 5 4
  ◇ 9 2           │ W     E │        ◇ 6 4 3
  ♣ A K 10 8 7 6  │    S    │        ♣ J 9 2
                  └─────────┘
                    ♠ K Q J 10 9 7 2
                    ♡ 3
                    ◇ A K 7 5
                    ♣ 4
```

"Remember that Papa suspects me of a singleton diamond and the bidding strongly inclines him to misplace the missing aces. How, then, would he play? How *should* he play?"

THE SCISSORS COUP

The Owl hooted softly.

"Exactly," agreed the Hog. "To a technician like Papa the situation presents no problem. He wins the diamond in dummy, leads the ♣Q and promptly discards his singleton heart, the Scissor Coup, severing, or so he thinks, communications between my hand and the Toucan's. Whatever I return, he will win and drive out the ♠A, *my* ace, remember, and I'll have no means of putting the Toucan in to give me a diamond ruff. That's how Papa will see it.

"Only, of course," went on the Hog, "when I win the third trick with my ♡A I produce out of the blue, my second diamond and when the Toucan comes in with the ♠A he gives me a ruff for which I have worked so hard."

My glass was empty, the Hog turned reluctantly to his own.

"As you can see," he added, "the scissors can snip both ways, and here you have a case of the snipper snipped, so to speak." The Hog smiled happily at the recollection of Papa's discomfiture.

FLIGHT OF THE ACES

Nothing is more maddening about Charlie the Chimp than his habit of concentrating on whatever he happens not to be doing at the time. No matter what hand he is playing, his attention is invariably riveted on another. He was at his very worst the other day in a rubber in which he and the Hideous Hog opposed Papa the Greek and Karapet the Unlucky.

On the first hand Papa made game. The next one he played in 1♠, an unbreakable contract, and to while the time away, the Chimp communed with a kibitzer about the Stock Market.

"I bought them at 86," he was saying, "that was before Consolidated Keyholes had even begun to bid for Voids and Vacuums. Diamonds? I sold my De Beers at . . . oh, sorry, yes, of course I have a diamond."

The next hand the Chimp was dummy. Turning to the next table, he was soon shaking his head as he followed the play with obvious disapproval.

"You had more than enough to make an effort," he told Walter the Walrus severely. "Why, partner's game rebid promised something like 20 points and . . ."

"4♡!" barked the Hog, who had by now completed the next deal:

Dlr. South
E/W Vul. & 30

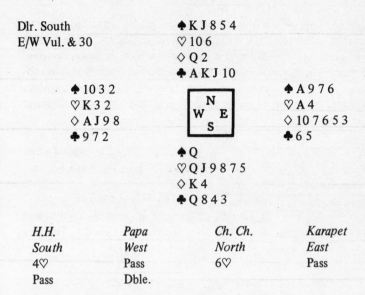

♠ K J 8 5 4
♡ 10 6
◊ Q 2
♣ A K J 10

♠ 10 3 2   ♠ A 9 7 6
♡ K 3 2   ♡ A 4
◊ A J 9 8   ◊ 10 7 6 5 3
♣ 9 7 2   ♣ 6 5

♠ Q
♡ Q J 9 8 7 5
◊ K 4
♣ Q 8 4 3

H.H.	*Papa*	*Ch. Ch.*	*Karapet*
South	*West*	*North*	*East*
4♡	Pass	6♡	Pass
Pass	Dble.		

The auction is less incongruous than appears at first sight. The Hog
was stretching, a long way, admittedly, in view of the vulnerability
and of the part-score. But the Chimp wasn't even stretching. His was
the right bid, though at the wrong table. Behind him, the Walrus
had opened 1♡ and rebid 4♡ over his partner's 1♠ response. That was
the sequence on which his attention had been focused the hand before,
so he felt far too good to pass on this one.

Papa doubled on two counts — as a mark of disrespect for the Hog,
and also because he expected to defeat the contract. Karapet sighed
in bewilderment. If Papa could double all on his own, two more aces
should prove useful in support, especially as one of them was the
ace of trumps. And yet a premonition, born of long and bitter experience, told him that something would surely go wrong.

No lead looked attractive to Papa. The choice lay between a trump
and the ♠2 and since the Hog's pre-empt suggested fear of spades,
the Greek selected the ♠2 as the more attacking opening.

The Hog inserted the eight and Karapet pondered. If Papa had led
from a four-card suit, as the two suggested, the Hog had none. If, on
the other hand, Papa had led a singleton, the ace wouldn't run away.
So Karapet put up the ♠9 and H.H. won with the bare queen. A low
diamond at trick two gave Papa a moment's thought, but it was really
no problem. The Hog, marked by now with the ♠A, would have hardly

opened 4♡ with an ace and a king in the side suit. Besides, even if he
did have the ◇K, the ◇A wouldn't run away. So he played low and
the queen won. The ♠K now forced the ace from Karapet. The Hog
ruffed and crossing to the ♣A promptly discarded his ◇K on the ♠J.
Next came the ♡10, Karapet played low and so did Papa, expecting
the Hog to repeat the finesse and so give him a count on the trumps.
The Hog, however, now ruffed a diamond and led a low trump towards
the table.

Tossed from horn to horn of a horrible dilemma, Papa gnashed
his teeth in anguish. The sound, like that of cicadas at night, heralding
a warm, sunny day, brought joy to the Hog's heart, for it told him
that the Greek was in dire trouble.

Should he go up with the ♡K? Dare he play low? Was it conceivable
that the Hog had pre-empted at the four level on a six-card suit headed
by the QJ? Conversely, was it likely that having seemingly brought off
a finesse, he would deliberately give up the chance of repeating it?
Could it be that Papa's double, a matter of lofty principle rather than
of high cards, had given away the position?

It was a guess either way and if Papa misguessed, the Hog would
jeer loud and long. But he would surely jeer louder and longer if Papa
failed to take a trick at all. Perhaps, after all, one of the dilemma's
horns was less sharp than the other. With a half-suppressed curse in
his native language, the Greek went up with the ♡K, quickly swallowed
by Karapet's ace.

Recriminations followed thick and fast across the table. "Why
didn't you take your ◇A and make sure of beating the contract?"
asked Karapet in injured tones.

"Do you suppose I was doubling for one down?" countered Papa
indignantly.

"Come, come, Karapet," jeered the Hog, "you can hardly blame
Papa for omitting to make his ◇A when you, yourself, failed to take
a trick with the ace of trumps! Ha! ha!"

"Curious hand," observed Oscar the Owl, our Senior kibitzer.
"Three aces vanish into thin air and neither side enjoys the ace of
trumps."

The Hog, in rare good humour, insisted on having the last word.
"How often have I told you, Themistocles," he said, winking at the
kibitzers, "that these light doubles of yours don't pay."

FIVE BOTTOMS BELOW AVERAGE

"We need a top," said Papa the Greek to his partner, Karapet, as the penultimate board of the weekly duplicate at the Unicorn was placed on the table. "Try to steer the contract into my hand. With match-point scoring, that extra trick may make all the difference."

"Do you think we have a chance?" asked Timothy the Toucan anxiously.

The Rueful Rabbit consulted his copious notes. "I make us four bottoms below average," he replied after some thought, "but I'm not sure what the average is, I mean, they keep on changing it, but we have four zeros fewer than last week when we finished halfway down, so if it's the same average ..." While the Rabbit was dithering, Papa, the dealer, bid 1♠.

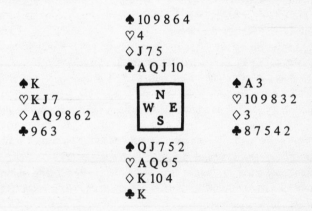

```
              ♠ 10 9 8 6 4
              ♡ 4
              ◇ J 7 5
              ♣ A Q J 10
♠ K                            ♠ A 3
♡ K J 7          N             ♡ 10 9 8 3 2
◇ A Q 9 8 6 2  W   E           ◇ 3
♣ 9 6 3          S             ♣ 8 7 5 4 2
              ♠ Q J 7 5 2
              ♡ A Q 6 5
              ◇ K 10 4
              ♣ K
```

It was hard to see how Papa could score his much-needed top on this board. With spades as trumps, all the Souths had made eleven tricks, though not all had bid game.

Against the normal club lead, every South had played the same way, going up with dummy's ace, continuing clubs and promptly discarding three diamonds. West ruffed, but the ace of trumps was the only other trick for the defence. The bidding at Papa's table followed the usual course.

Papa	T.T.	Karapet	R.R.
South	West	North	East
1♠	2◇	4♠	

While the Toucan was trying unsuccessfully to dispose of his coffee cup, in which Papa had absentmindedly put out his gold-tipped cigarette, the Rabbit reviewed the situation.

What were the prospects for the defence? He had reasonable expectations of three tricks — the ace of trumps, the ◇A and a diamond ruff. A club or a heart or maybe a second-round ruff by T.T. in one suit or the other, was the best hope of defeating the contract. Having completed his analysis, R.R. led the ♣4.

"Tournament Director!" called Papa, "lead out of turn." There was a triumphant gleam in his eye.

The startled Toucan dropped his coffee cup in Karapet's lap. The Rabbit apologised profusely, but nobody listened to him.

The Tournament Director read out the appropriate rule, with which everyone was already familiar, and the Toucan managed at last to find a resting place for his coffee cup.

Papa had no special objection to a club opening, but a lead into his heart tenace or up to his ◇K was what he really desired, so in a commanding voice he announced: "I prohibit a club lead."

Bouncing rhythmically in his chair, Timothy the Toucan began the search for a safe lead.

Either a heart or a diamond looked like costing a trick, and since clubs were banned, the king of trumps appeared to be the best of all available evils. It might even cut down declarer's tricks if he set about cross-ruffing. The Toucan led it.

Steadying himself with a sip of his favourite Cherry Brandy, the Rabbit looked at the ♠K and surveyed the scene. After his gaffe, could the defence still come to four tricks? As he studied the various possibilities, it never dawned on him, of course, that T.T. had led a bare king. The ♠Q was surely behind it and would inevitably crash with his ace. So, before it was too late, the Rabbit overtook the ♠K and shot his singleton diamond through the closed hand. The Toucan made his ace and queen of diamonds, and continued with a third diamond which the Rabbit ruffed.

"May I now lead a club?" he asked. He seemed to remember the Tournament Director reading something about ". . . or prohibit him from leading that suit for so long as he retains the lead."

"I rather think," observed Oscar the Owl, "that you have now scored your fifth bottom below average."

WEST V. SOUTH-EAST

"People sometimes wonder why I find it so tedious to win from my inferiors," soliloquized the Hideous Hog. "And yet it's simple. My artistry is wasted on an ignoramus. How can I execute a progressive squeeze against the Rabbit? Before I've squeezed him in one suit he's made suicidal discards in two others, so of course, he's always ahead of me, lying down before I can hit him.

"Or try to end play that Toucan. Since any card he plays is likely to be against his best interests, what's the point of stripping him of cards that he wouldn't play anyway?

"How different when you're up against Papa who is good enough to understand everything that happens — though only after it has happened to him, of course. Why, it's a pleasure to take his money. You must have enjoyed that er backward end-play yesterday, the one . . ."

It was the last rubber. The Hog winced when he cut the Rabbit, though it was a consoling thought that he had Papa and the Toucan against him.

Dlr. North   ♠ K Q 10
Neither Vul: ♡ 7 5 3
                    ◇ K Q 2
                    ♣ Q 10 3 2

```
        N
      W   E
        S
```

          ♠ 6 5 3
          ♡ A K J
          ◇ J 4 3
          ♣ A 7 6 4

H.H.	*T.T.*	*R.R.*	*Papa*
West	*North*	*East*	*South*
–	Pass	Pass	1♣
Pass	3♣	Pass	3NT

The Hog led the ♡2 to the Rabbit's ♡Q. Winning with the ♡K, Papa led the ◇J, then another diamond to dummy's ◇K. The Rabbit won the second time and returned the ♡8 to the ♡A.

A lesser declarer might have played on clubs. Not so Papa. He liked to play for split aces, reasoning that should R.R. have both, he couldn't have the ♣K as well, for that would give him 13 points and he had passed as dealer.

At trick five, then, after two hearts and two diamonds, Papa led a spade. The Rabbit rose at once with the ♠A and continued with the ♡6, setting up, at last, a heart trick for H.H.

Smiling confidently at the kibitzers, the Greek placed the ♣A firmly on the table. With the certain knowledge that the ♣K was where he wanted, he could almost spread his hand.

When, however, the ♣K fluttered unexpectedly on the ace, Papa frowned, for suddenly his ninth trick, a third club, had vanished into thin air. Now he would need the spade finesse — or so it seemed.

A moment's reflection, and his brow cleared. Looking around him for the admiration that was his due, he addressed the onlookers.

"A good hand for the newspapers," he began. "Call it, if you like, 'A simple play in an advanced situation'. I'll explain," and ignoring the groans round the table, he proceeded to do so.

"On his lead and on the play, H.H. is marked with four hearts. So he has no longer suit, for he would have surely led it had he possessed one, in preference to those anaemic hearts. He has a singleton club. Ergo, as the geometricians say, his shape must be 4-4-4-1 and that, if you count the suits, makes R.R.'s pattern 3-3-3-4. Simple isn't it?"

"All I need to do," went on Papa keeping up a running commentary as he played, "is to remove R.R.'s last diamond and lead the ♣3. Whether he returns a spade into dummy's ♠Q10 or a club into the ♣Q10 I'm . . ."

R.R. played the ♣8 on dummy's ♣3, but to everyone's surprise, the Hog produced the ♣J and proceeded to cash a heart and a diamond to break the contract.

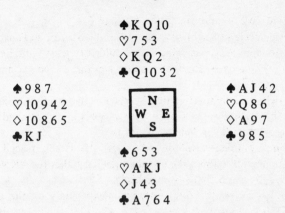

♠ K Q 10
♡ 7 5 3
◊ K Q 2
♣ Q 10 3 2

♠ 9 8 7
♡ 10 9 4 2
◊ 10 8 6 5
♣ K J

♠ A J 4 2
♡ Q 8 6
◊ A 9 7
♣ 9 8 5

♠ 6 5 3
♡ A K J
◊ J 4 3
♣ A 7 6 4

When H.H. finished gloating, he addressed the gathering.

"It was really a case of West versus South-East," he explained. "Had the Rabbit held up his ♣A, as he should have done, Papa would have stood no chance. Even if he had returned a third diamond, when he was in with the ◊A, we had the contract beaten.

"Alas, instead of profiting from Papa's 'wrong views', shall we say, he ensured the contract for him.

"How could I get the better of my opponents? Only by palming on Papa the image of a 4-4-4-1 pattern and the illusion of an end-play. And since R.R. wouldn't set up my fourth diamond, I had to get Papa to do it instead.

"What was that caption of yours?" jeered H.H. "A simple player in an advanced situation? Quite appropriate. Never mind, Themistocles," added the Hog with a patronising air. "At least you were good enough to be fooled. Thousands wouldn't."

PAPA'S DEAL WITH THE HOG

"All this nonsense about winning seats! It's so childish."

The speaker was Papa the Greek. Over canapés and Madeira at the Griffins Bar we were talking about the fuss H.H. so often made about the choice of seats. The Hog argued that apart from partner there were two other opponents to consider and either might be superstitious, and if so, it was only right and proper to inconvenience him from the start.

"What matters in an unbalanced game," explained Papa, "is that the stronger player should sit over his principal opponent. That's especially important when the Hog is at the table. By bluff and bluster and silly psyches, which shouldn't deceive a baby, he has built up some sort of reputation. So he trades on it to scare the weaklings and gets away with murder.

"That," went on the Greek, "is why I like to sit over him. I know his methods and I don't allow myself to be bamboozled as the others do.

"And then, of course, they are simply terrified of doubling him, though mind you," added the Greek contemptuously, "defending as they do they're probably quite right."

A loud guffaw interrupted the monologue. From behind a pillar appeared the pink, fleshy countenance of the Hideous Hog.

That same evening, towards the end of the session, Papa had the opportunity of demonstrating the superiority of his seating theory over the Hog's.

Papa cut the Rueful Rabbit. The Hog cut Timothy the Toucan.

"Where shall we sit?" asked the Greek with a meaning look at the Hog. "It's our choice."

"It always is," growled the Hog.

Papa gave him a superior smile. "I always forget. Seats are so important, of course. I'll tell you what I'll do, H.H., just to humour you I'll let you choose the seats if, in return, you position yourselves first, as in a match. How about it?"

"It's a deal," said H.H.

"No, please Papa," pleaded the Rabbit. "This line has won every rubber tonight. The cards are running . . . I mean . . ."

Nobody paid attention to him and he was still dithering and shaking his head as he dealt the first hand.

Dlr. East   ♠ A Q
Love All   ♡ A K 8
                              ◇ A Q 6 2
                              ♣ A K Q 4

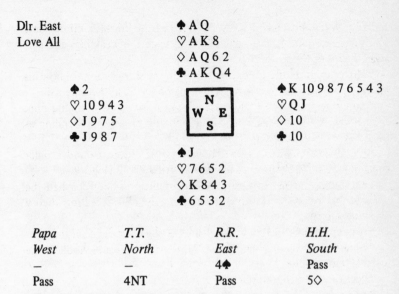

```
♠ 2                                          ♠ K 10 9 8 7 6 5 4 3
♡ 10 9 4 3          N                        ♡ Q J
◇ J 9 7 5        W     E                      ◇ 10
♣ J 9 8 7            S                        ♣ 10
                              ♠ J
                              ♡ 7 6 5 2
                              ◇ K 8 4 3
                              ♣ 6 5 3 2
```

Papa	*T.T.*	*R.R.*	*H.H.*
West	*North*	*East*	*South*
–	–	4♠	Pass
Pass	4NT	Pass	5◇

Papa led his singleton spade. The Hog went up with dummy's ace and
played the king and ace of diamond. On the second round the Rabbit
discarded a spade. Next, the Hog cashed two top clubs and when the
Rabbit showed out again, every card was marked.

"Three inescapable losers," whispered Oscar the Owl, our Senior
Kibitzer to one of his juniors.

"In the winning seats the hand should present no difficulty," scoffed
Papa.

"It won't," snapped the Hog. He cashed the ♡AK and led the ♠Q
to the Rabbit's K. Both H.H. and Papa threw hearts.

With only spades left, R.R. had to lead another, squeezing the
Greek in three suits, including trumps.

"Sitting over me," sneered the Hog letting go a club, "you should
have no difficulty in finding the right discard."

Papa considered his options.

If he ruffed, the Hog would throw a heart from dummy and score
the last two tricks by cross-ruffing.

If he discarded a club the Hog would ruff in dummy and park
his last heart on dummy's fourth club.

And if Papa threw another heart, dummy's eight would yield the
Hog his eleventh trick.

"I was squeezed in three suits," I heard the Rabbit tell the Toucan

later, "and that only left me with spades which were no good to
anyone."

"It's those seats," sympathised T.T.

A BOTTOM FOR EAST-WEST AND NORTH

Eyebrows were raised at the Griffins when it was rumoured that H.H.
and Papa would be playing together in the Unicorn's weekly duplicate.
Surely, that was carrying the detente idea too far.

But it was true. The Hog had been having a bad run. On some days
his winnings dwindled to single figures and he was growing restless.
"I'd rather lose matchpoints than money," he admitted frankly, "and
what better way can there be of getting rid of one's bad cards than
by playing with *him*? Two birds with one stone . . ."

"People have been grumbling," explained Papa, "that I always pick
strong partners. So, in a weak moment, I agreed to play with *him*. He
was delighted, of course."

The evening started amicably and they were still on speaking terms
after the first set of two boards, when, with the Hog sitting South,
this hand came up.

Dlr. North   *Papa*
Neither Vul: ♠ 9 4
                                ♡ J 10 9
                                ◇ K J 10 9
                                ♣ A K J 10

$$\begin{array}{c} N \\ W \quad E \\ S \end{array}$$

H.H.
♠ K 2
♡ —
◇ A 8 7 6 5 4 3
♣ Q 9 6 3

Papa dealt and bid 1◇. The Professor of Bio-Sophistry, better known
as the Secretary Bird, came in with 1♡ and it was up to H.H. If the
right cards were in the right places, slam prospects were bright. If they
weren't, even game couldn't be guaranteed. Did Papa have a fit in clubs

or would he have wasted values in hearts? To find out, H.H. made a probing bid of 2♣ and this sequence followed.

West	North	East	South
—	1◊	1♡	2♣
2♠	3♣	4♡	5♣
Pass	6♣	Dble.	

When Papa bid 3♣, H.H. asked to review the bidding. The last time that the Greek had raised his suit was in 1969 and history didn't repeat itself as often as all that.

One thing was certain. Papa's club support must be sensational if he could find no way of suppressing it. Spades having been bid over him, there was no longer a moral responsibility to hint at a fit in diamonds. The lead had to run up to his hand. So over 4♡ H.H. bid a confident 5♣.

Papa's raise to 6♣ was an example of matchpoints technique. Other pairs might end up in notrumps and some might make 430 or even 460. Bearing in mind that a minor suit game seldom leads to a good result, the Greek bid one more 'for the road'.

The Secretary Bird's sibilant double, the tufts of hair bristling belligerently over his ears, the gleam of his pince-nez, everything should have conveyed a message to the guileless Toucan sitting West. S.B. was demanding a diamond lead.

Oblivious of the environment, Timothy led the ♡5, just as he would have done without the double, the bristles or the gleam of the pince-nez.

The Hog ruffed S.B.'s ♡Q and paused for several seconds. "He'll go over to the table, ruff another heart and make all thirteen tricks on a dummy reversal," confided one kibitzer to another in a loud aside.

With a grunt of derision, the Hog cashed dummy's ♣AK, noting with relief that all followed, and came back to his hand with the ♣Q. Next he led the ◊3 and when T.T. followed with the ◊2, he finessed.

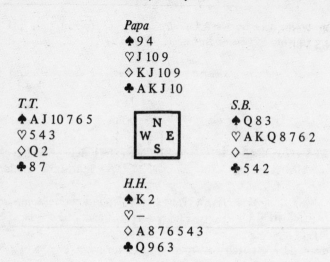

Papa
♠ 9 4
♡ J 10 9
◇ K J 10 9
♣ A K J 10

T.T.
♠ A J 10 7 6 5
♡ 5 4 3
◇ Q 2
♣ 8 7

S.B.
♠ Q 8 3
♡ A K Q 8 7 6 2
◇ —
♣ 5 4 2

H.H.
♠ K 2
♡ —
◇ A 8 7 6 5 4 3
♣ Q 9 6 3

"Why didn't you lead a diamond?" hissed the Secretary Bird. "Didn't you hear me double?"

"How could I guess," retorted the Toucan, "that H.H. hadn't mentioned his seven-card support for Papa's suit?" Then passing to the counter-attack, he went on: "If only you hadn't doubled, H.H. would never have finessed, the diamonds would have been blocked . . ."

"I should have gone down and you would have all been happy, especially Papa," jeered the Hog. "As it is, I score a top and you three share a bottom. How many extra matchpoints is that?"

AN UNUSUAL TRANSFER SQUEEZE

Whenever Papa and Karapet face the Hog and the Rabbit, the unpredictable always happens, so when fate brought them together again, a bevy of Griffins quickly gathered round the table. I found a seat between the Greek and R.R.

On the first hand the Hog bid 3NT, a fair contract against any lead except a spade, a heart or a club. Papa opened a diamond and the Hog made game on a finesse. Then this deal came up.

Dlr. West
N/S Vul:

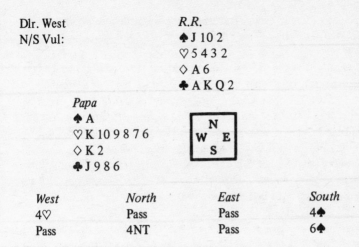

R.R.
♠ J 10 2
♡ 5 4 3 2
◇ A 6
♣ A K Q 2

Papa
♠ A
♡ K 10 9 8 7 6
◇ K 2
♣ J 9 8 6

West	North	East	South
4♡	Pass	Pass	4♠
Pass	4NT	Pass	6♠

The Rabbit's 4NT wasn't Blackwood or anything else in particular.
It was a purring noise, signifying pleasure, and the Hog evidently took
it as such.

Papa led the ♡10. Karapet played the jack and the Hideous Hog
won with the ace. Next came a trump and Papa was in again. I could
almost hear his brain ticking as he analysed the situation.

The Hog must surely have seven spades to have bid the slam. With
no more than six, missing the ace, jack, ten, even he would have settled
for game.

The play to the first trick marked him with the bare ♡A. That
came to seven tricks and dummy had four more. If the Hog had the
◇Q he couldn't fail to make his contract for Papa would be the victim
of an inevitable Vienna Coup. After taking the ◇A H.H. would reel
off his trumps and in the 4-card ending Papa couldn't retain his ◇K
and four clubs. The only hope was that Karapet had the ◇Q and the
only danger would then be that if he, too, had four clubs, he would
mistakenly discard the diamonds.

To make things easy for his partner, Papa led the ◇K, noting with
relief Karapet's ten on dummy's ace. Now Papa could keep four clubs,
leaving the Armenian to hold on to the two red queens.

The Hog played out his trumps at top speed, throwing hearts from
dummy on the fourth and fifth rounds.

The Greek's features, tense before the second heart discard, relaxed
in a smile.

"In your younger days," he told H.H., "you would have made this contract. It's too late now, I fear, for you have made a serious mistake."

"Really," said the Hog. "Perhaps you will tell me where I went wrong?"

"Certainly," rejoined Papa, not troubling to conceal his disdain. "Instead of throwing those little hearts from dummy, you should have ruffed one, both if you like. Now, Karapet, who can hardly have started with more than two hearts, could no longer guard the suit and I would have been inexorably squeezed in hearts and clubs. It's known as isolating the menace, a misleading expression, because . . ."

"Would you like a bet?" broke in the Hog. He tried to sound humble and meek, but there was a malevolent gleam in his beady eyes. "I'll say that the contract can't be made your way, but that I'll make it in mine."

"After one heart ruff the squeeze would be automatic."

"What will you wager?" pursued the Hog, who wasn't listening. "Already, owing to an earlier miscalculation, if that's the right word, you'll be sending me a case of vintage Bollinger. How about making it a case of magnums?"

The eyes of the kibitzers were focussed on Papa.

"You say that had you ruffed a heart, I wouldn't have been squeezed?" The Hog nodded. "And that you'll make the contract just the same?" The Hog nodded again. "I assume, of course, that you haven't the ◊Q," added Papa as an afterthought.

"I haven't," H.H. assured him.

"The bet's on," declared Papa. Thereupon the Hog spread his hand. This was the deal in full:

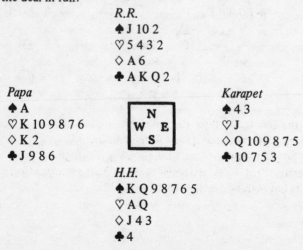

```
                      R.R.
                      ♠ J 10 2
                      ♡ 5 4 3 2
                      ◊ A 6
                      ♣ A K Q 2
   Papa                                  Karapet
   ♠ A                                   ♠ 4 3
   ♡ K 10 9 8 7 6       N                ♡ J
   ◊ K 2             W     E             ◊ Q 10 9 8 7 5
   ♣ J 9 8 6            S                ♣ 10 7 5 3
                      H.H.
                      ♠ K Q 9 8 7 6 5
                      ♡ A Q
                      ◊ J 4 3
                      ♣ 4
```

"You have the ♡Q?" exclaimed the Greek incredulously.

"True," agreed H.H., "but had I won the first trick with the queen, it would have been obvious that Karapet had a singleton, since he couldn't have the ace. So, when you came in with the ♠A you would have given him a ruff. The only way to stop you was to take the jack with the ace, 'marking' Karapet with the queen.

"Naturally," went on the Hog, winking knowingly at the kibitzers, "as the cards lay, I couldn't make the contract. I hoped against hope that Karapet would have the ◇KQ. Fortunately, Papa came to the rescue with that brilliant lead of the ◇K. Instead of keeping the red king himself and leaving Karapet to look after the clubs, he executed a cunning transfer squeeze, forcing Karapet to retain the diamond guard, so that neither of them could deny me dummy's last club.

"Now watch," went on the Hog. He led his sixth spade, then his seventh. This was the position:

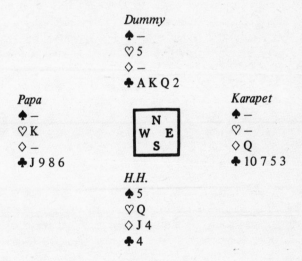

Dummy
♠ —
♡ 5
◇ —
♣ A K Q 2

Papa
♠ —
♡ K
◇ —
♣ J 9 8 6

Karapet
♠ —
♡ —
◇ Q
♣ 10 7 5 3

H.H.
♠ 5
♡ Q
◇ J 4
♣ 4

On the last spade Papa had to let go a club so as to retain his ♡K, exposing Karapet to a squeeze in the minors.

"So you thought that I had made a mistake?" observed H.H., severely. "Let it be a lesson to you, Themistocles. I may have my faults but making mistakes isn't one of them."

AN EMBARRASSING ENTRY

The Rabbit left the bar at the Griffins to get a stamp. He was away for barely a couple of minutes, but when he came back the letter he was going to post had gone.

"The very man I want," cried the Hideous Hog, moving over from an adjoining table. "You are East defending against . . ."

"Have you seen a letter," broke in the Rueful Rabbit, "a white oblong . . ."

". . . a contract of 4♠," went on H.H., brushing aside the interruption, "but it's not a double dummy problem, so let me cover up South and West." Deftly manipulating a tray of olives and a soda syphon, the Hog presented the Rabbit with this diagram.

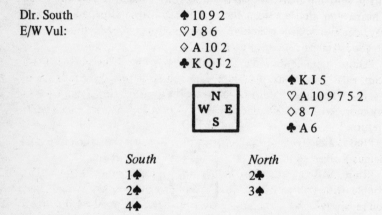

Dlr. South
E/W Vul:

```
                    ♠ 10 9 2
                    ♡ J 8 6
                    ◇ A 10 2
                    ♣ K Q J 2
                                    ♠ K J 5
                 N                  ♡ A 10 9 7 5 2
               W   E                ◇ 8 7
                 S                  ♣ A 6
```

South	North
1♠	2♣
2♠	3♠
4♠	

The Rabbit was taken aback. Unaccustomed to being consulted, he suspected a trap.

"A textbook case, really," went on the Hog, "only no textbook I know gives the right answer and I am curious to know what an ordinary paloo . . . what an er less sophisticated type of expert would do. I had this hand just now," he added reassuringly.

"Against whom?" asked R.R. suspiciously.

"The Walrus," replied H.H.

"But he's away on a cruise," objected the Rabbit.

"Well, then it was some other Walrus. What does it matter? Another name, no doubt, same IQ. Anyway, West leads the ♡Q. Proceed."

Timothy the Toucan came over with a glass of Madeira to join his friend the Rabbit and together they studied the situation.

"Obviously a singleton," said R.R., "so I go up with my ace and give partner a ruff. I still have the ♣A up my sleeve and every prospect of making a trump to get declarer one down. What's the catch?"

"Which heart do you lead back for partner to ruff?" asked the Hog.

The Toucan bounced excitedly in his chair. "A suit signal," he exclaimed. "Of course. I lead back the two, asking for the lower-ranking suit, and partner returns a club to my ace."

The Hog gave him a pitying look. "And having enjoyed your signal, what do you do next?" he asked. "Remember that declarer has at most 12 points, yet he managed to bid the fourth spade. He must surely have six trumps, in which case West has a singleton. If you lead a third heart, when you are in with the ♣A, he will have nothing to ruff it with and that will give the whole show away. If you don't lead a heart, you arouse suspicion, so it comes to the same thing. Either way, declarer will now double finesse trumps and make his contract. No good, Timothy. Over to you, R.R."

"Quite simple," declared the Rabbit. "Before giving my partner a heart ruff, I cash my ♣A, killing the entry to the dangerous hand, a sort of Merrimac Coup, if you see what I mean. Now I can't get in any more, so I can't do any damage and it doesn't matter which heart I return."

"But killing your own entry is unreasonable and therefore suspicious," objected the Hog.

"Unreasonable, yes. Suspicious, no," retorted the Rabbit. "The trouble with you experts is that everything you do has a reason, so you're always giving something away to somebody. But I do things without reasons, so nobody is any wiser than I am myself."

"What would a good player do, say, Papa?" asked the Toucan.

"I'll answer each of your questions in turn," replied H.H. giving T.T. a disapproving look. "First, Papa. He would return the ♡10, calling for a diamond. Slick, but not really clever, for an astute declarer would know that he couldn't possibly be anxious to have a diamond and that might put him on the right track. Now for the professional. He would lead the ♡7 an intermediate card which couldn't be a suit signal."

"But surely," protested R.R., "half the time partner would return a club, and as you've just explained, whether you played another heart or not, you would be giving away the trump position."

"By no means," rejoined the Hog, "for if a club is played, I don't take it. I haven't asked for a club, so no one need know that I have the ace."

"And is that what you did?" asked T.T.

"Certainly," replied H.H. "At least, that's what I caused to be done. But then I was West, you see. East was Papa and of course, at trick two, he returned the ♡10 for me to ruff. Since he asked for a diamond, I naturally played back a club . . ."

"And did he play low?" asked T.T. eagerly.

"Yes, he was just good enough to play the right card after I had virtually palmed it on him, but then he had the effrontery to pretend that he'd made a clever psychological play, asking for a diamond, because he knew that would cause me to lead a club and allow him to play low without arousing suspicion."

The Hog removed the now empty tray of olives and the syphon. "Here's the full deal, not that the other hands are really important," he added.

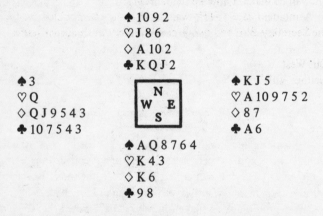

```
                    ♠ 10 9 2
                    ♡ J 8 6
                    ◊ A 10 2
                    ♣ K Q J 2
   ♠ 3                              ♠ K J 5
   ♡ Q            N                 ♡ A 10 9 7 5 2
   ◊ Q J 9 5 4 3  W   E             ◊ 8 7
   ♣ 10 7 5 4 3      S              ♣ A 6
                    ♠ A Q 8 7 6 4
                    ♡ K 4 3
                    ◊ K 6
                    ♣ 9 8
```

"But that's my letter," cried the Rabbit indignantly as the Hog began to screw up the paper into a little ball. "You've written that hand all over the envelope, you . . ."

"Well, you've found your beastly letter, so what's the panic?" rejoined the Hog testily. "Now, here's another curious hand. Give me a bit of paper, someone . . ."

THE HOG LIBELLED

"Oh well played, Papa." The Rueful Rabbit and Timothy the Toucan spoke in unison.

"Yes, a very pretty defence," echoed Charlie the Chimp. "What a pity it wasn't the Hog." The Secretary Bird agreed heartily.

"Perhaps we could set the hand up and goad him into betting," suggested the Chimp. "If we mention Papa . . ."

"No, no," broke in the Greek. "It's certainly high time to teach the Hog a lesson. But for heaven's sake don't tell him that I was West or he'll naturally expect something brilliant and that might put him on the right track. Better say that I was declarer and went down, but you wonder if, after all, there might be some play for it."

When, an hour or so later, the Hog entered the card room, the deal had been reconstructed and was waiting for him.

"We had a pretty hand just now," said the Chimp. "Papa, who went down on it, says that you would have fared no better, though double dummy, of course . . ."

"I play all hands double dummy," broke in the Hog, "and if this one can be made, I'll make it. Naturally."

A moment later, H.H. was declarer in 4♠, doubled by the Chimp, the Secretary Bird and two junior kibitzers, at the usual stakes.

Dlr. West
Neither Vul:

♠ A K 2
♡ K 5 4
◇ A K J 9 3
♣ 7 4

```
  N
W   E
  S
```

♠ Q 10 6 4
♡ A 6 3
◇ Q 10 4
♣ 8 5 3

The bidding was given as:

West	North	East	South
3♡	Dble.	4♣	4♠

As dummy went down, the Owl, who wasn't a party to the plot, walked into the room. After a look at the two hands and being told the bidding, he showed his disapproval. "Surely 5◇ would be a better contract," he observed thoughtfully.

The Hog shook his head in dissent.

"But you can't lose 5◇," persisted O.O. "West has almost certainly seven hearts. Anyway, one round will clear that up. When you've seen how often he follows in the minors you will know how many spades he has and finesse or not accordingly. You will have a complete count."

"A superficial analysis," objected H.H. "In diamonds, declarer would be some imbecile who can't count anything. Present imbe ... present company excepted, of course. In spades *I* am in charge. Play on."

West's lead was the ♣6.

East won the first two tricks with top clubs, West following, and continued with a third club on which West threw the ◇2.

"So, Themistocles went down," murmured the Hog softly.

Oscar frowned. "Why doesn't West uppercut? With only the deuce in dummy behind the tops, it should be easy enough."

"Precisely," agreed H.H. "It's a clever defence and will succeed against anyone but a virtuoso. You see what will happen, don't you? Declarer ruffs, lays down the ace and king of spades and must now get back to his hand to take a third round of trumps, for he can leave one trump out, but not two. If he tries to cross with a diamond, West ruffs and gives East a heart ruff. If South tries to get back with a heart, defenders ruff in reverse order. Very neat indeed," added the Hog with a surreptitious glance at his opponents. He was looking distinctly crestfallen.

"You forgot to redouble," hissed S.B.

"It's not too late," jeered the Chimp.

"I will gladly oblige," agreed the Hog with alacrity. The redouble was duly noted and now the Hideous Hog, having got what he wanted, proceeded to play like lightning. Ruffing the third club with the ♠A, he cashed the ♠K and crossing with the two to his queen, exited with a trump. The defence won that trick, but no other.

This was the full deal:

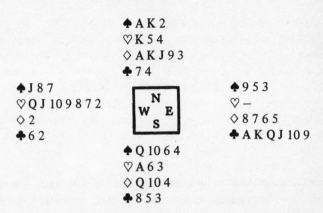

♠ A K 2
♡ K 5 4
◇ A K J 9 3
♣ 7 4

♠ J 8 7
♡ Q J 10 9 8 7 2
◇ 2
♣ 6 2

♠ 9 5 3
♡ –
◇ 8 7 6 5
♣ A K Q J 10 9

♠ Q 10 6 4
♡ A 6 3
◇ Q 10 4
♣ 8 5 3

"How did you guess . . ." began T.T.

"Surely it was against the odds to play for a 3-3 trump break," ventured R.R. "I mean, spades don't often break like that, do they?"

"That poor Papa." The Hog was in his element. "It's so easy really, if only you stop to think. On his bid and East's play, West must have seven hearts. He wouldn't have discarded a diamond if it were not a singleton, for then it would serve no purpose and the uppercut would be automatic. And if he has three cards in the minors – two clubs and one diamond – he must have three spades."

"We can now tell you," admitted the Rabbit, "that Papa wasn't declarer. He was the West who found this pretty . . ."

"What," broke in the Hog. "It was Papa who produced that silly defence?"

"But you were all for it just now," protested R.R. and T.T.

"Bah! That was before I saw the ♠J. With that key card he could make life really hard for declarer by upper-cutting. The second top trump is cashed and now declarer doesn't know whether to play East for three trumps or for four and finesse against the jack. He has no count on West, who might well have two clubs and two diamonds.

"I suppose that it was Papa who put you up to it," went on H.H. "Not only did he misdefend, but he would have misplayed the hand, too, and he thought that I could do no better. Me! Who does he think I am?" cried the Hog indignantly, "another Papa? It's defamatory. It's a libel. I'll sue . . ."

CHAPTER EIGHT

H.H. versus R.R.

The Guardian Angel wasn't away for long. Back in harness, he quickly seized the reins and moved into position beside his protegé, the Rabbit.

Was he, as Oscar believed, destiny's agent? Was the magic touch which crowned R.R.'s every gaffe with glory, a gift of the gods?

I looked for the answer in the records of clashes between H.H. and R.R.

A conversation we had over dinner long ago set the scene.

THE HOG PULLS THE WRONG CARD

Raising someone's glass of Romanée Conti, the last before the port, the Hog addressed us in philosophic vein.

"As the French say, *'la plus belle fille du monde ne peut donner que ce qu'elle a'*. Very true. The most beautiful girl in the world cannot give more than she has."

"Have you been playing in a Mixed Pairs event? enquired the Toucan.

"And so it is with bridge," pursued H.H., ignoring him. "The best player in the world cannot give what isn't there, not if the fates and furies conspire against him."

"Surprising how much H.H. has in common with the most beautiful girl in the world," chipped in Colin the Corgi, "for unless I'm mistaken, he and none other, was the victim of the fates and furies."

The Hideous Hog didn't seem to hear him. Clearing a space, he scribbled quickly on the tablecloth with his green ball-point pen.

Dlr. West
Neither Vul:

♠ K 6
♡ K Q J 10 9 3
◇ J 10
♣ Q 8 5

```
    N
  W   E
    S
```

♠ A Q J 10 9 2
♡ A
◇ 8 6 5
♣ A 4 2

West	*North*	*East*	*South*
Pass	1♡	Pass	4♠

"You are South. West leads the ◇K, then the ◇A, East echoing with the nine and two. Next comes the ◇Q. How do you play?"

"Those lovely hearts are blocked," observed the Toucan. "What a pity."

"If we ruff high," ruminated the Owl, "we lose our only entry to dummy. If we ruff low, East over-ruffs, and returns a trump. Either way, the hearts are dead, so our only hope is to find West with the ♣K, a 50/50 chance and . . ."

"Not one in fifty," broke in the Hog. "You see why, of course?" he asked, turning to R.R.

"Yes, naturally, I mean . . ."

"You don't? Then I'll explain. West passed as dealer and he is clearly marked with six diamonds, headed by the three top honours. With a king outside, he would have surely opened the bidding. So he can't possibly have the ♣K."

"What if we don't ruff that third diamond?" suggested Colin the Corgi.

The Hideous Hog was too busy with the port to interrupt, so C.C. pursued the theme.

"We win the fourth trick and must now make the rest, but things aren't as black as they seem. After laying down the ♡A, we cash the ♠A, cross to the ♠K and throw two clubs on dummy's hearts. All we need is to find East with four hearts and three trumps, which is likely enough since he is short in diamonds."

The Hog nodded approvingly. "Yes" he agreed. "West can't ruff because he has no trump left and East must follow, if, that is, he started with four hearts. It will work most of the time, but what if West knows his business?"

"He'll have a third trump?" suggested the Toucan.

The Hog gave him a withering look. "Having gathered three tricks," he went on "West will lead a fourth diamond. If you ruff with the king in dummy and throw a club, you'll still have a club loser. If you ruff low, East over-ruffs and you must win in your hand. You cash the ♡A, go over to the ♠K and try to get rid of your two club losers on the hearts. Alas, West ruffs the third heart, assuming, of course, that he began life with two hearts and two trumps. If he had three hearts, so had East and we are worse off than ever, for he will have thrown one on the third diamond which you didn't ruff. Now, whether he ruffs over the ♠6, or discards another heart, you're sunk either way. No, you'll have to do better than that."

Another glass of port gurgled down the Hog's capacious gullet, but still no one spoke.

"Your one precious asset is the ♠2," resumed H.H., "no one can crawl under it. So you ruff the third diamond with the ♠K, cross to your hand with the ♡A, cash two top spades and exit with the deuce. All you need is to find East with three trumps, which is likely enough as Colin has pointed out. With only hearts and clubs left, East is lost."

"And is that what happened?" enquired the Toucan.

"Where does that beautiful girl come in?" asked the Corgi.

The Hog turned to me. "Tell them," he said. Cracking nuts and sipping port left little time for story-telling.

This was the sad sequence of events. As happens sometimes when S.B., the Emeritus professor of Bio-Sophistry is at the table, the course of play was dictated by dummy.

Walter the Walrus was West, the Rueful Rabbit sat East and the Hideous Hog was declarer.

Unaccustomed to holding poor cards, the Rabbit's mind was wandering. He thought of Concorde. Why did people want to fly so fast when there wasn't anywhere to go? Next he turned to his horoscope, which reminded him that he had mislaid the trees to his new suede shoes.

Mechanically he played high–low to the king and ace of diamonds, and when the Walrus continued with the queen, he had his ♠7 all ready to over-ruff dummy's six. The king came as a surprise and the seven had left his hand and was well down on the way to the table before he could retrieve it.

The Secretary Bird was there in a flash. "Exposed card," he announced triumphantly.

"Certainly not." bellowed the Hog, who could see his carefully laid plan in ruins. "I couldn't see the card at all, not even that it was a trump, and neither could Walter."

"It was plainly visible," insisted S.B. "and the rule says . . ."

"I want no favours," cried the Rabbit indignantly, slamming the ♠7 on the king. "Mind you," he added with a touch of asperity, "it won't do you the slightest bit of good."

Try as he would, the Hog couldn't enforce the non-payment of a penalty and the odds, once so favourable, shrank to 50-50. After laying down the ♠A, he exited with the deuce, hoping that the Rabbit would be forced to win with the eight. It was not to be, for this was the deal:

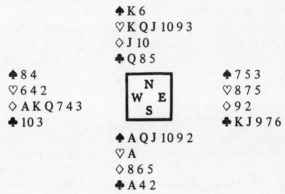

                    ♠ K 6
                    ♡ K Q J 10 9 3
                    ◇ J 10
                    ♣ Q 8 5
    ♠ 8 4   ♠ 7 5 3
    ♡ 6 4 2   N   ♡ 8 7 5
    ◇ A K Q 7 4 3 W   E   ◇ 9 2
    ♣ 10 3   S   ♣ K J 9 7 6
                    ♠ A Q J 10 9 2
                    ♡ A
                    ◇ 8 6 5
                    ♣ A 4 2

The Walrus snorted contemptuously as he scored an unexpected trick with his ♠8.

"They all think they are so good," he told me after the rubber was over. "First that Rabbit throws a trump away because his mind is wandering, then H.H. pulls the wrong card and lets me make a baby trump. And yet I'm a loser, you know. Amazing! And they say there's no such thing as luck."

COUP OUT OF THE BLUE

Having told his left-hand opponent how he should have played the previous hand and his partner how he should have bid the one before,

Charlie the Chimp had a moment or two to spare. Before picking up
his hand, his restless eyes wandered round the room.

"You've dropped a card," he told the Rueful Rabbit who was dealing at the next table. The Rabbit thanked him, picked up the ◊10 from
the floor and sorted his hand.

```
Dlr. South              ♠ 7 6 4
N/S Vul:                ♡ A 5
                        ◊ 7 6 5 3
                        ♣ K Q 5 4
```

```
                  ┌─────────┐
                  │    N    │
                  │  W   E  │
                  │    S    │
                  └─────────┘
```

```
                        ♠ A J 9
                        ♡ K 8 2
                        ◊ A 10 9 8
                        ♣ A 7 3 2
```

R.R.	T.T.
South	*North*
1NT (15–17)	2NT
3NT	

The Rabbit nearly passed 2NT, but that ◊10 gave him just a fraction
above the minimum and his horoscope for the day said distinctly:
'Be bold and resolute. Enterprise will be rewarded.' So he decided
to stretch a little.

The Hideous Hog and the Secretary Bird, sitting East-West, took
no part in the auction. S.B.'s lead was the ◊K.

Surveying his prospects, the Rabbit counted eight tricks – a spade,
two hearts, a diamond and four clubs. Fortunately, after the lead he
could set up a second diamond for his ninth trick. So, going up with
the ◊A he promptly returned the eight.

The Emeritus Professor won with the ◊Q and continued with the
jack, the Hog shedding the two and three of spades. At trick four,
S.B. played the ◊10 – and so did R.R., the two tens colliding in the
centre of the table, neither prepared to give way.

"*En carte*," called a junior kibitzer who had graduated from watching baccarat.

Timothy the Toucan bounced giddily in his chair. "What's the rule?" he asked. "The two tens are equals, so who takes the trick?"

Oscar the Owl, our Senior Kibitzer, shook his head gravely. "No," he said, "the red ten is more equal than the blue, the card from the right pack takes precedence. *Primus inter pares*."

S.B. turned up the cards. His ten was from the red pack, with which they were playing. The Rabbit's ten was from the blue pack.

"That's the card I picked up from the floor," cried R.R., "and without that extra half-point I would have passed 2NT. Besides, I wouldn't have played that way, I mean . . ."

"Quite irrelevant," hissed the Secretary Bird, "so kindly replace that card in the blue pack and substitute a card from the proper colour." As he spoke, S.B. waved a fifth diamond triumphantly in mid-air. This was the full deal:

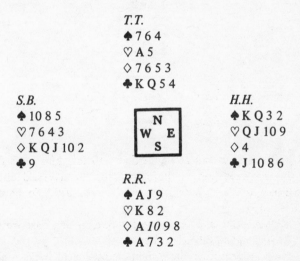

```
                    T.T.
                    ♠ 7 6 4
                    ♡ A 5
                    ◇ 7 6 5 3
                    ♣ K Q 5 4
S.B.                                        H.H.
♠ 10 8 5              N                     ♠ K Q 3 2
♡ 7 6 4 3        W         E                ♡ Q J 10 9
◇ K Q J 10 2          S                     ◇ 4
♣ 9                                         ♣ J 10 8 6
                    R.R.
                    ♠ A J 9
                    ♡ K 8 2
                    ◇ A 10 9 8
                    ♣ A 7 3 2
```

The Hog, who had been strangely quiescent, raised a fat forefinger. Putting on his most ingratiating manner, he said in a silky voice: "I don't think, Professor, that we should take advantage of an er overdeal, so to speak. Let's wash the hand out. With a bare 16 points, R.R. wouldn't have bid again, as he has just told us, so . . ."

There was a dangerous gleam behind S.B.'s pince-nez. "Who's side are you on, ours or theirs?" he asked angrily, the tufts of wiry hair over his ears bristling belligerently. "If R.R. over-valued his fourteenth card, misappropriating half a point which didn't belong to him, is

that any reason for presenting him with a bonus? Pray play to the
next trick."

The Hog, who had parted with the ♡9 on the fourth diamond, now
came under heavy pressure. Hoping that S.B. had the ♡8, he let go the
ten. R.R. discarded a spade and a club.

Having four tricks stacked neatly in front of him, the Secretary Bird
shifted to a heart. The Rabbit won in dummy and started to cash his
clubs. Then, when S.B. threw a heart on the second round, he shook
his head ruefully. A moment earlier he could see nine tricks and now
they had shrunk to seven. Maybe, if he contrived to throw someone
in with something, he could save a trick. Looking for the right exit
card, he came back to his hand with a heart, this being the 5-card
end position:

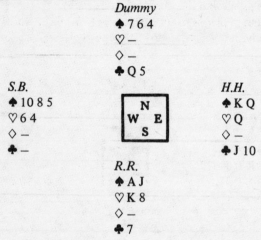

```
                        Dummy
                        ♠ 7 6 4
                        ♡ —
                        ◇ —
                        ♣ Q 5

        S.B.              ┌─────────┐        H.H.
        ♠ 10 8 5          │   N     │        ♠ K Q
        ♡ 6 4             │ W   E   │        ♡ Q
        ◇ —               │   S     │        ◇ —
        ♣ —               └─────────┘        ♣ J 10

                        R.R.
                        ♠ A J
                        ♡ K 8
                        ◇ —
                        ♣ 7
```

When the Hog produced the ♡Q R.R. looked at him suspiciously. The
Rabbit remembered seeing the jack and ten of hearts, but where was
the nine? It was just like H.H. to display flamboyantly the QJ10 and
keep the nine hidden. And yet, although R.R. couldn't be sure, there
was at least a chance that the ♡8 was good, but no chance at all that
the ♠J or dummy's last club could take the trick. Hopefully R.R.
tested the ♡8, squeezing the Hog, without malice-aforethought, in the
black suits.

The Toucan was shocked to see the Hog throw a club. "Only goes to
show," he said afterwards, "that even the best players make mistakes.
I suppose H.H. miscounted dummy's clubs. It's an easy thing to do."

The Hog snarled. "I congratulate you," he called to the Chimp at the next table. "For the first time in your life you've brought off a progressive squeeze — not at your own table, of course, but it's as near as you are ever likely to get to it."

HOW MANY WRONGS MAKE A RIGHT?

"Two wrongs may not make a right," began the Hog, "but three wrongs or four or . . ."

"You must be thinking of the Rabbit," interposed Oscar the Owl, our Senior Kibitzer.

"I am," agreed H.H., looking round for a bit of paper, "and just as the way to Hell is paved with good intentions, so in his case, the way to Heaven is paved with the worst."

Tearing out a picture from a volume of memoirs, which someone had carelessly left *en prise*, the Hideous Hog scribbled quickly on the back.

```
Dlr. East              ♠ J 9 7 3
N/S Vul:               ♡ 9 8
                       ◇ K 10 8 4 3
                       ♣ A 7
   ♠ A K Q 4 2        ┌─────────┐
   ♡ 4 3              │   N     │
   ◇ Q 9 3            │ W   E   │
   ♣ 6 4 3            │   S     │
                      └─────────┘
```

R.R.	W.W.	T.T.	H.H.
West	North	East	South
—	—	3♡	4♣
Pass	5♣		

"There," he told us, "you are West and the Toucan's East. I am declarer with the Walrus as my partner, if, that is, he falls into that category.

"You start with the ♠AK, to which all follow, and switch to the ♡4. The Toucan's card is the ♡10 and I win with the ♡A. Next I reel off seven trumps — the Toucan follows once — and then the ◇A. What do you keep?"

The Owl recapitulated. "Two spades have gone, the two red aces and seven clubs, leaving me with two cards. Correct?"

The Hog nodded and O.O. resumed.

"If you have a heart and a diamond left, it doesn't matter what I keep for there's an automatic double squeeze. Since I must retain my ♠Q, I have to bare the ◇Q. Dummy's ♠J goes and Timothy is squeezed in the red suits. I assume, therefore, that you have no heart and I promptly discard my ♡3 to give partner a count and . . ."

"Most unlikely distribution," broke in H.H. "At favourable vulnerability, with eight good hearts, the Toucan wouldn't have been so pusillanimous as to open 3♡. He would have made it 4♡. Anyway, I did have a heart and a diamond, so . . ."

"Then," broke in the Owl, "nobody can do anything about it."

"Except the Rabbit," retorted H.H.

"Do you mean," asked O.O. incredulously, "that he found a way to break the unbreakable contract?"

"I do," declared the Hog, "but the way he got there is even more remarkable than the end-product." Emptying the nearest glass, H.H. told the story.

"When he's playing with T.T., R.R. is at his best, that is his deadliest, for the Toucan is the weaker of the two, if that is possible, and the chivalrous Rabbit tries to protect him. So, instead of playing, as usual, the card nearest his thumb, he thinks and counts and calculates. Here he actually worked out that after nine black cards and two red aces had been played, I would have two cards left. What would they be?"

Silencing the Owl, who had half opened his mouth, H.H. continued.

"The Rabbit was certain that I hadn't started with ◇Ax, for in that case I would have given myself the chance of setting up the suit with one ruff. Then, if trumps broke 2-2, I would be home. You see the fallacy of that argument, of course."

H.H. paused and O.O. nodded assent.

"You can't see it? Then I'll explain. If I have only two diamonds, I must have a heart, so T.T. has seven. He has shown two spades, and has, therefore, four cards in the minors. So if he has three diamonds, he can't have two clubs and vice versa. In short, both minors can't break and no distribution would allow me to enjoy a third trick in diamonds.

"Next, R.R. considered my having three diamonds and no second heart. That didn't worry him. If I had the ◇J, I couldn't lose, for he would have to cling on to his ♠Q, and if T.T. had it he would keep the ◇Jx to the end and all would be well."

The Hog paused to refill his glass.

"As you were no doubt about to point out," resumed H.H., "that supposition is impossible. If I have three diamonds, the Toucan can't have more than two, for the Rabbit can see the other eight, three in his own hand and five in dummy.

"But then R.R. is no mathematician. His approach is essentially psychological. And so it was here.

"All along, he suspected me of having the bare ◇A and three hearts. It wouldn't have helped me to cash the ◇A and score the ◇K, while I was in dummy with the ♣A, since I would still have a heart to lose. So I was trying to bamboozle the opposition, and more especially, his friend the Toucan. To retain his useless diamonds, he would discard his precious hearts. That, he thought, was my idea.

"Some ten years ago," went on H.H., "the Rabbit was the victim of just such a coup and he has never forgotten it."

The Hog filled in the diagram.

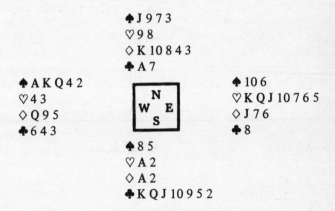

```
                   ♠ J 9 7 3
                   ♡ 9 8
                   ◇ K 10 8 4 3
                   ♣ A 7
    ♠ A K Q 4 2         N          ♠ 10 6
    ♡ 4 3          W        E      ♡ K Q J 10 7 6 5
    ◇ Q 9 5             S          ◇ J 7 6
    ♣ 6 4 3                        ♣ 8
                   ♠ 8 5
                   ♡ A 2
                   ◇ A 2
                   ♣ K Q J 10 9 5 2
```

"The Rabbit's first three discards were, therefore, the ◇5, the ◇9 and the ◇Q, to give T.T. a count on the diamonds. Now, willy nilly, he had to keep his ◇J7 and throw his hearts, the ♡K following dummy's ♡9.

"But you see what happened. So anxious was the Rabbit to shed his diamonds, that without malice aforethought, he kept his ♡3, the key card. No double squeeze now, for T.T. could let go his hearts with impunity. He was forced to do the opposite of what R.R. intended.

The Hog drained his glass and concluded bitterly. "That's what happens when you have a bad run. With his mind on a hand that came up ten years ago, assuming fourteen diamonds in the pack and expecting his partner's four cards in the minors to consist of three diamonds and two clubs, he produces, despite his best endeavours, a superb defence.

"How many players, do you suppose," asked the Hog rhetorically, "would realise, after the suit had been played once, that the 3 would be a master card?"

WOE TO THE WINNERS

"We all know," philosophised Oscar the Owl, over the post-prandial port, "that it's our other pair that loses the points. But badly as they play, they leave our vanity unpricked, our egos unruffled. Think how galling it would be if they played better than we did and stole the limelight. I wonder," mused O.O., "if in the last resort it isn't better to lose a match than to have them win it and bask miserably in their sunshine."

These reflections were prompted by the Hog's mortifying experience in the inter-club match between the Anchorites and the Sybarites.

With eight boards to go, the Anchorites, Papa's club, had a lead of 10 IMPs and when seven flat boards followed, it looked as if they were bound to win. Then came the last, fateful board. Spectators crowded round the table to watch Papa and Karapet as they faced H.H. and Colin the Corgi.

Dlr. West
Both Vul:

	♠ Q 9 7 2	
	♡ Q J 10 4	
	◇ A K	
	♣ K 7 6	
♠ J 10 8		♠ K 6
♡ A K 7 5 3	N	♡ 8
◇ 6 2	W E	◇ Q J 5 4 3
♣ A 8 3	S	♣ Q J 10 4 2
	♠ A 5 4 3	
	♡ 9 6 2	
	◇ 10 9 8 7	
	♣ 9 5	

Papa	C.C.	Karapet	H.H.
West	North	East	South
1♡	Dble.	Redble.	1♠
Pass	2♣		

Papa began with three rounds of hearts, giving Karapet a ruff. The ◇4 to dummy's ◇K followed.

The Hog played off the ◇A and continued with the ♡Q. When Karapet rose with the ♠K, the contours of the entire hand quickly took shape.

H.H. over-ruffed and led a club. Papa promptly went up with the ♣A and exited with another club to the ♣K.

Ruffing dummy's third club, the Hog brought about this four-card ending.

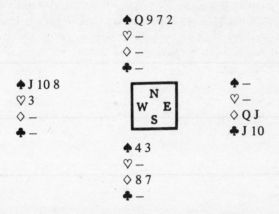

"If he had another entry and could play through West's hand," explained O.O., to a junior kibitzer, "he could score three of dummy's trumps. As it is, of course . . ."

At this point, the Hog led the ♠4, and when Papa inserted the ♠10, he allowed him to hold the trick, playing from dummy — the ♠7!

A trump return would spell instant defeat, so Papa played back the ♡3. H.H. ruffed in dummy with the ♠2 and over-ruffed in his hand with the ♠3. Having conjured up a previously unsuspected entry to his hand, he threw a diamond jauntily on the table and claimed the last two tricks.

"Same result in the other room, no doubt," said Papa. "The hand plays itself."

A loud guffaw was the Hog's only comment.

They were playing the last board in the other room and O.O. tiptoed across discreetly to look at the score.

"The Sybarites have won," he announced on his return. "That hand you've just had decided the match."

"Just as I thought," said the Hog, with a contemptuous look at Papa. "I expect they made 3♣ your way and . . ."

"No, no," broke in the Owl, "the match was won by your East-West pair who made game."

"Impossible!" declared Papa. "What in?"

"Spades," replied O.O., a faint smile showing through his usually inscrutable mask.

This is what happened.

Like Papa, Timothy the Toucan had opened 1♡ and like Colin the Corgi, Walter the Walrus doubled. Thereafter however, the two paths diverged. Not thinking that he was worth a redouble, the Rueful Rabbit bid 1♠. He had no thought of psyching. He expected to be doubled and intended to redouble, so as to force the Toucan to show his longer minor. How else could the Rabbit describe a weak, distributional hand with clubs and diamonds?

Alas, the Toucan didn't get the message and 1♠ redoubled became the final contract, after this sequence.

West	North	East	South
1♡	Dble.	1♠	Pass
Pass	Dble.	Redble.	Pass
Pass!			

Charlie the Chimp, who was sitting South for the Anchorites, led the ◇10. The Walrus cashed the ◇AK and exited with the ♡Q. After the ♡AK and a heart ruff, the Rabbit led the ◇Q, throwing a club from dummy.

The Walrus ruffed, and unable to visualise the trump position, switched to a club, a fatal move.

These were the last seven cards.

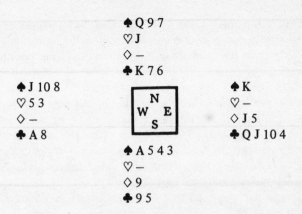

♠Q 9 7
♡ J
◇ —
♣K 7 6

♠ J 10 8
♡ 5 3
◇ —
♣ A 8

♠ K
♡ —
◇ J 5
♣Q J 10 4

♠A 5 4 3
♡ —
◇ 9
♣9 5

Coming in with the ♣Q, R.R. led another diamond, this time discarding a heart from dummy. Again the Walrus ruffed and again he couldn't bring himself to lead a trump. A club to the ♣A was followed by a heart and a deadly uppercut with the ♠K. Over-ruffing, the Chimp had to lead a trump, for he had nothing else, ensuring two trump tricks and the contract for a bewildered Rabbit. That came to 670 points, and a swing of 13 IMPs to the Sybarites, just enough to win the match.

The Hideous Hog was stunned.

"Do you mean," he repeated slowly, "that they won, that is, er we won, not through my fine play, but through their execrable bidding?"

The Hog's lofty moral principles were shattered.

"It's an outrage," he cried. "Cancel the board! Cancel the Toucan! Cancel the ..." The loud bang of the door as he stalked out of the room, drowned his last words.

SEVEN NOTRUMPS ON A TRUMP SQUEEZE

"You know," said the Rueful Rabbit, as we sat sipping liqueurs after dinner, "I sometimes think that the Hideous Hog isn't really as black as he is painted." Seeing the startled looks on our faces, R.R. hastened to explain. "Oh, I know that he gloats and jeers and abuses his partners, hand after hand — and his opponents, too, of course, for it wouldn't be ethical otherwise — but there must be a better side to him, as well. Here's an example. Lately every time Timothy and I have asked him if we could play together, instead of cutting for partners, he has agreed with alacrity. Rather decent of him, you know."

"Don't you think," asked Oscar the Owl, "that self interest could have something to do with it? He might take the view, for instance, that you two are less technically advanced than er some other people."

"I'd thought of it," replied the Rabbit brightly, "but it can't be that really. After all, it isn't as if he could avoid being saddled with a partner altogether, and what's the use of cutting, say, the Walrus instead of one of us? It's like falling out of the frying pan into the fire, isn't it? Yes, I know the Walrus thinks of himself as the third worst player in the club, but then we all over-rate our game, don't we? I'll say this for him, though? he, too, never minds playing set with the Hog against us. Very sporting, I call it."

"Could it be," ventured O.O., "that he prefers the Hog as a partner to either of you?"

"Ye-es, there's that," agreed the Rabbit a little hesitantly, "but there's another side to it, too, you know. It's rather tiresome to be told before even you've detached a card, that only a moron would think of playing it. The Walrus is rich and important, a director of banks and things, and he doesn't like being reviled all the time. But he puts up with the Hog, like the rest of us, and he told me why quite frankly. 'Whenever I sit down to play,' he said, 'I'm insulted anyway. At least when the Hog's my partner, I'm insulted by a much better type of player'."

R.R. and T.T. like to play together by way of practice for tournaments. Just at present their target is the Pairs Salver at the Rockall International Bridge Festival over the August Bank Holiday. "All those prizes on the Blue List reserved for non-experts are very tempting," he told me, "and we *are* non-experts, aren't we?" The claim could not be challenged.

The day after we had been discussing the Hog's new-found magnanimity, H.H. and W.W. found themselves once more at the same table with R.R. and T.T. Soon this hand came up.

Dlr. South
Love All

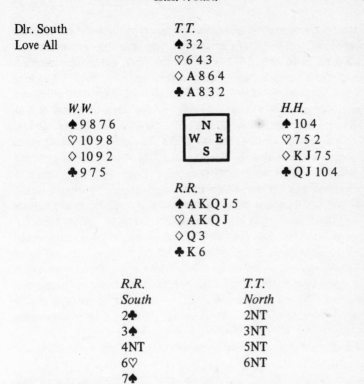

T.T.
♠ 3 2
♡ 6 4 3
◇ A 8 6 4
♣ A 8 3 2

W.W.
♠ 9 8 7 6
♡ 1 0 9 8
◇ 1 0 9 2
♣ 9 7 5

H.H.
♠ 10 4
♡ 7 5 2
◇ K J 7 5
♣ Q J 10 4

R.R.
♠ A K Q J 5
♡ A K Q J
◇ Q 3
♣ K 6

R.R.	T.T.
South	*North*
2♣	2NT
3♠	3NT
4NT	5NT
6♡	6NT
7♠	

The bidding sequence gave nothing away, East-West remaining as much in the dark as North–South themselves.

The Rabbit's 4NT was two-way, partly Blackwood, partly quantitative. The Toucan's 5NT response was a transfer bid — transferring the responsibility to partner. At this stage, the Rabbit could do no more than show his first four controls in hearts. Wondering whether this was a suit, a cue-bid or a grand slam force, agreeing notrumps, the Toucan signed off in 6NT. Thinking of his honours, the Rabbit closed proceedings with 7♠. After all, it was one more.

Walter the Walrus led the ♡10 and as T.T. tabled his hand, carelessly placing the diamonds on the right, the Emeritus Professor of Bio-Sophistry, commonly known as the Secretary Bird, walked into the room. In a wide tie of rich bilious yellow, his wiry tufts of hair standing up on either side of his bald domed-shaped head, he looked every inch a secretary bird.

"What are they in?" asked S.B., addressing an elderly Griffin, who

used to be a fair auction player in the twenties, but has never quite
succeeded in mastering the finer points of contract.

"7NT," replied the elderly Griffin. After all, notrumps had been
mentioned five times and spades only twice.

Impressionable by nature, and confused by finding the diamonds
on dummy's right, R.R. began to think instinctively in terms of notrumps. He could count four spades, probably five, four hearts, the ♢A
and the ♢K of clubs, at best twelve tricks. The thirteenth would need
a minor miracle, but then the Rabbit was a firm believer in miracles.

After the ♡A, he played off four spades. Was the fifth one good?
The Hog had thrown the ten on the first round, but had he followed
the next time? It was a black card without doubt, for had it been a
red one, the Rabbit, with his fine sense of colour, would have spotted
it at once. But was it a club or a spade? While he debated the issue,
he cashed the hearts.

The Hog's beady eyes contracted into narrow slits. Unless that
hair-brained Rabbit played off quickly his last spade, he might stumble
inadvertently on to a trump squeeze. Should he be alerted? Some
friendly remark like, "A hundred honours, I fancy," would create the
right ambiance. The Hog took the cigar out of his mouth and cleared
his throat, waiting only for W.W. to follow to the last heart. This was
the position:

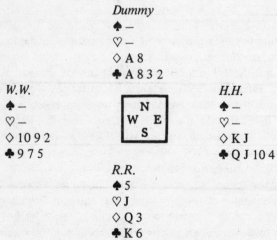

When the Walrus produced the ♣5 the Hog gave him the sort of look
he usually reserved for Papa and replaced the cigar in his mouth.

It was no use now inciting R.R. to play off his spade. If he did and if, as was to be feared, he had the ♢Q and the ♣K, H.H. would be caught in a criss-cross squeeze. In the four-card ending, dummy would retain the ♢A and three clubs, headed by the ace. The Rabbit would have the queen-small of diamonds and the king-small in clubs, and the Hog would have to unguard one suit or the other.

On the last heart a diamond was shed from dummy, while H.H. parted with the ♣10. Maybe R.R. didn't have the ♣K after all. It was a chance.

Suddenly the Rabbit saw a gleam of hope. If the Hog had thrown a club earlier on that second spade, maybe all the outstanding clubs would fall together. Breathing hard, he laid down the ♣K. The Hog followed with the jack, the Walrus with the seven. One more heave. If only the nine and queen would come down on the ace! Alas, the nine appeared, but the Hog calmly produced the four. Crestfallen, the Rabbit played a third club, throwing the ♠5 on the Hog's ♣Q.

"Sorry, Timothy," he murmured, "one down."

"Never mind, consoled the Toucan, "you had honours, didn't you? Well, we're still 50 up on balance."

"Honours?" hissed the Secretary Bird. "I thought you were in notrumps. If you were in spades, you've made your grand slam."

"I'm afraid I've conceded . . ." began R.R.

"Nonsense." There was a dangerous glint behind S.B.'s pince-nez. The jurist in him was fully aroused, and matching the Hog's snarl with a loud hiss, he recited Law 74. "If a trick cannot be lost by any sequence of play of the remaining cards, the concession is withdrawn. Sub-section (b), if my memory serves me right."

After a triumphant look at the Hog, who had so often been his tormentor, S.B. turned to the Rabbit. "I congratulate you, R.R. on a brilliantly timed trump squeeze."

"Ah well," said the Rabbit meekly, "it's something to have brought off a trump squeeze, even if only when playing in notrumps.

Could it be, I wondered, looking back on these hands, that the Guardian Angel was exceeding his instructions? Whenever his protegé was in danger, no stratagem seemed too cynical, too Machiavellian to be employed on his behalf. I began to suspect that the Angel had a cruel, vicious streak in him and that he positively enjoyed his part.

CHAPTER NINE

Enter the Ladies

A SQUEEZE WITHOUT A NAME

Since it was founded, long before bridge was born, The Griffins has been a man's club. Ladies have been welcome as members' guests in the restaurant, but none has ever been admitted to the cardroom — until this year. As a daring innovation, the first Thursday in every month has now been set aside as Ladies' Day, when the cardroom is open to both sexes.

The Hideous Hog was the first to give this revolutionary step his blessing.

"We are getting short of worthwhile losers," he told the committee. "Of course, your Walrus and your Toucan contribute their steady 500s and there's always the Rabbit, but the 800s and 1100s are getting scarcer every day. The girls will soon put that right. Let 'em come. I'm no male chauvinist pig, you know, not by any means."

Molly the Mule, one of the stars of the Mermaids Club, was the first member of the stronger sex to visit us. Her initiation was with the Rueful Rabbit as partner, facing the Hideous Hog and Timothy the Toucan.

"What do you like to play?" she asked R.R. "I prefer reverse signals, inverted minors, Roman Blackwood, South African Texas, a weak notrump throughout and anything else you say."

"A weak notrump is a bit dangerous, vulnerable, don't you think?" ventured the Rabbit.

"Not if you play your cards really well," replied Molly reassuringly.

Hoping fervently that he wouldn't get vulnerable, the Rabbit tried not to look apprehensive.

The rubber started inauspiciously. The Hog opened 1♣ and rebid 3NT over the Toucan's response of 1♡. Molly, sitting over the Toucan, doubled resonantly. She held: ♠J6 ♡AQJ10962 ◇104 ♣Q5.

The Hog promptly redoubled and quickly wrapped up eleven tricks. The Rabbit gurgled ruefully.

"It's no fault of mine if you've no heart to lead," Molly told him severely, "and if I can't double with six certain tricks in their suit, I should like to know when I *can* double. When it's my own lead, I suppose!"

"Not in this case," pointed out the Hog with a friendly leer. "I would have made an extra trick with dummy's ♡K."

"You didn't even have an entry," murmured the Rabbit reproachfully.

"I can't have everything," snapped back M.M.

Shortly afterwards, she made game. Then this hand came up.

Dlr. East
Both Vul:

T.T.
♠ 6 4 3 2
♡ 7 5 3
♢ Q 8 2
♣ A K Q

R.R.
♠ Q J 10 9
♡ 9 8
♢ 9 6
♣ 6 5 4 3 2

```
  N
W   E
  S
```

M.M.
♠ A K 8
♡ Q 4 2
♢ K J 10 5 3
♣ 10 9

H.H.
♠ 7 5
♡ A K J 10 6
♢ A 7 4
♣ J 8 7

R.R.	T.T.	M.M.	H.H.
–	–	1NT	Dble.
Pass	Pass	2◊	2♡
Pass	4♡		

The Rabbit feared the worst when Molly's 1NT was doubled and was much relieved when 2◊ wasn't.

The Hog's bidding wasn't exactly sound, but then neither were his opponents and he added 3 points from each, in turn, to his other values.

Against 4♡, R.R. led the ♠Q, then the ♠J, overtaken by Molly, who continued with a third spade. The Hog ruffed, laid down the ♡A and crossing to the ♣A, took the trump finesse. After another round of trumps, he cashed the ♣K, then the ♣Q, Molly discarding the ◇3.

She looked at her wristwatch. "Let's save time. I get two diamond tricks. One off," she announced.

"*One* diamond trick," corrected H.H. "I make the rubber come to eight points."

With a disdainful look, Molly showed the Hog her hand.

The Hog nodded. "Quite so," he said, "you're marked with these cards, except perhaps the ◇10, but when I throw you in, you will play a diamond away from . . ."

"I shall do no such thing and no one is going to throw me in," retorted Molly defiantly.

"I'll squeeze you first, of course," rejoined the Hog with a meaning wink at the kibitzers.

"Squeeze me? What in?" demanded Molly.

"Diamonds," replied H.H.

"And what other suit?" persisted Molly.

"Just diamonds. Diamonds and diamonds," replied the Hog.

"But that's ridiculous," protested Molly. "There must be at least two suits."

"It's customary," agreed the Hog "but when a second suit is lacking, I make do with one. Watch." This was the position.

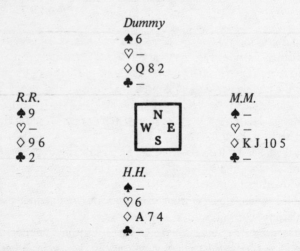

The Hog led dummy's ♣6. "This, my dear Molly, is how I squeeze you," he explained. "If you throw your low diamond, I duck a diamond into your hand and . . ."

"I unblock, obviously," countered Molly, throwing the ◊10.

The Hog ruffed and played the ◊4.

"Which card would you like from your partner?" he asked politely, and as M.M. said nothing, he went on. "If he plays low, I insert dummy's ◊8 and you have to lead away from your ◊K. If he goes up with the ◊9, I cover with the ◊Q and you have to play away from your ◊J while the ◊8 remains in dummy.

"To avoid the end-play," concluded the Hog, "you must retain the ◊KJ10 and a low one, as well — four cards in the three-card ending. That's why you are squeezed. You can see it, of course, R.R.?"

The Hog winked again at the kibitzers.

"Of course," replied the Rabbit, "and I am squeezed, too, in a manner of speaking, because I have to play the ◊9 or the ◊6 and both are wrong. I haven't got a card that isn't. I seldom do, you know. I am squeezed, as it were, from the start, before I discard anything at all. It's what they call 'a squeeze without a name', I suppose."

Molly had the last word. "If only you'd had the courtesy to lead my suit, all this wouldn't have happened. I did bid diamonds, you know, not spades." And with a scornful look she sailed out of the room.

MIXED BRIDGE

A Mixed Pairs, the first in the club's history, was the highlight of a gala Christmas party at the Unicorn. The Santa Claus Cup, and the rich prizes of scent, caviar and champagne that went with it, brought together the leading players and kibitzers in clubland.

Molly, nicknamed the 'Mule' and Dolly the Dove, the brightest stars at the Mermaids, as they were the first to admit, partnered the Hideous Hog and his rival, Papa the Greek.

Molly had her faults, but being wrong wasn't one of them and for any points she lost in play, she fully made up in the post-mortem.

Dolly owed her soubriquet to the gentle look in her eyes whenever she doubled opponents into game or conceded a hefty penalty. "I had to do it," she would coo softly, "didn't I?"

Chastened by the ministrations of their respective Mermaids, the Hog and Papa almost forgot how much they disliked each other when they met on the last set of boards.

"Doing well?" asked Papa, hoping for a bitter disclaimer.

"I reckon I need two tops or thereabouts," replied H.H., "and you?"

"About the same," said the Greek. "We've had our share of presents, but . . ."

"I know," sympathised the Hog, "some people," he added with a meaning look at Molly, "think it's more blessed to give than to receive."

On board 11, the first of the two they had to play, Molly miscounted the trumps and went one down in 4♠.

"It's not too bad really," she explained after glancing at the travelling score slip. "We would have only had an average had I made it. Everyone seems to have bid it and they all scored ten tricks."

"There are eleven on a criss-cross squeeze . . ." began the Hog, but got no further.

"Which is how I was going to play it," declared Molly, "if only that miserable waiter hadn't come up with the coffee I hadn't ordered just as I was about to draw trumps."

As H.H. picked up the next hand he reflected gloomily that even a cold top would no longer bring him the caviar and champagne which had been so nearly in his grasp.

They were playing in a small alcove, separated from the main cardroom, with Colin the Corgi, the facetious young man from Oxbridge, as the only kibitzer.

As will be seen from the diagram opposite, board 12, the last of the evening, had some unusual features:

Dlr. South   ♠ A Q 9
Game All   ♡ A 8 6
                              ◇ J 10 7 6 5
                              ♣ 10 2

```
        N
    W       E
        S
```

                              ♠ A Q 8 3
                              ♡ A 2
                              ◇ A K Q 6
                              ♣ J 9 2

H.H.	Papa	M.M.	D.D.
South	West	North	East
1◇	Pass	3◇	Pass
4♣	Dble.	4♡	Pass
4NT	Pass	5♡	Dble.
5NT	Pass	6♣	Pass
6◇			

Papa led the ◇10.

"Curious duplication of aces," observed Colin, as dummy came down. "I wonder if there's a third ♠A or ♡A lurking somewhere.

"You have two of my cards," said Dolly to Molly accusingly.

There was a stunned silence.

"I rather think," suggested the Corgi, "that the North hand was picked up inadvertently from board 19, presumably left behind after an earlier round and now out of play." He pointed to a set of boards on an adjoining coffee table.

"If they will strew wrong boards all over the place, what can you expect?" exclaimed Molly indignantly. "I wonder you bother to have tournament directors."

"The cards are of a different colour," pointed out Dolly. "My new curtains . . ."

"I can't see the backs of my cards," retorted Molly with spirit, "but you can and not one of you spotted anything. Amazing! Mind you, a more ridiculous colour than this wishy-washy pallid pink, it would be hard to imagine."

Having put the blame fairly and squarely where it belonged, on the

tournament director, the other three players and the parties responsible
for providing the cards, Molly replaced her hand in board 19 and took
out the one from the North slot on board 12. As she tabled it, this
was the picture.

♠ K 5
♡ K 8 7 6 5
◇ 5 4 3 2
♣ K 5

♠ A Q 8 3
♡ A 2
◇ A K Q 6
♣ J 9 2

"Fancy that," exclaimed Molly, looking at the new dummy, "I might
as well have made the same 3◇ bid here, starting with 1♡, perhaps,
then 3◇, and we should have reached 6◇ just the same."

"Identical hand," observed the Corgi, "just two aces missing."

"Yes, but three kings in their place," countered Molly, "so that's
9 points instead of 8."

"I suppose we'll have to call the tournament director," sighed Papa.
"One good result, after that last board, and we should have probably
won. Now we'll get an average, an adjusted score and..."

"They'll take hours over it," broke in Dolly.

"I'm starving," said Molly. "Why can't we play the hand as it is?"

Papa beamed at her.

The Hog, who had been meditating deeply, greeted the sugges-
tion with a derisive snort. "What, with that dummy?" he asked
contemptuosly.

After a pause, he cleared his throat and resumed in more ingratiating
tones. "I'll make you a sporting offer. Before the last bottom we were
probably winning and now we are not, so I've nothing to lose. How
would it be then if instead of calling the tournament director," the Hog
waited for the words to sink in, "I agreed to chance my arm in 6◇
with this miserable dummy and you, in turn, agreed that if I made it,
we would er rectify the result on the last board? That way one or other
of us would get two tops which would obviously serve the public
interest best."

No one could see any flaw in the argument.

"The scoring slip for board 11 is still here," said the Hog. "The result," he added with a meaning look, "is entered in pencil."

"Most irregular," remarked Dolly, "and I like to be regular, of course, but it would save a lot of fuss and no one, I am sure, would say anything." She looked appealingly at Colin the Corgi.

Colin was sympathetic. "It would be a worldly solution," he agreed, "in keeping with the season and the festive spirit. Besides the play in 6◇ could be of interest."

Molly supported the proposal enthusiastically. "It's only fair," she said. "After all, why should the result of the tournament be decided by a silly waiter? But for him I would have certainly drawn the last trump and worked that crossword squeeze as I had intended all along . . ."

"It's a deal," broke in Papa. "Neither of us wants an average, so I'll be generous. My lead stands, of course."

Before tempting Papa with his all-or-nothing offer, the Hideous Hog had made a quick assessment of his prospects.

Over Molly's jump raise of 3◇ he had made an inhibitory bid of 4♣, since any other lead would suit him better, and Papa had doubled. Clearly, dummy's ♣K was well placed. That was the key factor in his calculations.

Winning the first trick with the ◇A, the Hog led the ♣2. The Greek went up promptly with the ♣A and returned another trump.

The Hog now had ten top tricks — three spades, two hearts, four diamonds and the ♣K. On the face of it, he could score two more by ruffing a spade and a club in dummy. Without the trump lead and continuation, that is how he would have played. Now he no longer had the communications.

He could cash his ◇K, take the ♠K and ♣A and ruff a club. Coming back with the ♡A, he could ruff a spade, but there would be no way back to the closed hand to draw the last trump, except by ruffing a heart and Papa would undoubtedly over-ruff. For hadn't Dolly doubled the 5♡ response to Blackwood, indicating a safe lead? With three hearts only, the double would make no sense.

So the Hog devised another plan. Papa could surely be placed with the ♣Q. Without it, going up with the ♣A at trick two would have been a doubtful play.

If only Dolly had the ♣10, the caviar and champagne might still be his.

Back on play with the ◇K at trick three, the Hog took three rounds of spades, throwing dummy's ♣K!

This was the full deal:

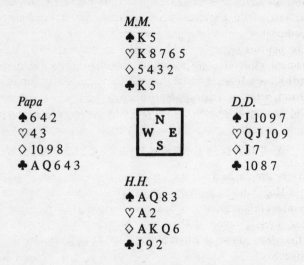

M.M.
♠K 5
♡K 8 7 6 5
◇5 4 3 2
♣K 5

Papa
♠6 4 2
♡4 3
◇10 9 8
♣A Q 6 4 3

D.D.
♠J 10 9 7
♡Q J 10 9
◇J 7
♣10 8 7

H.H.
♠A Q 8 3
♡A 2
◇A K Q 6
♣J 9 2

At trick seven came the ♣J, covered by the ♣Q and ruffed in dummy. Next H.H. led a diamond to his ◇Q, drawing the last trump, then his last diamond on which dummy shed a heart.

It was Dolly's turn. What could she do?

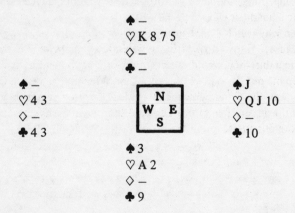

♠ —
♡K 8 7 5
◇ —
♣ —

♠ —
♡4 3
◇ —
♣4 3

♠J
♡Q J 10
◇ —
♣10

♠3
♡A 2
◇ —
♣9

After fingering every card in turn, she finally discarded the ♠J. The ♠3, now a master, applied the *coup de grâce*. If she gave up a heart, dummy's last heart would be a winner. If she parted with the ♣10, the ♣9 would yield the Hog his twelfth trick.

"Remind me to tell them Colin," said the Hog in a loud aside, "that I want those goods delivered before noon. My housekeeper . . ."

The rest of the sentence was drowned by an announcement over the loudspeaker.

"Competitors who played board 12 after the sixth round," said the tournament director, "are asked to note that they will be awarded adjusted scores. It is regretted that during the seventh round the East-West hands were accidentally inter-changed."

"Did you say before noon?" enquired Colin the Corgi solicitously.

A TRADE UNION FOR KIBITZERS

"Kibitzers should be paid the proper rate for the job," declared the Hideous Hog, putting down my glass. "Nobody should be expected to watch man's inhumanity to man at his own expense."

"But surely," objected Oscar the Owl, "that's in flat contradiction with the view you've so often expressed that kibitzers should pay for the privilege of . . ."

"Yes, yes," broke in the Hog impatiently, "and I agree with every word I said. Just as you pay to hear a virtuoso conduct an orchestra, so you should likewise pay to watch an artist perform at the bridge table." The Hog modestly dipped his eyelashes. "But," he went on, "art is one thing, butchery is another. To watch a quartet of ghouls massacre a hand trick by trick . . ."

"Then why watch?" interjected the Owl.

"Because," retorted the Hog, scribbling as he spoke, "if I strayed from the table they would cut again quickly at the end of the rubber and keep me out."

This was the hand which had caused the Hog so much anguish. It came up on another of our Ladies' Days, when Molly the Mule was once more our guest.

Dlr. West
Both Vul:

```
                        ♠ A J 7
                        ♡ K 4
                        ◇ A Q 10 8 6
                        ♣ A 4 3
  ♠ 9 8 5 4 3                              ♠ Q 10 2
  ♡ Q 7 6 5 2         ┌─────────┐          ♡ A 10 9
  ◇ 3 2               │    N    │          ◇ K 4
  ♣ 2                 │  W   E  │          ♣ Q J 10 9 7
                      │    S    │
                      └─────────┘
                        ♠ K 6
                        ♡ J 8 3
                        ◇ J 9 7 5
                        ♣ K 8 6 5
```

R.R.	Papa	M.M.	Ch. Ch.
West	*North*	*East*	*South*
Pass	1◇	Pass	2◇
Pass	3♣	Pass	3NT
Pass	Pass	Dble.	

"Not one of them put a foot right," went on H.H., deftly seizing two caviar canapés from a tray of assorted titbits which the barman had placed on our table. "Take Papa's silly bid of 3♣."

"But I've often seen you do it yourself," protested the Owl. "He bid clubs because he wanted some other lead against 3NT."

"Quite so," agreed the Hog, "but he should have foreseen that being one move ahead of him, partner would end up as declarer. No sense of timing. Do I let my partners get the better of me, like that?" asked the Hog rhetorically.

"Turn to Molly," continued H.H. "That fatuous double was the only way to present declarer with a contract which was otherwise destined to fail. See what happens if she has her wish. West, as ordered, leads a club and the king is driven out. Declarer loses the diamond finesse and the ♣A goes.

"Now East must find three discards on the diamonds. She lets go two hearts and is then squeezed. So she parts with a club. Declarer cashes his ♠K and exits with a club, end-playing her.

"Left to his own devices declarer looks to the spade finesse for his ninth trick and goes down like a gentleman. The double, pinpointing every card, allows him to play double-dummy.

"But," continued H.H., "Molly forgot that she was playing with the

Rabbit. He doesn't mind 'top of nothing' leads, as he explained later, but the ♣2 might give the impression that he had three or four to an honour. So he led the ♡5.

"Molly was furious," pursued the Hog. " 'Men are the most undisciplined sex I know,' she announced in a loud aside.

"But now it was the Chimp's turn to distinguish himself. He could see eight tricks. A heart would be the ninth, but before he could set it up Molly would get her clubs going. He thought, of course, that she had the ♡Q and would switch to a club at trick two.

"So the cunning Chimp decided to lure her into a trap and rose smartly with dummy's ♡K. No one, he reasoned, would do so with his actual holding. That would be crazy, so placing R.R. with the ♡J, Molly would cash the ace, then the queen and lead another heart. A typical monkey trick, but it misfired completely, for what do you think happened?"

The Hog looked round. No one said anything and there was no glass *en prise*. Reluctantly emptying his own, he resumed.

"Molly isn't known as the Mule for nothing. She had doubled for a club lead with two certain entries to set up her suit and she wasn't going to part with one of them to please the Rabbit or anyone else. With a vicious swish she slapped the ♡10 on the king.

"Observe the effect. Had she gone up with the ace, as any non-mule might have done, the suit would have been blocked — unless, that is, the Rabbit ducked the next heart. Would he have done? Unlikely, but it will never be known, for that spiteful swish produced a foolproof Rabbit-proof defence. When she came in with the ◇K even Molly realised that there was no future in clubs and the heart continuation killed the contract. No longer could even the Rabbit block the suit.

"Note that had Molly really started with the ♡AQx, the Chimp's crafty play would have been pointless. Without any hankypanky Molly would have been squeezed by dummy's last diamond in the same way as on a club opening.

"And if Molly had gone up with the ♡A, allowing the defence to win the first three hearts tricks, the Chimp, after giving up his natural trick in hearts, couldn't have failed to make nine others. He would win the club continuation, lose the diamond finesse and after winning the club return, run the diamonds, coming to this four-card ending.

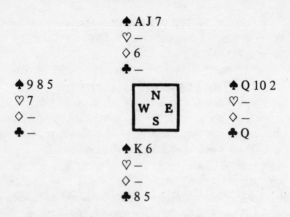

♠ A J 7
♥ —
♦ 6
♣ —

♠ 9 8 5
♥ 7
♦ —
♣ —

♠ Q 10 2
♥ —
♦ —
♣ Q

♠ K 6
♥ —
♦ —
♣ 8 5

On the last diamond Molly would have been inexorably squeezed."

The Hog cleared his throat. "And what do you suppose that Molly said when I congratulated her sarcastically on that bad-tempered swish withe the ♥10? Did she blush? Did she stammer? On the contrary. She informed me that it was intuition, something men didn't understand. What's more, she believed it."

The Hog concluded on a sombre note. "They all did their best to lose, but their blunders cancelled each other out and in the event I was the only loser. For twenty-seven minutes I had to endure this odious spectacle in silence — that is, in comparative silence. I have a right to compensation. There should be a Kibitzers' Trade Union to insist on fair fees for sufferers — a pound a minute for the first twenty minutes and double rates for overtime."

The introduction of Ladies' Day met with general approval and it wasn't long before it became a weekly event. The Hog, calling for new blood, to say nothing of the sheckels, was its most ardent advocate.

"Couldn't we be accommodating and admit them as members or something?" he suggested.

The Committee wouldn't hear of it. The Griffins had always been a men's club and so it would remain. Undoubtedly, Ladies' Day had proved a success and there was no need to be inflexible. So as not be unchivalrous, it was decided to designate Ladies' Days in retrospect — whenever a member of the stronger sex entered our portals.

And so, with the typical British genius for compromise, the Griffins remained a strictly men's club open to ladies.

CHAPTER TEN

The Hog goes Cruising

THE GENERAL AND HIS BIRD

When our secretary announced that the restaurant would be closed for extensive redecorations in November several of our most active members began to look for a suitable cruise. Papa was the first to book.

"That settles it. I'm going," declared the Hog when he heard the news. "If I stayed behind that odious Greek would tell everyone that he was the best player in London. What if someone believed him?

"Besides," went on H.H., "my doctor has been telling me for some time that I must slim down. I'm overweight, you know. It was bad enough before with pounds and stones, but now they've brought in kilos they've made it worse! I weigh more, much more and it was all so unnecessary. A cruise would be ideal and yet . . ."

The Hog paused to empty his glass.

"I wish you wouldn't always interrupt," he told Oscar severely as the Owl was about to open his mouth, "and yet, as I was saying, how can I shed kilos, or pounds for that matter, on a ship with the *haute cuisine* of the Souvoroff?"

"*Haute cuisine* on a Russian ship?" broke in Peregrine the Penguin. "You'll be lucky to get sausages and sauerkraut."

"No, no," rejoined H.H. "It's not a Russian ship. It's French, owned by the Messagerie Maritime Brillat-Savarin and France's finest chefs will be going."

"But Souvoroff was a Russian general," objected P.P. "He fought against the French. Why should they name a ship after him?"

"It's not named after the general, but after the pheasant, of course," rejoined H.H. "Pheasant Souvoroff is one of the most exquisite dishes devised by man. It's the glory of French gastronomy. The bird is cooked with foie gras inside a dome of flaky pastry so that nothing can escape and . . ."

"But Alexander Souvoroff was a Russian general," persisted the Penguin "so how . . ."

"Oh, I expect he, too, was named after the pheasant," retorted the Hog irritably. "Who cares about generals, anyway."

A few days later, after he had studied the brochure, I found H.H. in pensive mood. The Souvoroff was the most luxurious ship afloat and it was, of course, very expensive. The Hog's first idea was to set the cost of the cruise against capital gains tax. Unfortunately, he had omitted to declare any gains in the first place. "One can't think of everything," he confessed, "so I suppose those tax moguls are going to rob me yet again."

Before long, however, things took a turn for the better. First the Walrus, then the Rabbit and the Toucan booked on the cruise. The Hog worked out that his passage as far as Barbados, if not Antigua, would be taken care of. But the best was still to come. Wreathed in smiles, the Hog announced: "Papa has persuaded me," he paused for effect before adding, "to double our usual stakes. With that as collateral my financial worries are over. His credit is very good, you know."

"*He* has persuaded *you*?" asked the Owl incredulously.

The Hog chuckled. I had heard about it already. Taking me aside in the bar before dinner, Papa told me in confidence.

"You won't believe it but that Hog has actually been winning from me. Inexplicable? On the face of it, certainly, and yet there is a reason. I am apt to be careless. So I have persuaded him to double the stakes. He's so conceited that he thinks that he'll still win, even when I am concentrating. It's about time that he was taught a lesson."

It wasn't long before Papa and the Hideous Hog crossed swords at the new Souvoroff stakes, as they came to be known in the club. Their first encounter was preceded by a hand which deserves to be recorded in its own right. The Hog, waiting to cut in, was rooting against the Greek.

I saw the hand being played and heard about it again from the Hideous Hog, who gloated shamelessly as he told the story, with suitable embellishments, at a farewell party for the Rabbit on the eve of his departure for a holiday on the Riviera.

"You will recognise the hand, no doubt," began H.H., grinning maliciously at R.R.

The Rabbit didn't seem to hear him. He was too preoccupied looking for something.

"Excuse me" he muttered "I must have left it . . . I had it . . ." and rising hastily he made for the door.

"Give me a piece of paper, someone," went on the Hog, discarding the wine list and a theatre programme which allowed no room for the familiar diagram. In vain he searched his pockets and looked around. Finally, from under a newspaper he extracted a small bedraggled black book. Tearing out a page, he scribbled hastily.

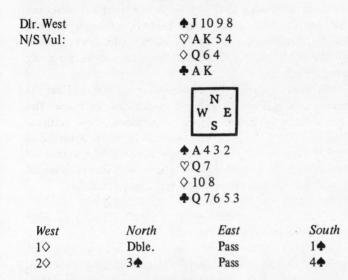

Dlr. West
N/S Vul:

♠ J 10 9 8
♡ A K 5 4
♦ Q 6 4
♣ A K

N
W E
S

♠ A 4 3 2
♡ Q 7
♦ 10 8
♣ Q 7 6 5 3

West	North	East	South
1♦	Dble.	Pass	1♠
2♦	3♠	Pass	4♠

"Who's who?" asked Oscar the Owl.

"A good question," replied H.H., "for the dramatis personae shape the play. So let me tell you. East was our friend the Rabbit. South was none other than Papa, facing that legal luminary, the Emeritus Professor of Bio-Sophistry. Walter the Walrus sat West, but his was only a walking-on part, so you can disregard him. He had done his bit when he led the ♦K, the Rabbit following with the ♦9, and then the ♦A."

The Hog broke off to empty someone's glass before putting the question.

"How do you play?"

We pondered.

"Since you have two diamond losers, you mustn't concede more than one trump," began the Owl. "The best chance is to play for split honours. East is unlikely to have both, but ..."

The Hog held up his hand. "Haven't you overlooked something?"

he asked. "Obviously the ◇9 is the beginning of a high-low signal, so at trick three the ◇Q will be ruffed and your other trumps being pygmies, you will have to over-ruff with the ♠A. Thereafter you will have two inescapable trump losers."

Noting with satisfaction that no one could think of a way out, the Hog continued. "Papa found an ingenious solution. On the ◇A he threw dummy's ◇Q! Now Walter had the master diamond and there was no need for East to ruff anything. Papa could ruff with the deuce in his hand, play for split honours and live happily 'til the next deal."

As he spoke H.H. filled in the other hands.

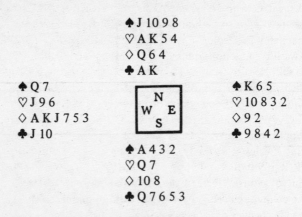

```
                      ♠ J 10 9 8
                      ♡ A K 5 4
                      ◇ Q 6 4
                      ♣ A K
      ♠ Q 7                             ♠ K 6 5
      ♡ J 9 6          N                ♡ 10 8 3 2
      ◇ A K J 7 5 3  W   E              ◇ 9 2
      ♣ J 10           S                ♣ 9 8 4 2
                      ♠ A 4 3 2
                      ♡ Q 7
                      ◇ 10 8
                      ♣ Q 7 6 5 3
```

"Very clever," said the Owl admiringly.

"Quite so," agreed the Hog, "but can you see how bewildering it was for the poor Rabbit? Why should Papa jettison dummy's ◇Q to promote Walter's ◇J? It made no sense. So when the ◇K appeared, R.R. frowned, shook his head and asked to see the last trick."

"Of course," said Papa with alacrity, only too glad to oblige.

"Certainly not," hissed the Secretary Bird. "The trick has been quitted and Section 67 of the Laws says clearly . . ."

"Under the new laws . . ." interjected a kibitzer.

"Under any law," retorted the Greek vehemently, "I can waive any penalty I like," and glaring defiantly at S.B., he thrust both previous tricks at the startled Rabbit.

R.R.'s head was in a whirl. He was much too confused to understand what was going on, but one thing seemed clear — Papa badly wanted him to know that after that vanishing trick with the ◇Q, the ◇J was master. Why? It could only be because he didn't want him to ruff his partner's winner. So he did. Papa was to be trusted and if he wanted R.R. to do something, it must be right not to do it, and vice-versa.

The Hog had barely finished the story and was still chortling over Papa's discomfiture, when the Rabbit suddenly reappeared. Looking distraught, his left ear twitching nervously, his pink cheeks aglow, he asked in an agitated voice:

"Have any of you seen my passport? I had it just now. I've looked everywhere. I . . ."

"Passport?" repeated the Hog. "So that's what it is! Here you are." Picking up the little black book, he handed it to the Rabbit, and with it the sheet with the diagram. "You may need this too," he explained "there are visas or something on the back. *Bon voyage*, all the same."

The hand had come up the previous afternoon, and though the Hog wasn't in action himself he had enjoyed Papa's discomfiture to the full. Next to winning his greatest pleasure was to see Papa lose.

When the rubber was over the Secretary Bird and the Walrus cut out. The Chimp and H.H. joined the table. A duel between the Hog and Papa was always worth watching, so I stayed on to kibitz. I wasn't disappointed.

"Would you mind if Papa and I play against each other?" asked the Hog. Seeing the Chimp hesitate, he added reassuringly, "I'll play with R.R. if you like and you . . ."

"But of course," agreed the Chimp with alacrity, relieved to think that he couldn't cut R.R. Papa didn't seem to mind.

Soon both sides became vulnerable.

Next, this hand came up:

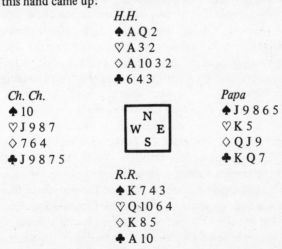

```
                    H.H.
                    ♠ A Q 2
                    ♡ A 3 2
                    ◇ A 10 3 2
                    ♣ 6 4 3
Ch. Ch.                               Papa
♠ 10                    N             ♠ J 9 8 6 5
♡ J 9 8 7          W        E         ♡ K 5
◇ 7 6 4                 S             ◇ Q J 9
♣ J 9 8 7 5                           ♣ K Q 7
                    R.R.
                    ♠ K 7 4 3
                    ♡ Q 10 6 4
                    ◇ K 8 5
                    ♣ A 10
```

"We would have got there playing Precision, you know," confided
Ch. Ch. to the Rabbit, "because . . ."

"It's your bid," said Papa irritably.

"No bid. Playing 5-card majors, I . . ."

"1◊," barked the Hog.

"I've often thought of taking up Precision," rejoined R.R. "only
I don't always get 5-card majors and . . ."

"No bid!" shouted Papa.

Eventually the Rabbit became declarer in 3NT after this sequence.

H.H.	R.R.
North	*South*
1◊	1♡
2♣	2NT
3NT	

The Hog glared. He had bid an inhibitory 2♣, all set to play the hand in
3NT, and now that scatterbrained Rabbit had bid notrumps first,
something he wasn't allowed to do except in an emergency.

Papa looked pleased. He was glad he had passed, concealing his
strength, and what better declarer could he have than R.R.?

Ch. Ch. led the ♣5 to Papa's ♣Q and the Rabbit ducked automatically.
One always did. Winning the next club, the king, he began to think
or rather to woolgather. What would he have bid, playing Precision?
He hadn't enough for 1NT, let alone 1♣, and playing 5-card majors
he couldn't bid 1♡. Yet he was surely too good to pass. The answer,
of course, was to open 1◊. Partner had more than enough for game,
though no suit except diamonds and . . .

"What's the state of the poll?" enquired Walter the Walrus walking
across to us. "I've just time for another rubber if you don't take hours
over this one."

"They're in a game contract and you're in if they make it," promptly
answered the Chimp, ready as always to join in a diversion.

The Rabbit frowned. It was all very well to be in game and, of
course, partner had to support diamonds, but how was he to make
eleven tricks out of that lot? How would the Hog set about it? On
such occasions, when he was two or three tricks short, R.R. envisaged
the only distribution that could give him his contract. That was the
recipe.

Papa fidgeted nervously, but the Rabbit didn't notice it. He was looking for the sort of distribution that the Hog would seek. Suddenly it came to him. One of the defenders would have to have a 3-4-3-3 pattern. He would be stripped of the black suits, thrown in on the third round of diamonds and forced to lead a heart away from the king. Since the Chimp seemed to have five clubs, Papa would have to be the victim and R.R. would come to eleven tricks with: four spades, two hearts, three diamonds, the ♣A and a club ruff in the closed hand.

The Rabbit's brow cleared and crossing to the ♠A, he led dummy's last club, 'ruffing' it with the ◊5. He was about to cash two more spades, proceeding with the elimination, when the Chimp gathered the trick and continued with another club.

"I'm afraid that's my trick, Charlie," said R.R. "I ruffed you know."

"An unusual manoeuvre in notrumps," jeered the Hog. "No wonder it took you so long to work it out."

The Rabbit dipped his ears in shame. It all came back to him in a flash. He wasn't playing in diamonds at all. It was all that talk about Precision. But what could he do now?

Gleefully, Charlie the Chimp cashed two more clubs. On the first one Papa threw a spade. Then he stopped in his tracks, for whatever he did next would be fatal.

This was the position.

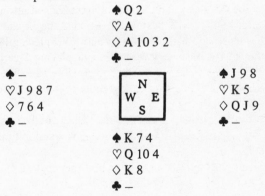

```
              ♠ Q 2
              ♡ A
              ◊ A 10 3 2
              ♣ —
♠ —                              ♠ J 9 8
♡ J 9 8 7        N               ♡ K 5
◊ 7 6 4       W     E            ◊ Q J 9
♣ —              S               ♣ —
              ♠ K 7 4
              ♡ Q 10 4
              ◊ K 8
              ♣ —
```

On Ch. Ch.'s last club R.R. shed dummy's second small heart, baring the ♡A, so Papa, in turn, bared his ♡K.

A heart came next and he could feel the sharp edge of the sword of Damocles scraping his neck. The Rabbit cashed dummy's ♠Q and came to his hand with the ◊K. The ♡Q inexorably squeezed Papa in spades and diamonds.

"Curious hand," observed Oscar the Owl, our Senior Kibitzer. "The only way to make 3NT is to play it in diamonds. Unbeatable. All it needs is a progressive suicide squeeze with a Vienna Coup thrown in."

"May I borrow your pen Themistocles?" asked the Hog politely, pulling out his Souvoroff notebook.

A SPLENDID PASSENGER

The Hog was looking forward to the cruise. All his favourite opponents were going, so that even when he wouldn't be playing himself Papa was certain to run into the most enjoyable misfortunes. Next to bamboozling the Greek the Hog's favourite pastime was watching him being bamboozled by others, notably by the Rabbit, for as he knew from bitter experience nothing could be more galling than to have one's best schemes brought to nought by an opponent who was at his deadliest when he didn't know what he was doing, which, in R.R.'s case, was most of the time. To be outwitted by the witless was surely the ultimate humiliation.

Two typical examples occurred during the run-up to the cruise. This was the first one.

```
Dlr. West              ♠ 2
Both Vul:              ♡ A Q 9 8
                       ◇ A 10 6 2
                       ♣ A Q 10 8
    ♠ A K J 10                              ♠ 5 4 3
    ♡ K J              ┌─────────┐          ♡ 10 7 3 2
    ◇ Q J 8           │   N     │          ◇ 9 7 5
    ♣ K J 9 7         │ W   E   │          ♣ 6 3 2
                       │   S     │
                       └─────────┘
                       ♠ Q 9 8 7 6
                       ♡ 6 5 4
                       ◇ K 4 3
                       ♣ 5 4
```

Papa	*T.T.*	*Karapet*	*R.R.*
West	*North*	*East*	*South*
1♠	Dble.	Pass	2♠
Pass	2NT	Pass	3♠
Pass	3NT	Pass	4♠
Dble.			

If the bidding appears somewhat unorthodox, it is because the Rabbit was a little confused. He had been trying to think where he had left the Toucan's car which he had borrowed while his own was being overhauled, and he was under the impression that it was his partner, Timothy, and not Papa, who had opened the bidding with 1♠. With so good a fit for opponents's suit, how could he fail to support it?

When Papa, unable to restrain himself any longer, doubled in a voice of thunder, Karapet asked to review the bidding. The Rabbit protested that it was the Toucan, not Papa, who had opened 1♠, but he was soon outvoted. That sort of thing had happened to him before, all through lack of concentration. Fearing the worst, he shook his head ruefully.

Then, just as Papa led the ♠A, he suddenly remembered where he had left the Toucan's car. So all wasn't lost after all. Go down he must, but at least he could now look dummy in the face.

After the ♠A came the ◊J. Winning in his hand, R.R. finessed the ♣Q, cashed the ace and ruffed a club. Next the ◊10 was finessed with confidence. After all, would Papa lead a true card? The ◊A and another club ruff followed. Then came the heart finesse, and after cashing the ace, the Rabbit exited with a heart.

Three cards only remained. Sitting with ♠KJ10 Papa couldn't help ruffing and leading a trump to present the Rabbit with his tenth trick.

"A masterly exhibition of the one-way finesse," siad the Hog, winking at the kibitzers.

"Why these speculative doubles?" complained Karapet. "You know that I never hold anything."

Not the least pleasing feature of the hand, from the Hog's point of view, was that Papa forgot to claim his hundred honours. The Hog reminded him several times, but only after the rubber points had been agreed.

VARIATIONS ON A CLASSICAL THEME

The Hog, as we all know, isn't one of nature's kibitzers. "Why should I watch others," he says, "when they could be so much better employed watching me?" And yet, this was a hand which the Hog wouldn't have missed kibitzing for anything.

Dlr. West   ♠ A Q
Neither Vul: ♡ 8 7
                   ◇ A 4 3
                   ♣ Q J 10 9 8 7

```
         N
      W     E
         S
```

                   ♠ J 10 9
                   ♡ A 3 2
                   ◇ K J 8 7
                   ♣ A 6 5

R.R.	Karapet	T.T.	Papa
West	*North*	*East*	*South*
Pass	1♣	Pass	1◇
Pass	2♣	Pass	3NT

Papa took a slight risk in responding 1◇, allowing Karapet to bid
notrumps first. The Free Armenian wasn't so presumptuous, however,
and the contract came to rest safely in Papa's capable hands.

The ♡5 was the opening, the Toucan produced the jack, and the
Greek quickly counted up to nine. Even if every card was wrong,
he had enough winners. The trouble was, that if the ♣K was offside,
he might also have too many losers. How could he prevent four
unstoppable hearts from descending on him?

A lesser player would have pinned his hopes on one of two things —
the club finesse or a 4-4 heart break. Not so Papa. A consummate
technician, he would ensure that if the club finesse lost, the Rabbit
wouldn't lead another heart.

Had Papa the ♡Q behind the ace, the situation would have con-
formed to a classical pattern. Concealing the queen, declarer wins the
first trick with the ace, and if the lead must then be surrendered to West,
he innocently leads low from his king, expecting to put partner in with
the queen.

Here, of course, East really did have the queen. It couldn't be otherwise, for his ♡J at trick one denied the 10, and from a suit headed by
the KQ10, the Rabbit would have surely led the king.

R.R. didn't know about the queen, however, and with no heart stop
other than the ace, he would expect declarer to hold it up.

So Papa boldly won the first trick with the ace, trying to look like a man who is hiding the queen. Then he crossed to the ◇A and took the vital finesse in clubs. The queen held. The ♣J followed and again the Toucan played low. So did Papa, but this time the Rabbit won with the king, and shaking his head gravely, continued with the ♠6. This was the full deal.

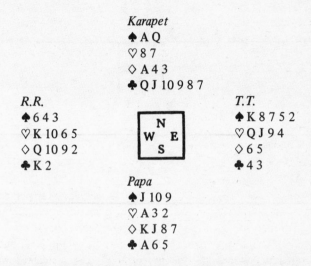

Karapet
♠ A Q
♡ 8 7
◇ A 4 3
♣ Q J 10 9 8 7

R.R.
♠ 6 4 3
♡ K 10 6 5
◇ Q 10 9 2
♣ K 2

T.T.
♠ K 8 7 5 2
♡ Q J 9 4
◇ 6 5
♣ 4 3

Papa
♠ J 10 9
♡ A 3 2
◇ K J 8 7
♣ A 6 5

Dummy's queen lost to East's king and the spade return killed the only entry to the clubs while the ace opposite still blocked the suit.

"Of course," explained the Rabbit, "I knew that Papa had the ♡Q. I mean he wouldn't have gone up so promptly with the ace if he had no other stopper. I've often seen this play in books and in reports of hands that might have happened in real life. Declarer tries to fool West, because he fears a switch to another suit, and what suit could it be but spades?"

"But weren't you afraid that you wouldn't make your ♣K at all?" asked someone. "What if Papa went up, the second time, with his ace?"

The Rabbit shook his head firmly. "With Kx you always hold up. The Hog does it all the time and of course the finesse is repeated. Why even with a singleton king there's a case, I mean you never know, do you?"

HIDING THE LADY

The very next day the hand below came up. This time, however, the
Hog was in action himself, playing at the Souvoroff Stakes.

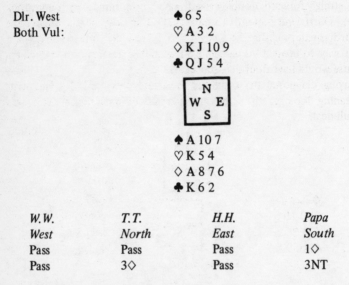

Dlr. West
Both Vul:

♠ 6 5
♡ A 3 2
◇ K J 10 9
♣ Q J 5 4

```
        N
    W       E
        S
```

♠ A 10 7
♡ K 5 4
◇ A 8 7 6
♣ K 6 2

W.W.	T.T.	H.H.	Papa
West	North	East	South
Pass	Pass	Pass	1◇
Pass	3◇	Pass	3NT

Walter the Walrus led the ♠3 to the Hog's jack which was allowed
to hold. So was the queen which followed. Next came the ♠8 to the
ace and Papa took note of W.W.'s cards, the four and the nine.

There weren't enough tricks without the clubs, so Papa's first
step was to lead low to dummy's queen. Going up with the ace, the
Hog returned the ♣3.

Papa took stock. The contract clearly hinged on the diamond
finesse. Where was the queen?

W.W.'s sequence in spades, the lead of the three followed by the
four, proclaimed a four-card suit. Had Papa been playing against
himself, he might have suspected a six-card suit or perhaps a doubleton, for it was beneath him to lead true cards, and on the theory of
restricted choice, if no false card was available, he tried another suit.
But an unimaginative pedestrian, like that Walrus, clearly had four
spades and that meant the Hog had four spades, too. Why, then, didn't
he play his last spade? The only possible reason was that he intended
to mislead Papa about the ◇Q.

The Hog knew that Papa knew that the Hog had another spade.

And each one, in turn, knew that the other was familiar with this particular manoeuvre in which East pretends to be out of a suit so as to make declarer think that West started with five, thereby inducing him to take the vital finesse the wrong way.

A straightforward double-cross," said Papa with a contemptuous smile. "Our friend pretends to have the ◊Q, so he pretends not to have a fourth spade, because he knows that I know he's pretending. It's a clever way to protect his partner's queen and against any other declarer the ruse would have doubtless succeeded."

Having diagnosed the situation, Papa laid down the ◊A and with a meaning look at the kibitzers, inserted dummy's jack. This was the full deal:

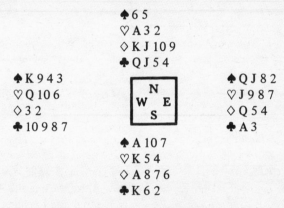

```
                    ♠ 6 5
                    ♡ A 3 2
                    ◊ K J 10 9
                    ♣ Q J 5 4
    ♠ K 9 4 3                        ♠ Q J 8 2
    ♡ Q 10 6          N              ♡ J 9 8 7
    ◊ 3 2          W     E           ◊ Q 5 4
    ♣ 10 9 8 7        S              ♣ A 3
                    ♠ A 10 7
                    ♡ K 5 4
                    ◊ A 8 7 6
                    ♣ K 6 2
```

The Hog slowly drew out the queen, gathered the trick in leisurely fashion and stacked it neatly in front of him. Then, after pretending to search through his cards, he produced the ♠2.

"Not a double-cross, Themistocles," he said with what was doubtless intended as a smile, "a treble cross. Why should I tell a lie when I can deceive you so much better by telling the truth?"

"An ideal opponent, that Greek," said H.H. as he looked back on the deal over a glass of port. "He'll make a splendid passenger."

THE HOG'S NIGHTMARE

The Hog admitted later that it was an error of judgment to have had a second portion of Lobster à l'Armoricaine before the Tournedos Rossini, especially as he was slimming. And yet, at the time, it seemed innocuous enough.

H.H. had had a pleasant day. He had booked the Strogonoff suite on the Souvoroff, the one nearest the Bar Perignon, and the dinner was by way of a celebration. It was just the right time of year to get into shape for the Christmas festivities, always a strenuous period for anyone with a healthy constitution.

The Hog liked luxury and he could afford to pay for it, at least, the Walrus and the Rabbit could, and so, of course, could Papa, and all three had booked already.

So long as the weather held up and they didn't run into too much sunshine, driving everyone out of the cardroom, it should prove a very inexpensive holiday.

As he turned out the light that night the lobster and the tournedos, the cream sauce and the foie gras, were still, technically, non-belligerents. The Hog began to dream happy dreams.

Papa was on his right, just where he wanted him, facing the inevitable Karapet. There was something about the sea, for the Free Armenian was barely looking miserable.

The ship's captain was his partner and years of bitter experience had taught the Hideous Hog that the devil you don't know is preferable to the devil you know.

Gliding smoothly over a rich carpet of modern design, white-coated stewards hovered benignly with trays of cool cucumber sandwiches and ice buckets with Riesling and Traminer. The ideal setting for a slam.

Dlr. East   ♠ 10 9 4 2
Both Vul: ♡ A K Q 4
                              ◊ A J
                              ♣ A K 2

```
        N
    W       E
        S
```

                              ♠ A Q
                              ♡ 5 3 2
                              ◊ K 9 8 6 3 2
                              ♣ 4 3

Karapet	Captain	Papa	H.H.
West	North	East	South
—	—	3♣	3◊
Pass	4♣	Pass	4◊
Pass	4NT	Pass	5◊
Pass	6◊		

Feeling that his vulnerable overcall at the three level had left few
values undisclosed, the Hog had been tempted at first to deny an ace.
The objection to responding 5♣, was, however, that partner might
rashly place him with all four aces. Reluctantly, the Hog decided that
it was a case where valour was the better part of discretion.

Karapet led the ♣8 and the Hog nodded approvingly at the sight
of dummy. A partner who could pick up a 21 count just when it was
wanted, was clearly the right man to put in charge of the ship.

The contract, however, was no certainty. Unless either defender
had the ◊Q10 bare, the slam would require the spade finesse or a
3-3 heart break or maybe a squeeze in the majors. Perhaps the captain
should have passed 5◊, but then he had doubtless allowed for the
Hog's dummy play to yield an extra trick or two. One could hardly
blame him.

Since the spade finesse had to be avoided, if possible, and the clubs
wouldn't stand up for three rounds, there was no good way of getting
to the closed hand to take the trump finesse. So H.H. laid down the
◊A and continued with the ◊J. Papa followed with the ◊4, then the
◊10, a revealing card.

Going up with the ◊K, the Hog could almost claim the contract,

there and then, on an end-play. First, however, he had to eliminate
Karapet's hearts and clubs. As he set about it, he felt a sharp twinge
in his midriff, then another. The lobster was clawing the tournedos.

At trick four, after the ♣A, the ◇A and the ◇K, H.H. led a club,
Karapet following. Next came the ♡A and the ♡K, and when Papa
followed suit both times, the Hog tabled his hand. He would lead
the ♡Q and ruff the ♡4, if need be. Whether Karapet over-ruffed or
not was immaterial, for if he didn't, he would be thrown in with
the ◇Q. Either way, he would only have spades left and the ♣AQ
would inevitably win the last two tricks.

"I'll save time," he announced, flicking the ♡Q to the centre of
the table.

"Certainly," agreed Papa with a mocking smile. "One down."
With a swish the Greek slapped the ◇Q on the ♡Q and exited with
a club. This was the full deal.

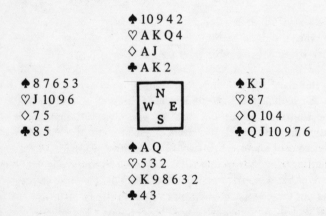

```
                    ♠ 10 9 4 2
                    ♡ A K Q 4
                    ◇ A J
                    ♣ A K 2
  ♠ 8 7 6 5 3                        ♠ K J
  ♡ J 10 9 6          N             ♡ 8 7
  ◇ 7 5           W       E         ◇ Q 10 4
  ♣ 8 5               S             ♣ Q J 10 9 7 6
                    ♠ A Q
                    ♡ 5 3 2
                    ◇ K 9 8 6 3 2
                    ♣ 4 3
```

The Hog was stifling. The internicine conflict within him was bringing
beads of perspiration to his forehead. Before his blurred vision steam
seemed to be rising from the ice bucket and those sandwiches, once
so inviting, looked more and more like big, ugly indigestion tablets.

"But, but," he spluttered, "you haven't, you can't have . . ."

"The ◇Q? Of course not," jeered Papa. "With the Q10 no one would
play the 10 on the jack. Just so. But then I had to create a little illusion
for you, since left to yourself you couldn't have found a way to go
down. The slam was foolproof, if that's the right expression. After
trying the hearts, you would have taken the spade finesse, just like anyone else. So I had to construct an end-play for you with the ◇Q as the

throw-in card. Rather neat, don't you think? Why, I might have fallen for it myself. Ha, ha!"

The Hog shuddered. Themistocles, his arch-enemy, had outwitted him and now he was jeering at him, throwing at him the contemptuous jibes he had so often thrown at Papa. He was even laughing in the same way.

A hideous fear sent a shiver down the Hog's back. Had some evil power cast a spell, causing him to change places with Papa? A transplantation of souls? Was he now Papa and Papa the Hog?

The horror of it was too much even for a nightmare and with a cry of pain H.H. woke up.

A CHEQUE BOUNCES BACK

The 'phone rang. "I hope I haven't disturbed you," began the Hideous Hog. It was five o'clock in the morning.

"I'm off to catch the boat train and I want you to stop a cheque for me, the one I gave at the Griffins last night. I've just remembered that I jotted a hand down on the back. I don't want to lose it, so get it back, pay for me or something and we'll settle later. Don't forget. Better make a note of it before you fall asleep again."

We had all been taken aback at dinner the previous night when the Hog picked up the bill, not to scribble a hand in the usual way, but with the avowed intention of paying. What's more, he wrote out a cheque there and then. Looking for a bit of paper later, as we sat chatting over coffee, he must have taken it up again absent-mindedly.

STORMS AT SEA

The wind was howling and the sleet was turning to snow when I made my way to the club the next day to recover the Hog's cheque. Putting it carefully in my wallet, I adjourned to the bar to share a bottle of pre-prandial Bollinger with Oscar the Owl.

"They are well out of it," said O.O. stirring the ice in the bucket, "though, mind you, I wouldn't like to be at sea in this weather. Tell me," he went on, "you've been on a cruise with the Hog, I believe. What's he like as a sailor?"

"Unpredictable," I replied. "We went to the Mediterranean together a couple of years ago. The Bay of Biscay was at its worst, but it didn't seem to affect his appetite at all and his game was the same as ever.

Yet a few days later, when we were lying off Cannes, in the Gulf of Juan, and the sea was as smooth as the proverbial millpond, he ran into a Force 10 storm. It was the 4th July and the Captain had invited on board a party of Americans to celebrate Independence Day. The soul of courtesy, as always, the Hog insisted on toasting each State in turn in alphabetical order. As we passed Pennsylvania it became painfully clear that the ship's stabilisers weren't functioning properly. On the way from Texas to Utah they broke down altogether." I was about to tell Oscar about a party in the Aegean we had later, when who should suddenly walk into the room but H.H. himself, closely followed by the Rabbit.

"Heavens!" I cried. "What are you two doing here? You should have left Cherbourg a couple of hours ago. What's happened to the Koutouzoff, I mean the Souvoroff?"

"You may well ask," replied H.H. bitterly. "At the last moment the crew called a strike. It all started, apparently, when a junior sommelier began to take round bottles of mineral water to the cabins."

"The cabin stewards claimed it was their prerogative," chipped in the Rabbit.

"The waiters supported the sommelier . . ."

"The laundry girls and the pools personnel backed the stewards . . ."

"The petty officers proclaimed solidarity with the catering staff."

"The engineers honoured their obligations to the electricians . . ."

"Then they all walked out."

"And so," said the Rabbit, bringing the sad story to a close, "twenty minutes before boarding we had to disembark."

"All over mineral water!" Angrily the Hog drained his glass and held it out for a refill.

"It will be some consolation to you, H.H., to see your cheque back. Here it is."

I remembered vividly the hand he had scrawled on the back for I had kibitzed it a couple of days earlier.

IMPROPER ADVANTAGE OF A PROPER PAUSE

Dlr. South
Both Vul:

	♠ 10 9 2	
	♡ K Q 2	
	◇ A 2	
	♣ K Q J 10 4	

```
         N            ♠ J 5 3
      W     E         ♡ A 9 6 3
         S            ◇ J 7
                      ♣ 9 7 6 5
```

H.H.	Karapet	R.R.	Papa
South	West	North	East
1NT	Pass	6NT	Pass
Pass	Pass		

The Hog's vulnerable 1NT showed 16-18, but that included points for
good play, as well as for high cards, and could, therefore, be flexible.

Karapet, the Free Armenian, led the ♣4. The Hog played the ♣9
from dummy and won Papa's ♣J with the ♣A.

At trick two, he led the ♡5 to dummy's ♡K, Karapet following with
the ♡4. Papa gave the matter some thought before playing the ♡6.
Undeniably he paused long enough to betray the presence of the ♡A.

H.H. snarled. Papa growled. Then, with a dreamy look, the Hog led
the ♡7 from the closed hand.

"You're in dummy," murmured R.R.

"Sorry, careless of me," apologised the Hog, and with a faint air
of reluctance he detached dummy's ♡Q.

Papa's long spatulate fingers beat a nervous tattoo on the table.
What was up?

The Hog knew that Papa had the ♡A. So he wouldn't have led a
heart at all unless he had the ♡J, and if he had it, why the pantomime
of playing from the wrong hand? Could it be . . .

Suddenly the scales fell from Papa's eyes. He could see it all. The
Hog didn't have the ♡J, but to steal a trick he was playing as if he had
it by pretending that he didn't. A brazen double-cross.

Curving his lips in disdain, Papa soliloquized *sotto voce*, just loud
enough for the kibitzers to hear.

"Not only is he trying to steal a trick, but he is hoping, at the
same time, to set the stage for an end-play. After three spades, two
hearts and five clubs, he intends to throw me in with the ♡A, forcing

me to lead a diamond. Even then he would have to guess, of course,
but if all went well, he would have brought off another of his ridiculous
contracts.

"Clever, but not clever enough against Papa," and with a swish the
Greek pounced with his ace on the ♡Q and promptly returned another
heart.

This was the deal:

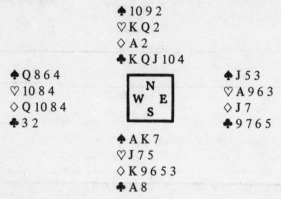

```
                ♠ 10 9 2
                ♡ K Q 2
                ◇ A 2
                ♣ K Q J 10 4
♠ Q 8 6 4                        ♠ J 5 3
♡ 10 8 4          N             ♡ A 9 6 3
◇ Q 10 8 4     W     E          ◇ J 7
♣ 3 2             S             ♣ 9 7 6 5
                ♠ A K 7
                ♡ J 7 5
                ◇ K 9 6 5 3
                ♣ A 8
```

The Hog cashed his ♠K and reeled off the clubs, coming to this four-
card ending:

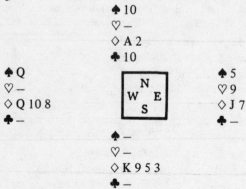

```
                ♠ 10
                ♡ —
                ◇ A 2
                ♣ 10
♠ Q                              ♠ 5
♡ —               N             ♡ 9
◇ Q 10 8       W     E          ◇ J 7
♣ —               S             ♣ —
                ♠ —
                ♡ —
                ◇ K 9 5 3
                ♣ —
```

On dummy's last club Karapet was inexorably squeezed.

"It was my only chance," gloated the Hog. "I had to find the same
defender with the ♠Q and four diamonds. But how could I rectify
the count for a squeeze or rather how could I persuade Papa to do
it for me?

"It would have been profoundly immoral to let him profit from his tell-tale trance. I could no longer conceal my ♡J legitimately by playing up to dummy twice, as if I hoped to find West with the ace, so I had to be er a little devious. A spot of hocus pocus, just enough to counter that deplorable hesitation, if you know what I mean. Ha! ha!"

On the agenda of the forthcoming meeting of our Ethics and Etiquette Committee is an item entitled: Taking improper advantage of a proper pause.

CHAPTER ELEVEN

Ethics, Etiquette, and Other Things

A FLURRY OF WRITS

Well founded rumours that the Club had commissioned a history of the Griffins quickly brought a flurry of threats of actions for libel. The first came from Papa. A letter from his solicitors, Sneezum, Satherthwaite, Prendergast and Sneezum, based on information from moles of unimpeachable character, complained that the whole exercise, thinly disguished as history, was inspired by a party known as H.H. and was intended solely and purely for his glorification, at the expense of better, worthier players, notably their client, Themistocles Papadopoulos.

Exception was taken especially to reports of proceedings before the Ethics and Etiquette Committee, precursor of the Monster Points Committee. In a quick glance at the document I noticed such phrases as ". . . conniving at gross misrepresentation, the Committee allowed H.H. to browbeat witnesses ... evidence fraught with malice ... defamation of character . . ."

A brief but pithy communication from The Friends of Justice reminded the Committee that it was not enough to prove that the wholly unfounded charges against their esteemed member, Charlie the Chimp, were true. Unless it were clearly demonstrated that it was in the public interest to bring them forward, the injured party could claim heavy damages.

Walter the Walrus made his representations in person. He played simple, commonsense bridge and was accustomed to be blamed for the blunders of illiterate partners, who could neither count, add, nor subtract. That he could take in his stride. But he had been credibly informed that the records contained such falsehoods as, "Having evidently miscounted his points and believing that he had 11 instead of 12, Walter passed as dealer ..." and, "In the post-mortem W.W. justified his bid, which cost 1100, on the ground that he had 19 points."

He could produce incontrovertible evidence, supported by sworn affadavits, that he had not 19 points, but 20½, and that but for a regrettable but understandable oversight the penalty would have been no more than 800.

Reflections on the numeracy of an accountant, one albeit who had retired before starting to practise, could not fail to do grave damage to his professional reputation. Unless all such passages were expurgated, he would sue.

More disturbing than overt threats was the ominous silence of the Emeritus Professor of Bio-Sophistry. Sightings had been reported from Lincoln's Inn and from the Middle Temple, and it was noticeable that his capacious briefcase was swelling from day to day.

That was the general picture put before me by Oscar the Owl, our Senior Kibitzer.

"We are taking legal advice, of course," he told me, "but I should like a layman's opinion. Besides, you were the Committee's rapporteur in most of the cases which came up before us. In several others you were the chief witness. Go over the records. See if there's anything which needs rewording. We don't want a flurry of writs."

I started at the beginning, going over reports I made many years ago.

This is one of the earliest which I reproduce verbatim.

MAN BITES CROCODILE

Criminologists aver that many a culprit would escape detection if he resisted the temptation to boast of his crimes. We were forcibly reminded of this dictum at the Griffins the other day when the club's Ethics and Etiquette Committee was convened to hear two serious charges against the Hideous Hog. The first was brought by his inveterate enemy at the table, Papa the Greek.

As I had witnessed the whole of the incident which gave rise to Papa's complaint, my evidence was taken first.

This, briefly, is what had happened.

The last table was about to break up at the end of the afternoon session. The Hog, however, had nearly an hour to go before the first of his dinner arrangements that night, so he wanted to play on.

"I can't," said Walter the Walrus. "I promised to be home before seven."

"Well, it's barely ten past," rejoined the Hog, "there's plenty of time for one more rubber."

The Walrus cut the Rueful Rabbit. The Hog faced Timothy the
Toucan. With his sleek, red nose standing out against the sheen of his
black mohair jacket, Timothy, bouncing jauntily in his seat, looked
more than ever like a Toucan.

Nothing much happened for the first few hands. Then, after a well-
contested auction in which T.T. bid clubs, diamonds and the majors,
while H.H. competed in notrumps, the Hog won and scored game.
And then came this deal which I watched sitting between the Rabbit
and the Toucan.

Dlr. West
N/S Vul:

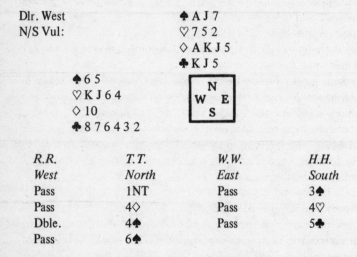

♠ A J 7
♡ 7 5 2
◇ A K J 5
♣ K J 5

♠ 6 5
♡ K J 6 4
◇ 10
♣ 8 7 6 4 3 2

R.R.	T.T.	W.W.	H.H.
West	North	East	South
Pass	1NT	Pass	3♠
Pass	4◇	Pass	4♡
Dble.	4♠	Pass	5♣
Pass	6♠		

The Rabbit led the ◇10, and as dummy came down, Papa the Greek,
walked through the room towards the bar.

"Excuse me," said the Hog after closely studying the hand for a
moment or two "I must have left my lighter in my overcoat."

"Have mine," began the Walrus, his ginger moustache bristling
with impatience, but H.H. was already out of the room.

No sooner was he back, than there was another interruption, the
steward coming in to announce a long-distance telephone call for
the Rabbit.

"Look here," protested W.W. "I really can't go on. It's nearly . . ."

"Let's ask Papa to take R.R.'s hand," suggested the Hog with his
most engaging leer.

The Walrus looked up in surprise. The Hog's unselfishness was quite
out of character. Fancy changing so desirable an opponent as the

Rabbit for a master of Papa's brilliance. In a slam, too. The Walrus acquiesced quickly, before H.H. could change his mind, and Papa was hastily summoned from the bar.

Having reviewed the bidding for Papa's benefit, the Hog proceeded to play like lightning. "We must consider poor Walter," he explained. "He has to be back home an hour ago."

Winning the first trick with dummy's ◇A, the Hog laid down the ♣A and drew two rounds of trumps. Then came the ♡A, followed by the ♡2. The Walrus, who had played the ♡9 on the ace, had his next card ready in his hand. Not so Papa. Sitting back purposefully, he studied matters with cold deliberation.

What was afoot? Both the bidding and the play pointed clearly to a six-card trump suit. With either the ◇Q or the ♣Q, therefore, the Hog would have not less than twelve top tricks. So W.W. had both. Everything, then, hinged on the hearts. If the Hog's hearts were headed by the AQ, he would have surely finessed. So Walter had the queen, too. But what was H.H. hoping to achieve by playing as he did?

It came to Papa in a flash. What would happen if Walter won that second heart trick? Having only clubs and diamonds left, he would have to lead into one of dummy's minor suit tenaces, presenting the Hog with his twelfth trick.

With a triumphant gleam in his eye, Papa addressed the Hog: "Well played, my friend," he said with a patronising smile, "but you have made one mistake. You should not have allowed me, Papa, to take the Rabbit's hand, for by now, of course, I can place every card. My partner started with the ♡Q9 and you propose to throw him in. Really? You have heard, no doubt, of the Crocodile Coup? Well, you are about to witness a demonstration. So! On your deuce I go up with my ♡K, swallowing my partner's ♡Q, just like a crocodile, and then . . ."

Dumbfounded, the Greek stopped in his tracks. With a swish, he had whipped the ♡K across the two, but instead of the queen, the Walrus followed with the ♡10.

This was the full deal:

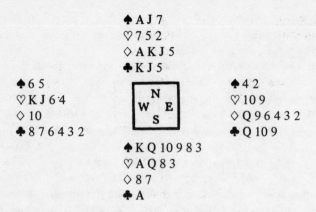

♠ A J 7
♡ 7 5 2
◇ A K J 5
♣ K J 5

♠ 6 5
♡ K J 6 4
◇ 10
♣ 8 7 6 4 3 2

♠ 4 2
♡ 10 9
◇ Q 9 6 4 3 2
♣ Q 10 9

♠ K Q 10 9 8 3
♡ A Q 8 3
◇ 8 7
♣ A

"Man bites crocodile," jeered the Hog, dissolving into fits of laughter. "The only player in the club I could rely upon to outwit himself. Ha! ha! ha!"

"They hung up on me. That is, they didn't answer. I mean . . ." The Rabbit was back in the room.

The episode would have had no sequel had the Hideous Hog stopped gloating there and then. But later than night, sipping Port after his dinners, he held forth at length in the smoking room.

"The ◇Q was obviously wrong and, of course, that Rabbit wouldn't have doubled 4♡ without the ♡K. So what hope was there? Only Papa. Who else could be baited with a crocodile? And he wasn't even in the room. I had to play for a transfer, so to speak. Ha! ha!"

"What a piece of luck for you, then," remarked one of our junior kibitzers, "that the Rabbit was called away and . . ."

"Luck, you call it?" broke in the Hog. "Technique, sir, technique and presence of mind. Do you know what that long-distance call cost me? A tenner, yes sir, that's what I gave the steward for his co-operation. Mind you, the sight of Papa's face was worth every penny. Ha! ha!"

Deplorable conduct, undoubtedly, but was it, strictly speaking, unethical? Postponing judgment, the Committee passed on to the next complaint against the Hog, brought by the Emeritus Professor of Bio-Sophistry. This was the evidence.

Dlr. South
Both Vul:

```
              ♠ Q J 10
              ♡ K Q 7 5
              ◇ Q J 9
              ♣ 8 5 3
♠ 9 5 4 2                      ♠ A K 8 7 6 3
♡ 6 4 3          N            ♡ A 10 9 8
◇ 4 3 2       W     E         ◇ 5
♣ Q J 10         S            ♣ 9 7
              ♠ —
              ♡ J 2
              ◇ A K 10 8 7 6
              ♣ A K 6 4 2
```

S.B.	H.H.	W.W.	R.R.
South	West	North	East
1◇	Pass	1♡	1♠
3♣	Pass	3◇	Pass
3♠	Pass	3NT	Pass
4♣	Pass	4◇	Pass
6◇			

The Hideous Hog led the ♣2. As the Professor detached dummy's ♠10, the Rabbit, who was re-arranging his hand to make the black suits alternate with the red, inadvertently dropped the ♠6, and the ♠A, which struck the edge of the table, fluttered to the floor.

"Exposed cards," snapped the Professor.

The Rabbit dived under the table to retrieve the two cards.

"Kindly place the exposed cards face upwards as specified in paragraph 50 of the Laws," insisted S.B.

"Shouldn't you waive the penalty?" began Walter the Walrus. After all, no one could see . . ."

"I name the ♠6 and ♠A," went on the Secretary Bird inexorably, "and I designate the ♠6 as the card to be played."

"But if I couldn't see the cards," persisted W.W. "I am sure that H.H. couldn't see them either, so . . ."

The Hog, who had been strangely quiescent, pensively stroking his chin, suddenly came to life.

"I fear," he said in his silkiest voice, "that I did catch a glimpse. Yes, I'm afraid that ♠6 is, as our friend says, a penalty card."

"I am only stating the law," said S.B. defensively. He knew all about Greeks bearing gifts and his experience told him that Hogs were just as dangerous.

"I had every intention of playing the ♠A," pleaded the Rabbit. "I mean, why should I . . ."

"That ♠6, dear partner, must be played," commanded H.H., the imperious note returning to his voice, and gathering the three cards together, he presented them to the Professor.

The Secretary Bird hissed venomously. The wild tufts of hair over his ears, which looked so much like quills, stood up belligerently. But on the spur of the moment, he could think of no law to invoke against himself. Whether he liked it or not, he had been presented with a wholly unexpected trick.

But what should he play on it from his hand. To throw a heart wouldn't help and a club discard would be pointless, unless he could get rid of two more. Two hisses later he conceded defeat.

The Hog winked meaningly at the kibitzers. "I am surprised, Professor," he mocked, "that a scholar of your distinction should have failed to find a better interpretation of the law, which was so clearly on your side.

"You could have called for the ♠A, you know, and made your contract. I don't have to tell you how the play would go," went on H.H., and proceeded to do so. "You ruff the ♠A, cross to dummy with a trump and lead the ♡5. If the ♡A goes up, you throw two clubs on dummy's hearts and another on a spade which you can set up easily enough. But, of course, R.R. plays low and your ♡J wins. You go back to the table with another trump and play the ♠Q. If it's not covered, you throw your losing heart. If it is, you ruff, cross to dummy on the third round of trumps and get rid of that heart on the ♠J which is now master.

"Yes, Professor, you should look up that paragraph 50 again, page 27, I believe."

That the Hog's behaviour had not been irreproachable was clear. But how was it unethical? The point was put to the Professor.

"To suggest a line of play to his partner, he told a lie. He couldn't possibly see those cards. He had no right to agree with me. Most improper."

"From your position, how could you see the cards?" Oscar the Owl, who was presiding, asked the Hog.

"They could be clearly reflected in the mirror," replied H.H.

"But there is no mirror," objected O.O.

"There used to be one for years," retorted H.H. indignantly, and swiftly passing to the offensive, he demanded to know who had given authority for its removal.

"I have a right," he cried, "I insist . . ."

A couple of weeks later *The Griffins Chronicle* carried this report.

A DUTY TO PARTNER

An unusual item on the agenda of the Ethics and Etiquette Committee was a charge by Papa, acting as an independent observer, against the Hideous Hog, and a cross-petition by H.H. against the Rueful Rabbit and Timothy the Toucan.

The complaints went back to a rubber, a couple of days earlier, in which R.R. and T.T. were partners against the Hog and the Walrus.

"We are playing together in Jill Gatti's Charity Congress this year," explained the Rabbit as they sat down, "so we are trying out some of the more sophisticated modern conventions, quite a wide range, in fact, including Blackwood, Gerber, Gladiator, Flint, Fisher, Fishbein, Forcing and Non-Forcing Stayman, South African Texas . . ."

The Rabbit was still reciting when the Toucan, who dealt the first hand, opened proceedings with 1♠.

```
Dlr. North              ♠ A Q J 9 8 2
Love All                ♡ 7 6
                        ◇ 5 4
                        ♣ A 10 9
     ♠ 5 4                              ♠ K 7 6
     ♡ A 9 5 3          ┌─────────┐     ♡ J 10 8 4 2
     ◇ K Q J 10 9 7 6   │   N     │     ◇ 8 3 2
     ♣ —                │ W   E   │     ♣ 7 3
                        │   S     │
                        └─────────┘
                        ♠ 10 3
                        ♡ K Q
                        ◇ A
                        ♣ K Q J 8 6 5 4 2
```

H.H.	T.T.	W.W.	R.R.
West	*North*	*East*	*South*
–	1♠	Pass	3♣
3◇	3♠	Pass	4♣
Pass	4NT	Pass	5♡
Pass	6♣		

The Hog led the ◇K to the Rabbit's bare ◇A. Fearing that if he drew trumps, H.H. would have a chance to signal in hearts, the Rabbit began by running the ♠10. If the finesse lost, there was a good chance that W.W. would return another diamond.

The Walrus won the trick with the ♠K and was detaching the ◇8, when the Hog stopped him with an imperious gesture. As he did so, he addressed the Toucan.

"Your partner," he said, "was giving us a list of your conventions just now, but I may have missed something. Are you using Blackwood or Gerber?"

"Both," replied the Toucan enthusiastically, "and negative and co-operative doubles, Kock-Werner, Drury . . ."

"Would you kindly explain your partner's response to your 4NT bid," persisted the Hog.

"As a strictly impartial and disinterested spectator, I protest," cried Papa, gesticulating wildly. "You are, as usual, directing your partner, suggesting improperly . . ."

"I don't require directions or improper suggestions," roared the outraged Walrus, slamming the ◇8 on the table. "I know exactly which card to play."

"Such conduct cannot be tolerated," declared Papa, as he described the incident to the Committee. "Declarer played well, testing the spades before touching trumps. It is true that a Papadopolous or any other great player," he added modestly, "would see through declarer's intentions and return a heart. But W.W. was going to play a diamond and for his partner to stop him, to er try to er . . . words fail me."

"Of course," declared the Hog, when Papa finally paused for breath, "my partner would have returned a heart unhesitatingly, but for that 5♡ bid, showing two aces. The Toucan, ready to play in 5♠, no doubt, enquired for aces in Blackwood. The Rabbit replied in Gerber. The question was 4NT. The response was to 4♣. It was gross, if unwitting deception and I had a duty to my partner.

"The section on the Proprieties," went on H.H., "states clearly that it is improper to use any convention the meaning of which may not be understood by the opponents. How much more improper," thundered the Hog, "to use a convention which you do not understand yourself?"

This argument was firmly rejected by the Committee.

"If the use of conventions were restricted to those understood by the players using them," warned Oscar the Owl solemnly, "we should be back in the Dark Ages when bidding was simple and intelligible.

The public would never stand for it."

Next I came across this report.

THE HOG PLAYS DOUBLE-DUMMY

An extraordinary meeting of our Ethics and Etiquette Committee was summoned urgently to discuss grave charges against the Hideous Hog.

His accusers, the Secretary Bird and Papa the Greek, alleged that the Hog, as dummy, had blatantly and flagrantly directed his partner's play.

The Hog's defence was simple and seemingly unanswerable. He had seen no card in anyone's hand but his own, exposed as dummy. How, then, could he have been in a position to influence the play?

Having witnessed the hand which caused all the trouble, I was called upon to give evidence. When asked for my personal opinion, I could only say: "I have no doubt that H.H.'s manoeuvres influenced decisively declarer's play. But I am satisfied that he didn't see, indeed couldn't have seen, any card in anyone else's hand."

"I made no attempt to reconcile the contradiction, but narrated the facts without comment. This was my story.

A new table was being formed.

"Scored any good points lately, Professor?" jeered H.H., who had cut the Rueful Rabbit as partner, "against yourself, that is, of course," he added with a leer.

"Are you going to tell us how clever you are," retorted the Secretary Bird, facing the Greek, "or may we deal first?"

The Hog brought home an uncertain 3NT, depending on the lead, a guess and a squeeze. There was, however, no other game contract. In hearts there were only ten top tricks and H.H. would not have been declarer.

Then this hand came up:

Dlr. South   ♠ 9
N/S Vul: ♡ Q 9 8 6 5 4 2
                              ◊ 7 5 3
                              ♣ A 3

```
        N
    W       E
        S
```

                              ♠ A Q 10
                              ♡ A K J 10 7
                              ◊ A Q 2
                              ♣ 7 5

R.R.	*S.B.*	*H.H.*	*Papa*
South	*West*	*North*	*East*
1♡	1♠	4♡	4♠
Dble.	Pass	5♡	

S.B. led the ♣J. The Rabbit went up with dummy's ♣A and paused
to think the hand out, a step he usually postponed till the end-game.

His best chance, he decided, as he told us later, was to play East
for the ♠J. He would finesse the ♠10, and if it lost to the ♠K, two
of dummy's diamonds would go on the ♠AQ.

First, of course, he had to remove the outstanding trump. So, doing
what comes naturally, the Rabbit laid down the ♡A and continued
with dummy's ♠9.

For a few seconds no one said anything. Then, just as Papa was
detaching a card, the Hog held up imperiously a fat, pink forefinger.

"Stop!" he commanded. "The lead's in dummy. "No," he went on,
as R.R. waved a trump in mid-air, "you must play the same suit."

With a sigh the Rabbit laid down the ♠A and continued with the
♠Q covered by S.B. with the ♠K.

What card the Rabbit would have played from dummy, had he
been left to his own devices, will never be known, for it was at this
point that the Hog committed the first of the more serious trans-
gressions reported to the Committee. Picking up the ♣3, he scooped
an invisible speck of ash from the table and replaced it an inch or so
in front of dummy's other cards, its edge caressing the ♠K.

The Rabbit played it automatically.

"You are deliberately directing your partner!"

"You have palmed that club on to him!" the Professor and Papa cried out in unison.

"Ridiculous," spluttered the Rabbit. "It just happened to be nearest my thumb and it can make no difference whether I lose a spade or a club. I can't lose two tricks in one, can I?"

Hissing, as was his habit when aroused, the Secretary Bird gathered the trick and exited with the ♣10.

The Rabbit ruffed, returned to his hand with the ♡K and continued with the ♠10. His intention, he explained later, was to eliminate spades and lead the ◇7 from dummy in the hope that S.B. would have to win.

Once more, however, H.H. sprang to life. No sooner had the Professor covered the ♠10 with the ♠J than the Hog began to 'tidy up' the dummy, to use his own expression. In so doing, he pushed aside unceremoniously the three little diamonds and spread out with loving care the hearts.

"Will you leave dummy alone!" protested S.B., the wild tufts of hair over his ears bristling angrily.

"And leave the table, too," cried Papa in exasperation.

The Rabbit's cheeks turned from pink to crimson, then to magenta. "I suppose," he said in a voice vibrating with emotion, "that if I dared to ruff, you would accuse me of succumbing to hypnotism. Well, take the beastly trick. I don't want it." And with a savage swish he banged the ◇7 on the Professor's ♠J.

The Hog sat back grunting euphorically. The contract could no longer be lost.

This was the deal in full:

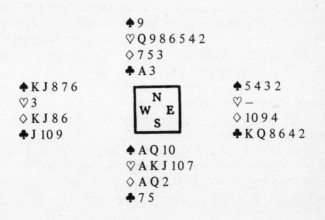

```
                    ♠9
                    ♡Q 9 8 6 5 4 2
                    ◇7 5 3
                    ♣A 3
  ♠K J 8 7 6                           ♠5 4 3 2
  ♡3                  ┌─────────┐      ♡—
  ◇K J 8 6            │   N     │      ◇10 9 4
  ♣J 10 9             │ W   E   │      ♣K Q 8 6 4 2
                      │   S     │
                      └─────────┘
                    ♠A Q 10
                    ♡A K J 10 7
                    ◇A Q 2
                    ♣7 5
```

"Disgraceful!" hissed the Secretary Bird.

"Scandalous!" fumed Papa.

"The defence, you mean? Yes, shocking," said H.H., nodding vigorously. "If, instead of that wanton club, the Professor continues with the ♠J, the contract is unmakeable. Declarer must ruff and play diamonds himself and . . ."

"What!" cried S.B. "Risk giving him a ruff and discard? Or was I to know that Papa raised me to 4♠ on five miserable points and four pigmy trumps headed by the deuce?"

"So it's my fault!" exploded the outraged Greek. "You . . ."

Having sown dissension and distracted attention, as he hoped, from his own peccadilloes, the Hog withdrew gracefully.

A couple of nights later, I caught H.H. in a mellow, expansive mood and over a bottle of Taylor '27, I asked him to explain something which was baffling me.

"Between ourselves, H.H.," I told him candidly, "you directed the Rabbit's play shamelessly from start to finish. But how could you tell . . ."

"The lie of the cards?" interrupted the Hog. "You are surprised? And yet I have told you often enough that I can play better as dummy without seeing the cards, than do most declarers — and all Rabbits, needless to say.

"Consider. The Rabbit plays from the wrong hand and that Secretary Bird, who is always invoking the laws and demanding penalties, lets him do it. Papa concurs. Clearly, they want R.R. to play from dummy. So, since it's in their interests, it's against ours and it's my duty to intervene.

"Of course, by the time R.R. has produced the ♠A and ♠Q, the whole picture is clear. On the lead, Papa is marked with the ♣KQ, so to justify the flimsiest overcall S.B. must have the ♠KJ and the ◇KJ, if not the ◇AQ.

"I admit," went on H.H., "that I er facilitated the play of that ♣3, leaving S.B. on play, but you can't blame me for tidying up the dummy. I knew that after all that hoo-ha, the Rabbit would do the opposite of anything I appeared to suggest. He wouldn't dream of taking advantage of my — guidance, shall we say.

"And, naturally, I wanted a diamond to run up to the closed hand. So, playing double-dummy, as it were, I end-played the Professor. Is that unethical?" asked the Hog rhetorically, raising my glass.

A PACK WITHOUT A KING

Next I came across this report:

A case of unusual complexity came up before Thursday's Committee meeting. Accusations of improper conduct were brought by Walter the Walrus against Charlie the Chimp, by the Chimp against the Hog, by Papa the Greek against the Chimp, the Walrus and the Hog, and by the Hog against Papa.

All charges arose from the same hand, and as I was kibitzing at the time, I was called upon to give evidence. The events themselves were not in dispute.

On the first hand of the rubber the Walrus opened 1♠. Judging that unless the hand were played intelligently 4♠ could go down, the Hog, his partner, preferred the safer contract of 3NT. The second best lead, a faulty discard by the Chimp and a pseudo-squeeze, and he was home.

Then, this deal came up:

```
Dlr. West    ♠ 5 4            ┌──────────┐
N/S Vul:     ♡ J 6 2          │    N     │
             ◊ 8 5 3          │  W   E   │
             ♣ A K 6 4 2      │    S     │
                              └──────────┘
             ♠ A Q 10 9 8 6 3
             ♡ K 8
             ◊ J
             ♣ Q 10 7
```

Papa	W.W.	Ch. Ch.	H.H.
West	North	East	South
Pass	Pass	1◊	1♠
Pass	Pass	Dble.	Pass
2♣	Pass	3◊	Pass
4◊	Pass	5◊	

No lead looked attractive, so after toying with the ◊J, the Hog picked on the ♠A. The Walrus followed with the deuce and the Chimp with the ♠7.

Charlie the Chimp, whose mind appeared, as usual, to be far away and who had just reproved a kibitzer for failing to spot an overtaking squeeze on a previous deal, turned to the Walrus.

"Do you play ace or king from AK?" he asked.

"The king," replied W.W. Then, as the implications of the question sank in, his tone changed. "You know perfectly well that we play the king," he said sharply. "Why do you ask? Does it mean that you haven't the king yourself?"

"No, no, it doesn't mean anything. Nothing at all," the Chimp hastened to assure him. "I was er thinking of something else . . ." His voice trailed off.

Fixing him with a malevolent look, the Hog switched, at trick two to the ♣Q. Declarer, he explained later, was marked wtih not more than two clubs and if it happened to be the Jx, the lead of a low club might be catastrophic, whereas the queen was safe, since it would cause the suit to be blocked.

At the sight of the ♣Q the Walrus spluttered angrily, registering intense disapproval.

The Chimp went up with dummy's ♣A, cashed the ♣K and ruffed a club, noting with a grunt of satisfaction the 3-3 break. Next came the ◊A, then the ◊K. When the Hog showed out, he paused and frowned.

Slowing down appreciably, he played out the rest of his six-card diamond suit.

This was the deal in full:

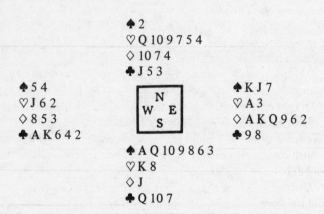

```
                    ♠ 2
                    ♡ Q 10 9 7 5 4
                    ◊ 10 7 4
                    ♣ J 5 3
  ♠ 5 4                              ♠ K J 7
  ♡ J 6 2          N                ♡ A 3
  ◊ 8 5 3        W   E              ◊ A K Q 9 6 2
  ♣ A K 6 4 2      S                ♣ 9 8
                    ♠ A Q 10 9 8 6 3
                    ♡ K 8
                    ◊ J
                    ♣ Q 10 7
```

On the last trump the Hog jettisoned his ♡K and when the Chimp continued with the ♡A and ♡3, hoping to end-play the Hog, the trick went to the Walrus who had two more hearts to cash. Two down.

The Walrus was still brooding on the Chimp's invidious question.

"What did you mean," he asked him suspiciously, "by enquiring whether we played the king or ace from AK? Didn't you know that you had the king yourself?"

"As I've already told you," replied the Chimp with an air of bravado to hide his embarrassment, "I was thinking of something else, but it didn't make the slightest difference and had H.H., misled by my unfortunate remark, played a second spade, you would have ruffed and . . ."

"And you would have made a very poor contract," broke in the Hog. "You were marked on the bidding with six good diamonds, so once Walter ruffed, dummy's ◊8 would have been an entry, and with the lucky 3-3 club break you would have had eleven tricks.

"Mind you," the Hog went on magnanimously, "I am not accusing you of working it out. I took several seconds over it myself. It was just that a spade continuation looked unattractive and . . ."

"Are you suggesting that I was trying deliberately to mislead your partner? That's a most improper allegation," protested the Chimp.

"You are all three improper," declared Papa, unable to restrain himself any longer. "Of course Charlie's remark was reprehensible but Walter was just as much out of order in asking him if he had the ♠K. He had exposed a card, yes, one he didn't have, it is true, but he had exposed it nevertheless. And you H.H.," he went on, turning indignantly on the Hog, "took full advantage of information to which you were not entitled. Had you thought that your partner had the ♠K, as you would have done without his improper remark, you would have led another spade, instead of hazarding that risky play in clubs, and we would have made our contract.

"As for you," pursued Papa, shaking his finger at the luckless Chimp, "you are doubly or rather trebly at fault. We should have been in 3NT, of course, and yet, as things were, you should have made 5◊.

"At trick three, when you were in dummy with the ♣A, you should have led a spade, you could see from Walter's expression of disapproval — most improper, needless to say — that he was dying to ruff a spade. Why didn't you let him die?"

All tried to speak at once, but the Hog, his voice loud and resonant, held the floor.

"I am prepared to make allowances for Papa," he began. "He has had a trying afternoon. He cut the Rabbit twice, then the Toucan, and now Charlie. Not once has he played with me. Of course it's bad luck, which explains, though it doesn't excuse, his bitter outburst.

"For my part," continued the Hog with quiet dignity, "I studiously refrained from taking advantage of anything. Both Charlie and Walter had announced, albeit in different ways, that they didn't have the ♠K.

Neither had I, nor was the ♠K in dummy. So, with scrupulous regard
for the niceties of etiquette, I played as if there were no ♠K in the
pack. Could I do more?"

The Committee meeting has been adjourned for a week to allow
further time for deliberation. A well-informed source, wishing to
remain anonymous, has indicated that all the accused are likely to be
found guilty, though not in equal measure.

BLACK IS WHITE

An unusual feature of the proceedings at Thursday's meeting of the
Ethics and Etiquette Committee was that the complaint was brought
not by one of the players involved in the dispute, but by a spectator
acting *pro bono publico*. The Emeritus Professor of Bio-Sophistry,
better known as the Secretary Bird, charged Charlie the Chimp and
the Hideous Hog with sharp practice, sharper in one case than in
another, but deplorable in both.

The Professor laid this hand before the Committee.

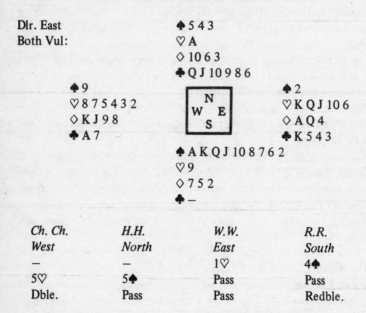

```
Dlr. East              ♠543
Both Vul:              ♡A
                       ◇1063
                       ♣QJ10986
        ♠9                          ♠2
        ♡875432      N              ♡KQJ106
        ◇KJ98      W   E            ◇AQ4
        ♣A7           S             ♣K543
                       ♠AKQJ108762
                       ♡9
                       ◇752
                       ♣—
```

Ch. Ch.	H.H.	W.W.	R.R.
West	North	East	South
—	—	1♡	4♠
5♡	5♠	Pass	Pass
Dble.	Pass	Pass	Redble.

"I don't want to seem pedantic," observed Peregrine the Penguin,
our vice-chairman, "but wouldn't it be more symmetrical to have as

many clubs as there are spades?"

The Professor explained that the hand was played as in the diagram, the Rueful Rabbit having seconded the ♣2 to the spades.

As I had kibitzed the hand from start to finish, it fell to me to describe the sequence of events.

The bidding called for little comment. Charlie the Chimp felt that a slow double over 5♠ was the best way to describe his hand. "A transfer double," was the comment of Colin the Corgi, "transferring the final decision to partner."

The Rabbit's redouble was eminently sound. With him as partner, no one, and least of all the Hog, would think of sacrificing. "Even if I have honours and the hand's a washout," H.H. would say, "it's too high a price to prolong the rubber, for how can you tell what he will do to you on the next deal?"

So the Hog actually expected him to make 11 tricks, something which didn't often happen to R.R. To be so confident the Hog had to be pretty good. The logic was irrefutable.

The Chimp considered his opening lead with care. Reasoning that if declarer had a losing heart, it wouldn't run away, he decided to retain the initiative until he saw dummy and opened the attack with the ♣A.

The Rabbit ruffed with the ♠6, carefully preserving the spurious two as a link with dummy, drew trumps in one round and crossed to the ♡A. Next came the ♣Q which brought the king from Walter the Walrus.

There was nothing to gain by playing low and a chance that, as in the actual deal, R.R. had no more hearts and would be unable to get back to dummy.

Ruffing high, the Rabbit now produced what he firmly believed to be the ♠2. As it landed on the table, however, it shed its mask and revealed for all to see the naked face of the ♣2.

"Revoke!" cried in unison the Chimp, the Walrus and a passing kibitzer.

"Oh dear, oh dear," lamented the Rabbit, "it looked just like the ♠2, same colour and everything. What shall I do?"

The Chimp told him. "You've revoked twice, so four tricks are transferred from your side to ours and though you now make the rest, you are two down. That's 1000 less 150 honours, 850 net."

Dipping his ears in shame, the Rabbit mumbled something inaudible.

"We're wasting time," snapped the Chimp tabling his hand. "I concede the rest."

There was a sibilant hiss from the direction of the Secretary Bird, whose table had broken up and who had come over to join in our argument.

The Hog, strangely silent up to now, held up his hand calling for attention.

"I rather think, Charlie," he told the Chimp, "that the Professor would like to remind you of the Laws relating to revokes. May we, sir," he added, turning to S.B., "have the benefit of your learning?"

S.B. drew himself up, as in his old days in court, and proudly recited. "Law 64, sub-section (b). There is no penalty if the revoke was a subsequent revoke in the same suit by the same player."

"So, you see," said the Hog, "you take two tricks only for the revokes and the contract, therefore, is duly made."

"But that's outrageous!" cried the Chimp, "surely no profit should accrue to a player through a breach of the Laws."

"No, no," declared the Rabbit, "I wouldn't dream of accruing, I mean I would rather not revoke at all than profit, that is . . ."

"Is there anything in the Laws, Professor," asked the Hog, "to say that a player may not derive benefit from a revoke?"

The aura of the lawyer's wig draped S.B.'s bald, domed head as he rose to reply.

"Though the position is not the same as in duplicate," he explained, "there is nothing in the Laws governing rubber bridge to prevent a player from benefiting from a revoke. It's against the spirit of the game to do so, but not against the letter of the Law, and," added S.B., "there's no tournament director to adjust the score."

The Chimp had been growing more and more despondent. Suddenly there was a gleam of hope in his eyes. "How would it be," he suggested, "if we turn a blind eye to those revokes, allowing them to unhappen, so to speak?"

"Most irregular," protested S.B., walking away in disgust.

"We could regard that ♣2 as being to all intents and purposes a little spade" pleaded the Chimp.

"Not the two," objected the Walrus. "I had it and *I* can tell one card from another," he added with a scornful look at R.R.

"Of course," agreed the Chimp, "the ♣2 becomes a spade, any spade other than Walter's two and since there's no longer a black two, officially, R.R. can't lead it, so he can't get to dummy's clubs and loses three diamonds. One down."

"Do you mean," asked the Rabbit ruefully, "that I must lead a diamond?" He would have preferred to enjoy himself a little longer reeling off his spades.

"May as well get it over quickly," coaxed the Hog in his silkiest voice.

Reluctantly R.R. led a diamond.

"One down," announced the Chimp, "that's 400 less the honours, which . . ."

"Play on!" commanded the Hog.

"I'm only claiming three diamonds," insisted the Chimp.

"Declarer's remaining diamonds are discarded on dummy's clubs," retorted the Hog.

"But I'm on play," protested the Chimp, "and you don't suppose that you are going to talk me out of taking our diamonds, do you?"

"Watch him," murmured Colin the Corgi.

There was no trace of bonhomie in the Hog's manner as he replied in icy tones, "You seem to forget, my friend, that you have exposed your hand." Holding up a podgy imperious finger, H.H. went on, "If you take the trouble to look up Laws 49 and 50, you will see that all your cards are penalty cards and declarer may designate which is to be played. So now your heart is ruffed in dummy . . ."

"But, but . . ." The Chimp was about to protest when the Hog turned on him.

"You mustn't abuse any further our patience and good nature," he told him sternly. "First you try brazenly to claim a penalty to which you are not entitled. Next you bend the Laws to deprive R.R. of his revokes. We give in. We accommodate. But, never satisfied, you now want to call our cards, when it's yours that are exposed, and so rob us of our overtrick. That's too much."

From the far corner of the card room, came a prolonged hiss, but the Chimp could think of no suitable reply. Black was white, after all.

"You know," I told the Hog as we left the card room, "you were entirely in the wrong. The Law says that the right to penalise an offence is forfeited if a member of the non-offending side consults his partner before . . ."

"Irrelevant," broke in the Hog, pressing the button for the lift. "The Chimp claimed four tricks, bending the Law one way. I claimed two, bending it the other. What's sauce for the goose is sauce for the Chimp. As for all this unilateral disarmament . . ." the end of the sentence was lost as the Hog disappeared into the lift.

AN UNDISCLOSED CONVENTION

". . . against a person or persons unknown," read the indictment.

The Hideous Hog was appearing before the Ethics and Etiquette Committee of the Griffins Club to give expert evidence. He had strong likes and dislikes, especially the latter, and to have identified the parties might have led to suspicions — or prejudice.

This was Exhibit 'A'.

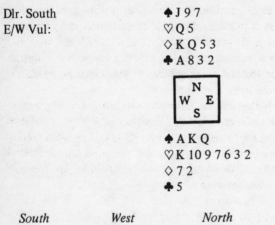

Dlr. South
E/W Vul:

♠ J 9 7
♡ Q 5
♢ K Q 5 3
♣ A 8 3 2

♠ A K Q
♡ K 10 9 7 6 3 2
♢ 7 2
♣ 5

South	West	North	East
1♡	2♢	Dble.	3♣
3♡	Pass	4♡	

The first three tricks were recorded as follows:

'West led the ♢A to which East followed with the ♢9. A second diamond was ruffed by East with the ♡4 and the ♣Q came back, West playing the ♣K. Dummy's ♣A won the trick.'

"How do you continue, H.H.?" asked Oscar the Owl, our Senior Kibitzer, who was presiding.

"I protest," cried the Hog. "First you blindfold me, then you tell me to point the way. Without knowing the guilty parties, how can I say which of them is innocent? Who was East?"

The Owl conferred with Peregrine the Penguine, his senior colleague on the Committee.

"Very well," he resumed. "To meet your objection, without revealing the identity of the players, I will invite you to consider several Easts in turn. Let's say it was Timothy the Toucan."

"That's easy," rejoined the Hog. "The contract depends on not losing two trumps and the AJ8 are still out. West must have the ♡A for his vulnerable overcall. But did he start with three hearts or two? That's the burning question. So, after the ♣A, I lead the ◇K. If the Toucan has another trump, he will ruff. If he doesn't, it's because he hasn't, so I get back to my hand and run the ♡10, playing West for ♡AJ8."

"Would you play the same against the Emeritus Professor of Bio-Sophistry?" enquired the Owl.

"That Secretary Bird!" scoffed the Hog. "No, I wouldn't. He's not bad enough to fall into that trap. He would reason that if I wanted a discard, I would first draw two rounds of trumps. If I didn't, it could only be because I was missing the ace or king, in which case I would surely have no spade losers. Guessing what I was up to, he wouldn't ruff, especially with the jack.

"There's a much better way to go about it against S.B. or any other player in the average or better bracket," went on H.H. "After the ♣A I lead the ♠7 — quickly, needless to say. East will signal to show whether he has three spades or four. Everyone signals automatically these days. It's a reflex, like putting trumps on the right, or blaming partner when you make a mistake. Which side will benefit is of secondary importance. Signalling is an end in itself.

"Here," pursued the Hog, "declarer, as so often happens, is the sole beneficiary. The signal solves his problem for him. If East shows four spades, West must have three. He is known to have six diamonds and his ♣K is obviously a singleton. So he must have three hearts. I lead the ♡10 and run it, knowing that it will win.

"Conversely, if East shows three spades, West has four, and therefore, two hearts only, in which case the jack will come down.

"Observe," concluded the Hog, "that East can't have five spades, for if West had two, he would have four hearts and we know that only three are out."

"And which of these methods would you adopt?" asked O.O. "if East were Walter the Walrus?"

"Either will do," declared the Hog. "The Walrus is thoroughly reliable. You can depend upon him to do the wrong thing in any situation."

"We'll have the Rueful Rabbit next," persisted the Owl. "Technically there's little to choose between him and the Toucan, so would you resort to your first manoeuvre, the ◇K to see if he ruffs?"

"No" the Hog shook his head. "Unlike the Walrus, the Rabbit isn't to be trusted. Besides he wouldn't stop to work it out and might refrain from ruffing, not for any technical reason, but because declarer seems to expect it of him and he likes to do the unexpected.

"However," continued H.H., "the Rabbit loves gadgets and conventions of every sort and he is an enthusiastic signaller. He even signals to himself, I am told, when he plays patience. So I lead a spade, waiting for the semaphore."

"Let's say," said O.O., "that the Rabbit plays the ♠8 and West the ♠4. What next?"

"Just to make sure, I cash another spade," replied the Hog.

"West's card is the ♠3 and the Rabbit's the ♠2," said the Owl with a smile.

The Hog frowned. "They can't both have four spades and neither can have a doubleton. Who's West?" he asked suspiciously.

"The Toucan" replied O.O. "He was at the table, after all, you see, and he does signal, doesn't he?"

"Ye-es, in a way," agreed H.H "but all the cards below the 8 or 9 are much the same to him, so I prefer to trust the Rabbit. Since he has shown four spades, he can't have a heart left, so I run the ♡10 and . . ."

The Owl finished the sentence for him: "The Rabbit wins with the ♡J. One down."

This was the deal in full:

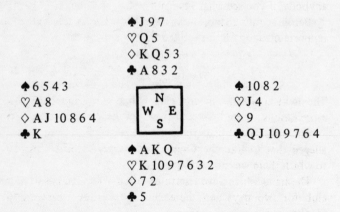

```
                    ♠ J 9 7
                    ♡ Q 5
                    ◇ K Q 5 3
                    ♣ A 8 3 2
  ♠ 6 5 4 3                              ♠ 10 8 2
  ♡ A 8              ┌─────────┐         ♡ J 4
  ◇ A J 10 8 6 4     │    N    │         ◇ 9
  ♣ K               │ W     E │         ♣ Q J 10 9 7 6 4
                    │    S    │
                    └─────────┘
                    ♠ A K Q
                    ♡ K 10 9 7 6 3 2
                    ◇ 7 2
                    ♣ 5
```

"I've never known the Rabbit give a false signal before," said the Hog in surprise. "It's much too subtle for him. Now had it been Papa . . ."

"But that's just it," retorted O.O., "It wasn't a false signal. The Rabbit was playing what he calls Descending Signals, high–low with an odd number of cards in ascending order with an even number. He maintains," went on O.O., reading from R.R.'s sworn statement, "that it is superior to the usual method, because while there's nothing to choose between the two if you want to show a doubleton, three cards or four, only Descending Signals enable you to distinguish between three and five. With three, the first card is the second lowest, with five, the third lowest. When you have to discard on a long suit, the information, he says, may be invaluable to partner."

"I'm not sure that it's an important contribution to science," observed P.P., "but are we to understand that this unusual convention hadn't been disclosed to declarer? That's the complaint, isn't it?"

"Yes" agreed the Owl. "Papa the Greek, who was declarer, reasoned exactly as H.H. did just now and he was taken in completely by the false signal."

The Rabbit was summoned before the Committee and was asked to give an explanation.

O.O. put the question: "Did you not think of informing declarer that you were using a special convention?"

"But I wasn't actually using it," protested the Rabbit. "I was practising. It's still in the blue print stage and I was only trying it out by myself. It wouldn't have been proper, would it, to announce a convention which hadn't been disclosed to partner? I didn't want to mislead anybody, if you see what I mean."

Before pronouncing judgment, the Committee has appointed a rapporteur to look into precedents.

The Judgment of Solomon

The next complaint to come up before the Committee was of a far more serious nature.

Themistocles Papadopolous, who was once more the plaintiff, alleged that Charlie the Chimp had invented a new form of cheating to which there was no known antidote.

The hand which gave rise to the accusation had been the talk of the club for two days and there was no mystery, therefore, about the identity of the parties concerned.

Dlr. South
N/S Vul:

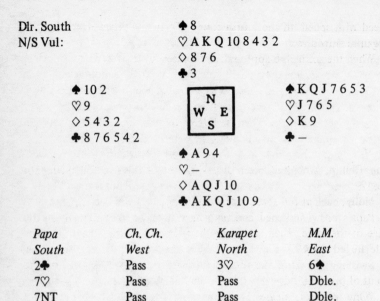

Papa	Ch. Ch.	Karapet	M.M.
South	*West*	*North*	*East*
2♣	Pass	3♡	6♠
7♡	Pass	Pass	Dble.
7NT	Pass	Pass	Dble.

Karapet, the Free Armenian, who still awaits official recognition as
the unluckiest player of the century, knew that evil was afoot when
Papa opened 2♣ and he saw what looked like eight cast-iron tricks
in his own cards. It was unlikely that Papa would let him play the
hand, but he did his duty by bidding 3♡, a jump in a forcing situation
to show a solid suit.

Molly the Mule's leap to 6♠ put Papa in a quandary. He would
either have to be dummy or miss a grand slam. Bearing in mind the
vulnerability, he bowed to his fate.

Of course 7♡ was just what Molly hoped to hear and she doubled
triumphantly. The note of jubilation was unmistakable and Papa
quickly guessed the reason. Because Karapet had advertised a solid
suit — which had clearly sprung an unexpected leak — it didn't follow
that he couldn't have the ◊K or even conceivably the ♠K. While, therefore, 7♡ would be doomed from the start, 7NT might be unbeatable.

Molly doubled out of self-respect, but the joyful note had gone
out of her voice.

Several kibitzers testified about the course of the play. This was
the broad picture which emerged from their evidence.

The Chimp led the ♠10, overtaken by Molly's jack and won by Papa
with the ace. Six clubs followed in quick succession, Molly matching

speed with speed 'til the fourth round. Then, still throwing spades, she began to slow down.

When the sixth club appeared, she was left with:

♠ K
♡ J 7 6 5
◇ K 9
♣ —

The Chimp, who had been observing her anxiously, followed with the ♡9.

Molly, back at full speed, discarded the ♡5.

Papa's brow darkened and his fingers beat an angry tattoo on the edge of the table. Then, gathering the trick and setting it neatly on one side, he led the ♠9.

Swishing the king victoriously through the air, Molly was on the point of bringing it down, when the Chimp stopped her.

"One moment, please. May I see the last trick? I find that I have a club er sticking to a spade. I suppose my ♡9 now becomes an exposed card. Sorry partner. Very careless of me. The light is . . ."

Exactly what followed isn't clear, for everyone spoke, screamed or shouted at once.

It emerged from the hubbub that Papa would report everyone to the Committee, that Molly had never been so insulted in her life, and that the Chimp, who could hardly plead the same, had been injured in his best feelings.

The Hog was asked for a brief technical appraisal. Since he disliked all concerned in roughly equal measure, he wasn't expected to show bias.

The Chimp, explained H.H., could see from the start that Papa had no heart. Otherwise, with the ♠A and six clubs, he could count fifteen tricks. But Molly couldn't be at all sure. It must have seemed unlikely to her that Papa would bid 7NT with a void, so she could hardly be blamed for holding on to her hearts.

In the event, she was destined to be the victim of a progressive pseudo-squeeze. Hoping that the Chimp had the ♠9 — and why shouldn't he — she would have surely thrown her ♠K on the last club, if, that is, destiny had had her way. Then, on Papa's ♠9 she would have shed her ◇9 hoping that the Chimp had the ◇Q. Even the ◇J would be enough if Papa didn't have a third spade.

"All in all," concluded the Hog, "Molly had a very difficult problem, until she saw that ♡9. That, of course, told her everything."

Asked for an explanation, Molly was indignant at the mere thought that she had been influenced by the sight of the ♡9. It was purely incidental, she told the Committee, for she had known all along that Papa had no heart.

"But how could you tell?" asked O.O.

"Intuition," declared Molly. "I just know these things. How did I know," she asked rhetorically, " that the ◇K would drop in that 6♠ contract which won us the annual match between the Mermaids and the Butterflies? How did I find the only lead to beat the unbeatable 6♡ in Sunday's Charity Match between the Forward Girls and Backward Boys? I sense things. You men," concluded Molly defiantly, "have a lot to learn when you play with women."

This last contention wasn't challenged. No one, except the Chimp, believed Molly's defence. No one, except Molly, believed the Chimp.

The Committee called on the Hog for expert advice.

"There's no adequate penalty," said H.H. "Treating the ♡9 as an exposed card is absurd, for to expose it was the Chimp's intention, the only way, in fact, to defeat the grand slam.

"The letter of the law won't help us. We must invoke the spirit. What would Solomon have done?"

No one on the Committee seemed to know, so the Hog gave his own authoritative interpretation.

"All the witnesses agree that Molly's ♠K was within a couple of inches of Papa's ♠9. It had all but been played. Solomon would have treated it, I think, as a card that actually had been played, establishing a revoke.

"So Molly wins the trick, but is now end-played. Papa makes the rest and one trick from the offending side is duly transferred to the other, in accordance with the rules.

"Themistocles becomes the first man to make a grand slam by means of a throw-in and, of course, gives the money to charity. Molly's Forward Girls is eminently suitable. All the guilty parties are pronounced innocent and everyone is happy."

The Solomonic solution is still being studied. Meanwhile, the Committee has recommended Karapet for the annual award to the Unluckiest Man of the Year.

It's an ill-wind . . .

THE COUP OF THE GREEN CHARTREUSE

"One might call it an inspired accident, I suppose," said Oscar the Owl doubtfully.

"Or maybe a well co-ordinated lapse," suggested Peregrine the Penguin.

"There's nothing to cover the case in the Laws," sighed O.O.

"Or in the proprieties," added P.P.

Our Ethics and Etiquette Committee had been discussing a charge of grave misconduct brought jointly by the Professor of Bio-Sophistry and Charlie the Chimp against the Hideous Hog.

Papa the Greek, who had been kibitzing, came forward to give evidence *pro bono publico*, that is to say against the Hog.

This was the hand which gave rise to the complaint.

```
Dlr. South            ♠J 7 2
Love All              ♡Q 7 6 3 2
                      ◇A K
                      ♣J 3 2
                         N
                      W     E
                         S
                      ♠K 8 3
                      ♡5 4
                      ◇J 7 6 5
                      ♣A K Q 4
```

R.R.	S.B.	H.H.	Ch. Ch.
South	*West*	*North*	*East*
1♣	Pass	1♡	Pass
1NT	Pass	3♡	Pass
3NT	Pass	Pass	Dble.

The bidding is explained by the system, known at the Griffins as the Pragmatic Notrump. This reflects the vulnerability. The Rabbit, being acutely vulnerable, is under orders to bid notrumps only in extremis. The Hog usually does it for him and so steers the contract into the right hand.

The system bid on the Rabbit's hand was 1◇ with 2♣ as the intended rebid.

The diamond suit being distinctly porous, however, the Rabbit opened unthinkingly 1♣ and found himself with no permitted rebid. Hence 1NT.

The Hog tried to restore the situation by jumping in his six-card suit — five in the hand and one more in the play — but it was to no avail.

The Chimp doubled, partly to rattle the Rabbit, and partly for a heart lead, and the Professor duly began with the ♡A. At trick two he switched to the ♠6 which went to the Chimp's ace. The ♣9 came back.

The Rabbit wondered why the defence was so erratic, but not always certain what made him do things himself, he didn't like to enquire too closely into the motives of others. His main concern was to go down as little as possible.

Going up with the ace, he crossed to the ♣J in dummy and continued with the ◇AK. The Professor followed smoothly the first time, then he paused and pursing his thin, bloodless lips began to meditate.

Avoiding an End-Play

I had been observing the play from a seat between the Rabbit and the Chimp, and to see what was bothering him I walked round the table. This is how the cards had been dealt.

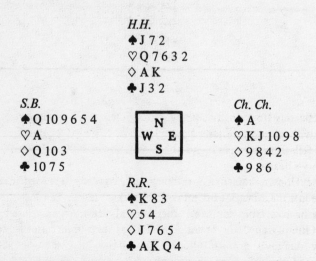

```
                      H.H.
                      ♠ J 7 2
                      ♡ Q 7 6 3 2
                      ◇ A K
                      ♣ J 3 2
   S.B.                                      Ch. Ch.
   ♠ Q 10 9 6 5 4          N                 ♠ A
   ♡ A                   W   E               ♡ K J 10 9 8
   ◇ Q 10 3                S                 ◇ 9 8 4 2
   ♣ 10 7 5                                  ♣ 9 8 6
                      R.R.
                      ♠ K 8 3
                      ♡ 5 4
                      ◇ J 7 6 5
                      ♣ A K Q 4
```

The Professor's problem was self-evident. If R.R. removed his last club

and threw him in with a diamond he would have to play a spade away
from his queen. So, after due reflection, he jettisoned the ◇Q, hoping
that the Chimp had the jack.

This cheered up the Rabbit visibly for he could now see himself
going only one down, always a good result in a doubled contract.

With a carefree air he came back to the ♣K, cashed the queen and
then the ◇J, discarding hearts both times from the table. The Secretary
Bird followed with the ◇10 and the Chimp with the nine.

The Rabbit sat back and shutting his eyes the better to concentrate,
tried to recall what the Chimp had thrown on the ♣Q at the previous
trick. With his keen sense of colour he knew that it was a red card.
But was it a heart or a diamond? Was his ◇7 good?

Experts can tell such things at a glance, but the Rueful Rabbit was
far from sure. One thing, however, was certain. He had everything to
gain and nothing to lose by trying it out. As he led the ◇7 this was
the 4-card position.

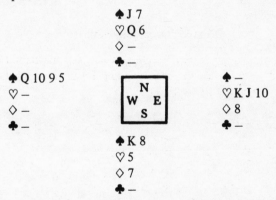

       ♠J 7
       ♡Q 6
       ◇ –
       ♣ –

♠Q 10 9 5   ♠ –
♡ –   N   ♡K J 10
◇ –   W E   ◇ 8
♣ –   S   ♣ –

       ♠K 8
       ♡5
       ◇ 7
       ♣ –

The Hideous Hog, slowly sipping a green chartreuse, was following the
play with close attention. Now, just as S.B. played to the trick the
glass fell from his hand and the sweet, viscous liqueur spread over
dummy's hearts.

The Hog apologised. "Sorry. It's that unsteady table leg. Careless
of me just the same. I'll get another pack."

As he rose from the table, the Secretary Bird hissed venomously.
The Chimp gasped for breath. The Rabbit, his mind on other things
threw dummy's ♠7 and shook his head ruefully when the Chimp
produced the ◇8. With hearts only left, however, he couldn't avoid
presenting R.R. with his ninth trick.

Declarer's Threat to Dummy

Called by the plaintiffs as an expert witness, Papa interpreted the play from a technical point of view.

"Such was the distribution," he began, "that the contract was at all times unbeatable. If the Professor retained the $\Diamond$Q he would be obliged to concede a trick in spades. If he jettisoned it, as in fact he did, Charlie would be forced to concede a trick in hearts. An end-play against one defender or the other was, therefore, pre-ordained. The contract was foolproof. But was it Rabbit-proof?"

Papa paused for effect and resumed slowly, giving weight to every word.

"The Rabbit, of course, had no idea of the distribution and no thought of an end-play, and so his last diamond became a squeeze card against dummy. Being as likely to throw a heart as a spade, the contract was no better than a fifty–fifty chance, less than that, perhaps, for he had thrown hearts on the two previous tricks and had got into a heart-throwing rhythm."

Clearing his throat and looking sternly at the Hog, the Greek pressed home the charge.

"To break up the threatened squeeze H.H. chose this critical moment to spill the contents of his glass over dummy's hearts. A split second before it was, as I've explained, an even-money chance which card the Rabbit would play. Now, having to choose between a wet and sticky heart and a crisp, dry spade, the result was no longer in doubt. I have yet to see," concluded Papa, "a viler defence against a potential squeeze."

"No one in the club, perhaps no one in the country," declared the Secretary Bird indignantly, "has greater control of a glass or more practice in exercising it than H.H. That he should let it slip at this particular moment was certainly no coincidence."

The Hog turned this neatly against the Professor.

"If it is true," he argued, "that I always have a glass in my hand then it follows that sooner or later I am likely to drop it. I haven't had a mishap like this for years, so surely I was due for one, nay, overdue. Why, it was an odds-on chance . . ."

The Hideous Hog was again the defendant in the next case recorded in *The Griffins Chronicle*.

This was my report.

CYNICAL SUIT SIGNALS

A meeting of the Ethics and Etiquette Committee was summoned urgently last night to hear grave charges brought by Papa the Greek, severally and jointly, against Charlie the Chimp and the Hideous Hog.

Papa, who believed that had fate not called upon him to own ships, he would have made a great advocate — or a great gynaecologist, a great astronomer or a great lepidopterist — presented his own case.

This was Exhibit A.

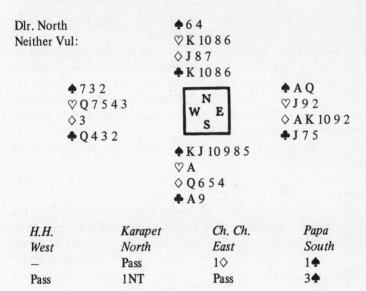

Dlr. North
Neither Vul:

	♠ 6 4	
	♡ K 10 8 6	
	◊ J 8 7	
	♣ K 10 8 6	
♠ 7 3 2		♠ A Q
♡ Q 7 5 4 3		♡ J 9 2
◊ 3		◊ A K 10 9 2
♣ Q 4 3 2		♣ J 7 5
	♠ K J 10 9 8 5	
	♡ A	
	◊ Q 6 5 4	
	♣ A 9	

H.H.	Karapet	Ch. Ch.	Papa
West	North	East	South
—	Pass	1◊	1♠
Pass	1NT	Pass	3♠

"A simple contract, gentlemen," he began. "I was sitting South, and as you can see, only a diamond ruff stops 4♠.

"However, Karapet, my partner, who always expects the worst in life and is seldom disappointed, passed cautiously and we stopped in the unbreakable contract of 3♠ — unbreakable," repeated Papa, "by honourable means. The defence, I regret to say, adopted other methods.

"Sitting West, H.H. led his singleton ◊3. The Chimp cashed the ◊K, the ◊A and . . ." Papa paused for effect.

"Which card," he resumed, "should he lead for H.H. to ruff? The ◊10? That would surely call for a heart return. The ◊2? That would ask for a club, and of course the Chimp wanted neither. Only a trump, a most unlikely play, could beat the contract. On any other return,

I would have time to cash the ♡A, cross to the ♣K and throw my last diamond on the ♡K. Thereafter, I could ruff a diamond high in my hand without any risk of being over-ruffed.

"Naturally," pursued the Greek, "the Chimp could see that. He knew by my jump to 3♠ that I had six spades. I had shown up with four diamonds, and to bid as I did, I needed the two other aces. Every card was marked and he could defend double-dummy.

"Should he, then, lead back the ◇9? That would disclaim interest in hearts and clubs, but it would hardly call for a trump. And so," went on Papa, a note of indignation creeping into his voice, "Charlie the Chimp coldly, deliberately and with malice aforethought, found another signal, dropping the ◇10 and ◇2 on the table *simultaneously*.

"The implications were unmistakeable. He had no interest in hearts or clubs, but he had an entry. It could be, indeed it had to be, in trumps, for one of the diamonds, an exposed card, would have to be played at the first opportunity and what good would that do him?" asked the Greek rhetorically, "if I had time to draw trumps first?"

"Of course," continued Papa "an ethical partner would never take advantage of such improper information. H.H. alas, didn't even pause. Ruffing the ◇10 with the ♠3, he promptly returned the ♠2, a cynical trump signal, advertising a third spade.

"The Chimp went up with the ♠A, of course, and observing brazenly 'I suppose I have to lead this now,' he pushed forward the ◇2 to give the Hog another ruff."

With a low bow to Oscar the Owl, who was presiding, Papa sat down.

"I do not know," began the Hog, "whether, as Papa says, the two diamonds inadvertently dropped by Charlie touched the table simultaneously. Maybe. Unlike some people," he went on with a scathing look at the Greek, "I consider it bad form to watch my partners as they draw their cards.

"But whichever card the Chimp intended to play first, and whether or not it had preceded the other by a split second, I was determined not to take advantage of it. And how could I make certain of that, except by leading a trump? Yes," continued the Hog, warming to his subject, "it was a *beau geste*, though I say it myself. I knew that partner had an ace and I deliberately gave up the chance of finding it. Could I guess, could I imagine that it was the ace of his own suit that Papa was missing?"

With a lofty look and a courtly bow, the Hideous Hog walked out.

The Chimp spoke for less than a minute. "No one, he declared indignantly, "has accused me of doing anything underhand for more than a fortnight. Would I allow my reputation to be tarnished for a part-score — against non-vulnerable opponents at that!"

CHAPTER TWELVE

Monster Points

MULTIPLE VANDALISM

As a counterpart to Master Points at duplicate the Griffins award Monster Points at rubber bridge. To qualify it isn't enough, of course, to commit an ordinary blunder. Were it so, most of the Griffins would have long ago acquired the status of Life Monsters. Only outstanding iniquities earn monster points, carrying a penalty of champagne round the table for players and kibitzers alike.

The conception behind monster points, the Hog's insistence that if master points are awarded for merit, iniquity and moral turpitude, should in turn, be punished, together with the early deliberations of the Monster Points Committee, all are fully reported in *Masters and Monsters*. A history of the Griffins would not be complete, however, without a mention or two of outstanding cases which came before us. *The Griffins Chronicle* records:

At Wednesday's meeting of the Monster Points Committee, Timothy the Toucan was arraigned on two charges brought by Papa the Greek.

Opening his case, the Greek told the Committee: "I do not expect my partners to play like Garozzo or Belladonna or er like I do. But neither do I expect vandalism – *multiple* vandalism," added Papa with a withering look at the Toucan.

This was the first hand of the rubber in which both the alleged offences occurred.

Dlr. South
Love All

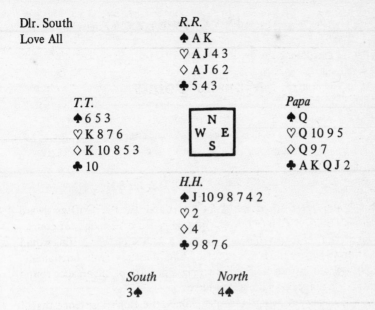

R.R.
♠ A K
♡ A J 4 3
♢ A J 6 2
♣ 5 4 3

T.T.
♠ 6 5 3
♡ K 8 7 6
♢ K 10 8 5 3
♣ 10

Papa
♠ Q
♡ Q 10 9 5
♢ Q 9 7
♣ A K Q J 2

H.H.
♠ J 10 9 8 7 4 2
♡ 2
♢ 4
♣ 9 8 7 6

South	North
3♠	4♠

The Toucan led the ♣10. Papa overtook it with the ♣J and laid down the ♣A. Seeing T.T.'s ♡8 the Greek had no difficulty in visualising the entire deal.

If the Hog had eight spades or either red king, he had ten top tricks. Even he, however, wouldn't open 3♠ on a six-card suit headed by the jack, so the defence had to be predicated on the assumption that he had seven spades. If so, he had nine tricks — seven trumps and two aces — and a club ruff would be the tenth. At trick three, therefore, Papa led the ♠Q to dummy's ♠A.

The Hog led dummy's ♣5.

"If I won the trick," explained Papa, "there would be no way of breaking the contract, since I didn't have another trump. So I very carefully played my deuce under dummy's five. The Toucan marked with two more trumps — if the Hog had seven — would be forced to ruff and his trump return, removing dummy's ♠K, would kill the club ruff, declarer's tenth trick. You will agree, I think," added Papa, "that I make things easy for my partner."

Pausing for effect, the Greek proceeded to unfold the sorry sequel to his subtle defence.

The order of play to the first two tricks having clearly established that Papa had the four top honours in clubs, it didn't dawn on the

Toucan that he was expected to ruff. Dreamily, with a far-away look, he discarded the ◊8.

The Hog gathered the trick with alacrity, ruffed his last club and duly wrapped up eleven tricks.

"Bad psychology, Themistocles," he told Papa, rubbing salt in his wounds. "You should have won the first trick with the king. That jack–ace sequence was too flamboyant. Enough to confuse anyone."

A pithy summary of the Toucan's short-comings took up the next seven or eight minutes and he was still squirming when this hand came up.

Dlr. North
N/S Vul:

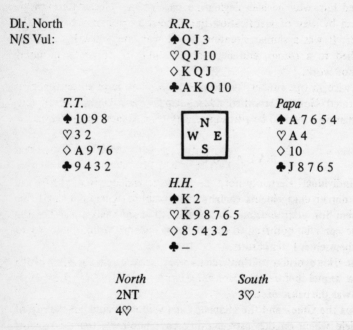

R.R.
♠ Q J 3
♡ Q J 10
◊ K Q J
♣ A K Q 10

T.T.
♠ 10 9 8
♡ 3 2
◊ A 9 7 6
♣ 9 4 3 2

Papa
♠ A 7 6 5 4
♡ A 4
◊ 10
♣ J 8 7 6 5

H.H.
♠ K 2
♡ K 9 8 7 6 5
◊ 8 5 4 3 2
♣ —

North	South
2NT	3♡
4♡	

The Toucan led the ♣10 to Papa's ♠A, the Hog following with the ♣2.

"It was immediately apparent to me," Papa told the Committee, "that unless the Toucan had the ◊A the contract was unbeatable. If I returned the ◊10, however, it wouldn't be obvious to him that it was a singleton. With three diamonds only on the table it might well be a doubleton, and if so, it would be right for him to hold up the ace 'til I came in with the ♡A and played my second diamond. Even T.T.," went on Papa, "would realise that I must have the ♡A to beat the contract.

"How, then, could I convey to him that my diamond was a singleton?"
Before anyone could hazard a guess Papa gave the answer himself.

"I laid down my ♡A. Then, and then only, did I lead that diamond.
As I told you just now, gentlemen, I like to make life easy for my
partners."

As he went on Papa looked sternly at the unhappy Toucan. "Though
I found partner with the ◇A, though I had devised a way of informing
him that I had no further entry, I did not get a ruff. Far from it. Slowly,
with purposeful deliberation, he returned a trump, yes, a trump!"

Papa waited for the words to sink in before he resumed. "When
I asked him why he had singled me out for this piece of sadism, he
recalled by way of justification the atrocity on the first hand of the
rubber. It was a similar situation. I had won the first trick and had
switched to a trump, and he had been told off for not continuing
the good work.

"Twice in one rubber," concluded Papa, "my inspired defence was
desecrated. Nothing less than a Jeroboam, if not a Methuselah of vintage champagne would be a fitting penalty for such acts of vandalism."

BALANCED FREAKS

"An Individual? Certainly not," declared the Hideous Hog. "I have my
usual dinner engagements tonight and I wouldn't give up a single one
of them for your precious Individual. All those freaks, just because
people can't be bothered to shuffle. They seem to think it's funny to
deal themselves 11-card suits."

The Hog's dislike of Individuals went back to an occasion which
had a sequel before our Monster Points Committee. A spectacular
freak was the cause of it.

Papa the Greek and the Hideous Hog were well ahead of the rest of
the field when, on the last set of boards, they came together against
the Rueful Rabbit and Timothy the Toucan. They eyed each other
with mutual dislike.

"I hope I can afford a couple of bottoms," murmured the Hog in
a loud aside.

"When he was younger," confided Papa in a resonant whisper to
no one in particular, "they used to think he was quite good. The
standard was much lower in those days, of course."

As dealer on the first board, Papa had the chance to bid notrumps
first and bought the contract. Then this hand came up:

Dlr. East   *Papa*
E/W Vul: ♠ A K
                                 ♡ Q J 10 9 8 7 6 5 4 3 2
                                 ◇ —
                                 ♣ —

```
        N
    W       E
        S
```

H.H.
♠ Q 10 2
♡ —
◇ A K Q J 10
♣ A K Q J 10

T.T.	*H.H.*	*R.R.*	*Papa*
East	*South*	*West*	*North*
Pass	2♣	Pass	2♡
Pass	2NT	Pass	5♡
Pass	6◇	Pass	6♡
Pass	7♣	Pass	7♡
Pass	7♠	Dble.	Redble.

When the matter was brought up by Papa before the Monster Points
Committee, the Hog's bidding came in for sharp criticism.

Peregrine the Penguin, reared on the classics, questioned the
propriety of the 2NT rebid which proclaimed, according to the text-
books, a balanced hand. "Was 3-0-5-5 a balanced hand?" asked
P.P. rhetorically.

"Maybe not," conceded the Hog, "but text-books leave out of
account the personal factor. Given the chance, Papa would have bid
notrumps first, as he always does. Nothing so trivial as a 2-11-0-0
shape would have stopped him treating the hand as strictly balanced.
First I had to make sure that the hand wouldn't be played from the
wrong side. Then I could show my distribution. Of course," went on
H.H., "I couldn't foresee an immediate leap to 5♡, by my er partner.
But observe the smooth, simple sequence which followed — that
is, from my side. Knowing that we had a cold grand slam in either
minor . . ."

"Aren't you forgetting those three losing spades?" broke in Peregrine.

"I had *no* losing spades," retorted the Hog heatedly. "I bid, as I play, looking through the backs of the cards and I could see clearly the ♠AK in Papa's hand. For what did he mean by his direct 5♡ over my 2NT? The manoeuvre is, these days, quite conventional, inviting partner to bid six with one of the two top honours and seven with both. So Papa couldn't have the ace or king of hearts, yet he had given me a positive response to 2♣, promising a trick and a half. The only trick and a half he could have were the ♠AK.

"But, of course," went on the Hog, "I looked beyond the cards into the mind — the unstable, devious mind, I fear — of the player holding them. If I bid the grand slam straightaway, would Papa accept as trumps a suit of which he was void, when he had an eleven-card suit of his own? Never. So I bid 6◊ first, knowing that I would hear 6♡. Then I bid 7♣. Now surely, even a purblind megalomaniac like Papa should have realised that I had two solid suits, a 7-6 shape as far as he was concerned. There are limits to iniquity," declared the Hog "and Papa went beyond them when, in a fit of vicious egotism, he wantonly took me out into 7♡, missing the AK. All he was asked to do was to give simple preference, choosing the void he liked best."

"Does that excuse your bid of 7♠?" asked Oscar the Owl, who as Senior Kibitzer, was presiding over the Monster Points Committee.

"Since we couldn't make 7♡," replied the Hog with simple dignity, "we were booked for a frigid bottom. Our bottom couldn't have been more frigid in spades than in hearts. As you know, gentlemen," went on the Hog in loftier tones, "I believe that nothing so befits a player, even the greatest, even a genius, as modesty, and with the utmost humility I venture to submit a consideration to which you may see fit to give weight.

"Whatever the superficial drawbacks of a 2-3 trump fit in a high-level contract, the grand slam in spades is unbeatable, without a double-dummy lead. As you know, I am no result merchant, but . . ."

Whereupon the Hog invited us to study the records. This was the full deal:

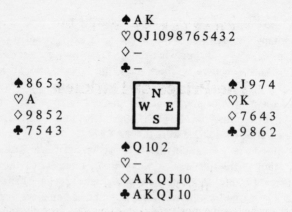

♠ A K
♡ Q J 1 0 9 8 7 6 5 4 3 2
♢ —
♣ —

♠ 8 6 5 3
♡ A
♢ 9 8 5 2
♣ 7 5 4 3

♠ J 9 7 4
♡ K
♢ 7 6 4 3
♣ 9 8 6 2

♠ Q 10 2
♡ —
♢ A K Q J 10
♣ A K Q J 10

The Rabbit led the ♡A. As he put down his hand, stretching the hearts right across the table, Papa addressed an empty space over the Hog's right shoulder.

"No doubt," he told the space, "my partner has more spades than I have hearts and since he could bid seven all on his own, with the ace-king of trumps over and above my bid, I was entitled, I feel, to redouble."

Shocked by a bidding sequence so highly charged with ill-feeling and emotion, the Rabbit gave the Toucan a meaning look.

"I don't think, Timothy," he said with a disarming smile, "that we would like to score a top or inflict a bottom because of er temperamental differences. I am quite willing to accept an average."

The Toucan nodded vigorously to signify assent.

"With *him* a cold bottom *is* an average. Play on," commanded the Hog.

Ruffing the ♡A, H.H. cashed four diamonds, then four clubs. Having gathered nine tricks, he ruffed his fifth diamond — he had kept the ace for the occasion to make it more spectacular — with dummy's ace of trumps. Now a heart, ruffed, over-ruffed and under-ruffed in turn, took him back to the closed hand. The ♣A was ruffed with the ♠K and it only remained to score the ♠Q for the thirteenth trick. To the last four tricks, the Rabbit and the Toucan, studiously under-ruffing, contributed eight trumps.

Having gone through the motions, the Hog bowed low to the Committee and in icy tones demanded:

"Pray, tell me, gentlemen, whether you find fault with my bidding or my play?" With a flourish he put out the stub of his cigar in Peregrine's coffee cup and walked out majestically.

CHAPTER THIRTEEN

The Prince of Darkness

HOG V. SATAN

I have left to the last the most remarkable episode in the club's history. The fateful date was 30th April, Walpurgis Night, when the witches ride forth on their broomsticks for a tryst with their master, the Devil. Owls hoot eerily, toads croak and the rustle of bats' wings seeps through the night air.

We had a partnership at the Griffins. As darkness fell our chief steward, Balthazar, announced the arrival of two distinguished visitors, Lord de Ville and Lady Greymalkin, who hoped to join in a few friendly rubbers.

The Rabbit and the Toucan, waiting for a game, courteously welcomed the strangers.

With pursed lips, lank grey hair and a hooked, beaky nose, Lady Greymalkin had nothing about her of the proverbial sex kitten. Tall, slim, commanding in appearance, her escort had a pitiless look in his cold, magnetic eyes.

At every table that night the cards were bewitched. The best contracts went down, the worst succeeded. No distribution complied with the odds, nothing was where it should be, as spellbound, dancing to some unearthly tune, the cards mocked the players.

From the first, the visitors held overpowering cards. During the first hour's play the Rabbit and the Toucan scored only twice.

The first time was when R.R. bid 1♠ out of turn. With T.T. unable to show his 20 points, a good-looking slam on which the partnership might well have reached game, was played at the one level. The defenders won the first six tricks on a cross-ruff, so 1♠ was just made.

A little later, T.T. and R.R. brought off an unusual defensive coup on this deal:

Dlr. South
N/S Vul:

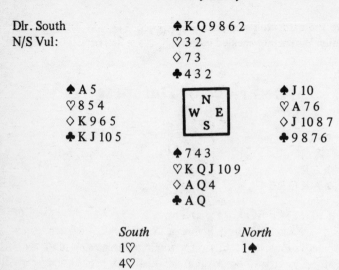

```
Dlr. South              ♠ K Q 9 8 6 2
N/S Vul:                ♡ 3 2
                        ◇ 7 3
                        ♣ 4 3 2

    ♠ A 5                             ♠ J 10
    ♡ 8 5 4          N                ♡ A 7 6
    ◇ K 9 6 5     W     E             ◇ J 10 8 7
    ♣ K J 10 5       S                ♣ 9 8 7 6

                        ♠ 7 4 3
                        ♡ K Q J 10 9
                        ◇ A Q 4
                        ♣ A Q
```

South	North
1♡	1♠
4♡	

"What flair," observed an admiring kibitzer, "against the best defence — a heart lead and a club back — 3NT is unmakeable, whereas even double dummy no defence can beat 4♡."

Looking for a ruff, the Toucan opened the ♣A and continued hopefully with the ♣5. The Rabbit ruffed and switched to the ◇J.

Going up with the ◇A, Lord de Ville proceeded cunningly with the ♡9.

The Rabbit rose with the ♡A and shifted to what he took to be the ♣10. On closer inspection this proved to be the ♠10. The Toucan, who was beginning to lose all hope of scoring that little trump, bounced happily and ruffed, killing the contract, for in no way could declarer now dispose of his three losers in the minors.

Viciously stabbing out her cigarette, Lady Greymalkin muttered an unladylike oath under her breath. The flower in Lord de Ville's buttonhole suddenly shrivelled.

Cut off from dummy, he was helpless. At duplicate, the tournament director can adjust the score, but there's no such remedy at rubber bridge. Two tricks for the revoke were transferred from the offending side to the injured party and the result then stood.

Soon after, however, R.R. and T.T. lost another rubber, and on the next deal, yet another game was made against them.

"The reading shows," announced Walter the Walrus, consulting his pocket points-programmed computer, "that our visitors have held 74.375% of the points on the last sixteen deals.

"Maybe the cards will now turn," suggested Lord de Ville with a sinister smile. His partner cackled mockingly as she dealt the next hand.

Dlr. North
N/S Vul:

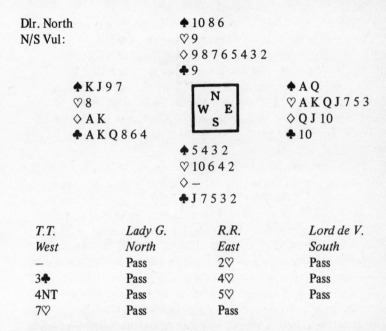

♠ 10 8 6
♡ 9
◇ 9 8 7 6 5 4 3 2
♣ 9

♠ K J 9 7
♡ 8
◇ A K
♣ A K Q 8 6 4

♠ A Q
♡ A K Q J 7 5 3
◇ Q J 10
♣ 10

♠ 5 4 3 2
♡ 10 6 4 2
◇ –
♣ J 7 5 3 2

T.T.	Lady G.	R.R.	Lord de V.
West	North	East	South
–	Pass	2♡	Pass
3♣	Pass	4♡	Pass
4NT	Pass	5♡	Pass
7♡	Pass	Pass	

Timothy the Toucan bounced high in his chair when he heard the Rabbit open 2♡.

"That shows eight playing tricks and a distributional hand," he explained unasked.

"And that," he went on when the Rabbit called 4♡, "promises a solid suit."

His heart thumped loudly against the scarlet silk lining of his shiny alpaca jacket as over the Rabbit's response to Blackwood, showing two aces, he heard himself bid 7♡.

He had never called a grand slam before. The Hog had warned him: "The pack has only 40 points. Allowing for your style of play, that's not enough to yield thirteen tricks, so don't throw away a small slam which you should have a 50–50 chance of bringing home."

And yet, tonight it was somehow different. Looking more than ever like a Toucan, his long crimson nose aglow, his arms flapping like wings, he leant over to the Rabbit.

"If you have what I think you have," he chirped excitedly, "we have eighteen tricks. Let me see," and bouncing up and down he exchanged hands with the Rabbit.

"Nineteen tricks!" he declared triumphantly.

"Wouldn't it be as well to wait until the bidding is over?" asked Lord de Ville coldly. "I haven't yet spoken you know."

The Toucan and the Rabbit looked dumbfounded.

"7NT," called out Lord de Ville in a loud metallic voice.

R.R. and T.T. stared at him incredulously. "But you are vulnerable," spluttered the Rabbit. "The sacrifice will cost much more than our grand slam. Umpteen hundreds more. How much is thirteen down Walter?" asked R.R. turning to the Walrus. "Get your computer to work it out."

"I can't double. It wouldn't be fair," declared T.T. "We wouldn't dream of it," agreed the Rabbit. "One doesn't, I mean, one cannot . . ."

The Toucan led the ♣A.

Lord de Ville's pointed left eyebrow rose a fraction of a millimetre. With a downward curve of his lips and a sardonic smile, he addressed his opponents.

"I fear that you do not appreciate the position. Your cards, *all* your cards are exposed. To refresh your memories would you care to look up Law 50 of the International Bridge Laws? No?

"Very well. Let me, however, recite one sentence from the second paragraph. 'If a defender has two or more penalty cards that can be legally played, declarer may designate which is to be played.' So, if it's not too much trouble, would you be so good as to lead the ♣8."

This was how the play proceeded.

Winning the first trick with the ♣J, Lord de Ville continued with the ♣7 and ♣5, West underplaying and East having to shed his ♠A and ♠Q.

Next came the ♠2 to dummy's ♠10, followed by the ♠8, West underplaying both times while East discarded the ♡QJ.

Declarer now switched to hearts — the ♡9, overtaken by the ♡10, then the ♡6 and ♡4. East followed with the ♡7, ♡5 and ♡3, while West parted with his ♠KJ.

The discard of dummy's ♠6 unblocked the ♠3 and ♠2 in the closed hand, declarer calling for West's ♣AK and East's ♡AK.

The ♡2, now master, compelled West to let go his ♣Q, allowing the ♣2 and ♣3 to score the twelfth and thirteenth tricks.

"With 39 points between them," exclaimed the awestruck Walrus, "they didn't make a single trick!"

"I don't feel terriby well," said the Toucan shakily. "If you'll excuse me, I'll stop playing."

"Pity," said Lord de Ville, "we would have enjoyed a few more hands."

The Hideous Hog, delayed by two seven-course dinners, was at last back at the Griffins. He had been a silent specator of the last few hands, but now he stepped forward, and with a courtly bow to the visitors, offered to partner the Rabbit.

"As this most enjoyable evening is coming to an end," suggested Lord de Ville, "shall we double the stakes for the last rubber?"

"By all means," agreed H.H. with alacrity, "and how about having a double or quits on whatever it is that my friends have lost? Ask your computer what it comes to Walter," added the Hog with a wink.

The Walrus didn't hear him. He had asked the computer to calculate the penalty in going down thirteen doubled. What would it have been? Looking at the tape for the answer, he shook his head. "It can't be right, not 256,984,673," he muttered. "Maybe it isn't programmed for penalties or perhaps it needs oiling. I must . . ."

"I seem to detect a whiff of sulphur in the air," observed the Hog, sniffing with distaste, and drawing a long Havana from his case, he looked around. "Where's my cigar piercer?" He searched his pockets in vain.

"I must have left it in my overcoat. Excuse me for just a moment." Rising, the Hog made for the door.

"Shall I cut for you?" asked the Rabbit.

"No, no, certainly not," replied the Hog. "You know how super-stitious I am."

He was away quite a while and once or twice our visitors glanced at the ormolu clock on the mantlepice.

"Sorry," apologised the Hog on his return. "Can't find it anywhere. Must have left it at home. Had to use a pin. Infernally careless of me," he added, cutting the pack for Lady Greymalkin.

Suddenly, just as she had completed the deal, the lights went out and the room was plunged in darkness.

A bat beat its wings against the windows. An owl hooted. A toad croaked. Brushing against Lord de Ville's elbow, a glass fell to the floor breaking into fragments. Thrusting out his leg under the table, the Hog's foot came into sharp contact with Lady Greymalkin's ankle. It all happened at once.

"I do apologise profusely," began H.H., when, just as suddenly as

they had gone out, the lights came on again and the players picked up
their cards.

Lady Greymalkin frowned. Biting at her bloodless lips, she was
muttering inaudibly. But it wasn't her ankle that seemed to be worrying
her. She was looking in bewilderment at her cards.

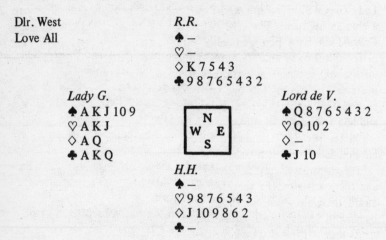

Dlr. West
Love All

R.R.
♠ —
♡ —
◊ K 7 5 4 3
♣ 9 8 7 6 5 4 3 2

Lady G.
♠ A K J 10 9
♡ A K J
◊ A Q
♣ A K Q

Lord de V.
♠ Q 8 7 6 5 4 3 2
♡ Q 10 2
◊ —
♣ J 10

N
W   E
S

H.H.
♠ —
♡ 9 8 7 6 5 4 3
◊ J 10 9 8 6 2
♣ —

Finally, staring at her partner, she bid 2♣. Gulping down his fourth
Cherry Brandy and biting nervously at a chocolate almond biscuit,
the Rabbit called 2NT.

"What do you understand by that bid?" enquired Lord de Ville,
looking no less perplexed than his partner.

"The usual unusual notrump," replied the Hog easily. "Clubs and
diamonds, that sort of thing."

"4◊," snapped out Lord de Ville. There was nothing suave about
his manner now.

Looking the picture of evil in distress, his pointed eyebrows seemed
to be oscillating, while the corners of his lips curled downwards almost
at right-angles.

The smell of sulphur was now unmistakeable.

The Hog overcalled 4◊ smoothly with 6◊. There was a shrill, hys-
terical note in Lady Gremalkin's normally low-pitched cackle as she
doubled.

This had been the sequence.

Lady G.	*R.R.*	*Lord de V.*	*H.H.*
West	North	East	South
2♣	2NT	4◊	6◊
Dble.			

Lady Greymalkin led the ♠A. The Hog ruffed in dummy and trumped a club in his hand. The ◊10 at trick two brought the ◊A from Lady Greymalkin who persisted with another spade. This time the Hog ruffed in his hand and continued wtih the ◊2 to dummy's ◊K, picking up the ◊Q on the way. Another club ruff in the closed hand and a heart ruff in dummy left one trump on each side of the table. A third club ruff with the Hog's last trump set up five club tricks and dummy still had a trump as an entry.

"Sorry partner," gloated the Hog. "I played too quickly. I should have made an overtrick. Ha! ha!"

The visitors were not amused. The temperature had suddenly dropped and there was almost a snarl in Lord de Ville's voice as he said: "I am afraid there's no time to finish the rubber. Lady Greymalkin has to be back in Scotland before dawn."

As they left the Hog rang the bell.

"Well done, Balthazar," he said to the steward, handing him a ten pound note. "You timed those lights perfectly. I had no trouble at all in changing the cards round, but would you believe it," he added turning towards us "I couldn't for the moment lay my hands on a glass to knock over and I nearly missed Lord whatnot altogether. Still, that thump I gave his girlfriend under the table created, I fancy, a suitable diversion."

Sipping his cognac, the Hog was in jubilant mood. "Prince of Darkness, indeed, flummoxed when the lights go out! Just because the cards are switched round a bit, he can't trust his own incantations."

"Do you mean that you and R.R. were meant to have the grand slam?" asked the Toucan who was slowly regaining consciousness.

"We were meant to have all the cards and they would make the slam," explained H.H. "Maybe he would have bet on it, too. The poor devil couldn't cast his spells accurately enough to be sure that there were thirteen cold tricks the other way. Neither could I, of course. All I knew, after seeing the last hand, was that we were to be at the wrong end of some sensation on this one, so I decided to change places, as it were.

"Pathetic, that 4◊ bid," went on H.H. "Did he expect to put me off, or was it an advance cue-bid? With her? Bah!"

The Hog shook his head. "The Powers of Darkness are not what they used to be in my day," he said with a sigh. "Evil may still get the better of virtue, but it's no match against technique — not when I'm in charge, anyway."

With a broad grin the Hog pulled out of his pocket a silver cigar piercer.

CHAPTER FOURTEEN

Epilogue

When I handed him my notes and he came to the events on Walpurgis Night, Oscar the Owl smiled.

"So, in the end, free will came out on top," I suggested.

"Not really," rejoined the Owl. "Our visitors have never settled their account, you know. All our communications have been returned with 'unknown at this address', and that, I fear, was predestined."

I tried again: "Would you say, then, Honours Even?"

"So far," agreed the Owl, "but the battle goes on and at the Griffins, as you know, both sides always win. There are no losers. That is our unique prerogative and therein lies the secret of our success."

Other books by
VICTOR MOLLO

MASTERS & MONSTERS
The Human Side of Bridge
(now in paperback)

New heroes and new villains join the allegorical Griffins to make this, the sequel to *Bridge in the Menagerie* and *Bridge in the Fourth Dimension*, the best of the original trilogy.

You will recognise your friends and foes alike and see maybe a fleeting picture of yourself in the exclusive club you are about to join. The members differ from lesser mortals only in being more colourful, more vibrant, more clearly defined in their ways. All have the same frailties and commit the same follies and are as comic in their vanity and their pretensions as the rest of the human race.

Advanced technique and simple psychology, closely linked, are the salient features of the many brilliant plays described. The Hog, insufferable and all but insuperable, brings off one coup after another and seldom fails to triumph over his hated rival, Papa the Greek. Both are experts but neither is a match for the Rueful Rabbit, for though R.R. rarely knows what he is doing or why, he is invariably saved from himself by the most accomplished guardian angel in the business.

YOU NEED NEVER LOSE AT BRIDGE
Happy Days in the Menagerie

'You may find us a little larger than life, but that is only because life at times is apt to be drab and dreary. So we infuse some colour into it. We like to see it sparkle.'

So spoke the Hog, introducing a Young Kibitzer to the Menagerie's club, the Griffins, where colour and sparkle weave the twin motif of everyday life. Against a rich background of subtle bids and brilliant plays every member does his own thing with gusto, which is why all are winners. Papa dazzles, often blinding himself in the process. Karapet savours every particle of endless misfortune. The Walrus counts his points, wondering why they are not as good as other people's. The Secretary Bird hisses and hates. The Rueful Rabbit does the right thing, of course, but invariably for the wrong reason. Molly the Mule, a rampant feminist, joins the cast. The reader will recognise them all and himself, too, perhaps, as he sits down to play — and to sparkle — at the Griffins, the club with no losers.

TOMORROW'S TEXTBOOK

That ubiquitous will o' the wisp, the average player, has learned a lot. Conventional methods of instruction and absorption have served him well — so far. The next stage in the advance to expertise calls for a new approach. It isn't enough to acquire the basic skills, to memorise points and tables and signals, and so find the right bid or play. More important by far is the ability to grasp what *makes* it right. Therein lies the way ahead.

In opening wide the window on tomorrow we will not treat bidding and play as separate subjects (the practice in standard textbooks) for they are one and indivisible, two sides of the same coin — neither being valid without the other. As Hamlet might have said, 'A contract is neither good nor bad but playing makes it so.'

In these pages you will be asked 230 questions, first on how you would bid, then on how you would play the same hands. You will soon see how, and above all why, the answer to each question is so often the answer to both.

THE COMPLEAT BRIDGE PLAYER

Bridge, says Victor Mollo, is the ideal medium for self-expression, allowing extroverts and introverts alike to release their egos. The bold, the cautious, the impetuous, the well-disciplined, the schemer, the dreamer — all are members of a cast in which each actor is a star.

With fascinating hands from top-class tournaments and the big money game as a background, the author examines the skills that make up the art of bridge, isolates and identifies each one in turn, and allows the reader to recognise where lies his weakness and where his strength, to correct the one and to nourish the other, to find himself, as it were, in the scheme of things — and so realise his full potential.

Approaching each theme subjectively, the reader will learn more about himself and so find the key to playing better and — more important — to enjoying the game even more than he does already.